IDEAS IN ECONOMICS

Recent Section F publications include

Kenneth Boulding (*editor*) THE ECONOMICS OF HUMAN
  BETTERMENT
Roy Jenkins (*editor*) BRITAIN AND THE EEC
R. C. O. Matthews (*editor*) ECONOMY AND DEMOCRACY
Jack Wiseman (*editor*) BEYOND POSITIVE ECONOMICS?
Lord Roll of Ipsden (*editor*) THE MIXED ECONOMY

SERIES EDITOR: David Reisman

Series Standing Order

If you would like to receive future titles in this series as they
are published, you can make use of our standing order
facility. To place a standing order please contact your
bookseller or, in case of difficulty, write to us at the address
below with your name and address and the name of the
series. Please state with which title you wish to begin your
standing order. (If you live outside the UK we may not have
the rights for your area, in which case we will forward your
order to the publisher concerned.)

Standing Order Service, Macmillan Distribution Ltd,
Houndmills, Basingstoke, Hampshire, RG21 2XS, England.

IDEAS IN ECONOMICS

Proceedings of Section F (Economics) of the British
Association for the Advancement of Science,
Strathclyde, 1985

Edited by R. D. Collison Black

Formerly Professor of Economics
The Queen's University of Belfast

MACMILLAN
PRESS

First published 1986

Published by
THE MACMILLAN PRESS LTD
Houndmills, Basingstoke, Hampshire RG21 2XS
and London
Companies and representatives
throughout the world

Photoset in Times by
CAS Typesetters, Southampton

Printed in Great Britain by
Anchor Brendon Ltd,
Tiptree, Essex

British Library Cataloguing in Publication Data
British Association for the Advancement of Science.
Section F (Economics). Meeting (1985: Strathclyde)
Ideas in economics: proceedings of Section F
(Economics) of the British Association for the
Advancement of Science, Strathclyde, 1985.
1. Economics
I. Title II. Black, R. D. Collison
330.1   HB171
ISBN 0–333–40885–3 (hardcover)
ISBN 0–333–40897–7 (paperback)

Contents

Notes on the Contributors

R. D. Collison Black was Professor and Head of the Department of Economics at The Queen's University of Belfast from 1962 until his retirement in 1985. He has held a number of visiting appointments abroad and is the editor of *Papers and Correspondence of W. S. Jevons*, also published by Macmillan.

Anthony Brewer is a Senior Lecturer in Economics at the University of Bristol. He is the author of *Marxist Theories of Imperialism: A Critical Survey*, *A Guide to Marx's Capital* and a number of articles in learned journals.

Bernard Corry is Professor of Economics at Queen Mary College, University of London. He is the author of *Money, Saving and Investment in English Economics, 1800–1850*, and of a number of papers on macroeconomic theory and the history of economic thought.

Walter Eltis is a Fellow of Exeter College, Oxford. He is the author of *The Classical Theory of Economic Growth* and (with Robert Bacon) of *Britain's Economic Problem: Too Few Producers*.

Samuel Hollander is University Professor and Professor of Economics at the University of Toronto, and Fellow of the Institute for the History and Philosophy of Science at the University. He is the author of *The Sources of Increased Efficiency: A Case Study of Du Pont Rayon Plants*, *The Economics of Adam Smith*, *The Economics of David Ricardo*, *The Economics of John Stuart Mill*. He was elected Fellow of the Royal Society of Canada in 1976, and held a Guggenheim Fellowship in 1968.

Terry Peach, B.A., B.Phil., D.Phil., was educated at Corpus Christi College and St Anthony's College, Oxford. Since 1980 he has been a Temporary Lecturer in Economics at the University of Manchester.

John R. Presley is Professor of Economics and Director of the Banking Centre at Loughborough University. He is the author of *European Monetary Integration* (with P. Coffey), *Currency Areas: Theory and Practice* (with G. E. J. Dennis), *Robertsonian Economics* and *The Saudi Arabian Economy*. He is joint editor (with D. P. O'Brien) of *Pioneers of Modern Economics in Britain*, and has also published many articles in learned journals.

Pedro Schwartz is Professor of the History of Economic Doctrines, University of Madrid, and the author of *The New Political Economy of J. S. Mill*.

Andrew Skinner holds the Daniel Jack Chair of Political Economy at the University of Glasgow, where he has taught since 1964. Professor Skinner has edited Sir James Steuart's *Principles of Political Economy* and also contributed to the Glasgow edition of the *Works and Correspondence of Adam Smith*.

John Whitaker is currently Professor of Economics at the University of Virginia and was previously Professor of Economic Theory at the University of Bristol. He edited *The Early Economic Writings of Alfred Marshall* and is at present preparing an edition of Alfred Marshall's correspondence. He has published a number of papers in learned journals on economic theory and the history of economics.

Introduction

R. D. COLLISON BLACK

All the papers in this volume were presented to Section F of the British Association for the Advancement of Science at its 1985 meeting in the University of Strathclyde. The general theme of that meeting was 'Putting Science to Use'. It might seem that Section F had chosen to ignore this fact, or even to fly in the face of it, by selecting for its own theme that of 'Ideas in Economics'. For, as a glance at the Contents List of this volume will show, all the papers are concerned with the ideas of the great economists of the past. Now what use can it be at the present time to investigate the ideas of the past? Would it not have been more appropriate to try to show how the latest developments in economic analysis might be put to use in moving towards solutions of those practical economic problems of which the world in general seems to have no shortage?

In fact, it was to some extent the recent application of economic doctrines in economic policy which stimulated this examination of the role of ideas in economics, and in particular of the persisting influence of past ideas in determining approaches to present problems. In both Britain and the United States the present governments are in an unusual degree committed to a specific economic doctrine as the basis of their policies. Yet that doctrine by no means commands universal assent and in consequence debates on economic issues have come to form part of the everyday content of newspapers, radio and television to a much greater extent than was normal, say, 25 years ago. In these debates competing views of how the economic system operates, and should or should not be controlled, are strenuously presented, but there is no unanimity as to which is correct. In these circumstances an examination of the intellectual origins of our present understanding of economic affairs could, it seemed, contribute to a clearer appreciation of the nature of Economics as a discipline, its potentialities and limitations. Hence economists might in the end be in a better position both to put it to use themselves and to interpret critically the ways in which it is used by others.

It was with these purposes in mind that the programme for the 1985 meeting of Section F was prepared. In attempting to realise them two approaches seemed possible – one concentrating on the work and influence of major thinkers, the other selecting major areas of policy and looking at the development of ideas about them. The programme which was finally presented combines both of these, although not in equal measure. In the first seven papers following my own attempt to set the scene, the authors have dealt with the work and influence of seminal thinkers for our time – Steuart, Smith, Bentham, Ricardo, J. S. Mill, Marx and Marshall. In the final two papers, however, the emphasis shifts to the area of monetary theory and policy, whose current importance seemed to warrant a separate attempt to bring out its historical origins and their significance.

Each of the authors was given a general brief but left free to develop their subject independently and in accordance with their own perceptions and interests.

I am most grateful to all my friends and colleagues who contributed the papers now brought together in this volume, and also particularly to Dr David Reisman, Secretary of Section F, for his invaluable support and help throughout the preparation of the programme and its subsequent conversion into book form.

In conclusion, I should like to put on record my thanks to the Officers and Committee of Section F of the British Association for the Advancement of Science for inviting me to serve as Section President for 1984–85 and giving me the opportunity to develop this view of the place of the past in the present in Economics.

The Queen's University of Belfast

1 Dentists and Preachers

R. D. COLLISON BLACK

The economic problem . . . should be a matter for specialists – like dentistry. If economists could manage to get themselves thought of as humble, competent people, on a level with dentists, that would be splendid! (J. M. Keynes, 1930–1972 edn, p. 332).

The first, probably the most important, and possibly the most surprising thing to say about the economist-preachers is that they have done very little preaching. I suppose that it is essential to state what I mean by preaching. I mean simply a clear and reasoned recommendation (or more often denunciation) of a policy or form of behaviour by men or societies of men. (G. J. Stigler, 1982, p. 3).

Many scientists – non-social scientists, that is – as well as many laymen, seem to have a view of how economists ought to operate which is not too different from that expressed by Keynes in the passage quoted above. Economists should be humble competent specialists who can diagnose an economic problem, prescribe the appropriate remedy for it or carry out the appropriate treatment, using well-understood and accepted techniques to produce an answer which is in some objective sense 'correct'.

Unfortunately, the non-social scientist will often go on to add, this is not the way in which he or she has usually found that economists do operate. Rather they seem to disagree about the nature of fundamental relationships in the economies they study, to advance theories which have low predictive power, and to offer conflicting advice on policies, as philosophers and theologians offer conflicting advice about the path to salvation.

Implicit in the scientist's view of how economists ought to behave is a view of Economics itself – as a positive science whose propositions about the real world are open to testing and falsification – and thus

1

more closely comparable with the 'hard' natural sciences such as physics than with the 'softer' disciplines of the humanities. Now the view of Economics as a science akin to the natural or experimental sciences is one which its practitioners have been trying to establish and promote for something like a century and a half, with varying degrees of success.

Already in the 1820s and 1830s Senior and John Stuart Mill were distinguishing between the science and the art of political economy, the one positive, the other normative.

> Science is a collection of truths; art, a body of rules, or directions for conduct. The language of science is, This is, or, This is not . . . The language of art is, Do this; Avoid that. Science takes cognizance of a *phenomenon*, and endeavours to discover its law; art proposes to itself an *end*, and looks out for means to effect it (J. S. Mill, 1844, p. 124; and compare Blaug, 1980, chapter 3).

Whether political economy in fact lived up to these methodological principles came to be widely questioned in the 1860s and 1870s – and some of the key discussions of the issue took place in meetings of the British Association.

One hundred and eight years ago Sir Francis Galton put before the Council of the Association his 'Considerations Adverse to the Maintenance of Section F'. Galton contended that

> usage has drawn a strong distinction between knowledge in its generality and science, confining the latter in its strictest sense to precise measurements and definite laws, which lead by such exact processes of reasoning to their results, that all minds are obliged to accept the latter as true . . . It is believed that the general verdict of scientific men would be that few of the subjects treated of [in Section F] fall within the meaning of the word scientific (Galton, 1877, p. 471).

Galton's challenge to 'the right of Political Economy and Statistics to citizenship in the commonwealth of science' was taken up by the President of Section F for 1878, John Kells Ingram (1823–1907), reputed in his day to be one of the most widely learned men in Europe, but now best remembered as a follower of Auguste Comte and the leading advocate in English of the historical method in political economy. Not surprisingly, while Ingram freely conceded the need for reform in the study of economic science, his main recommendations were 'that the study of the economic phenomena of society ought to be systematically combined with that of the other aspects of social existence' and 'that the *a priori* deductive method should be changed for the historical' (Ingram, 1878, reprint 1962, p. 68). But for all the skill and style of Ingram's address, which his contemporaries adjudged one of the best ever given before the Section, the methods which he advocated were not the ones which came to be generally adopted.

W. S. Jevons, whose own Presidential Address of 1870 has proved of less permanent significance than his first 'Brief Account of a General Mathematical Theory of Political Economy' read to Section F in 1862, showed himself a much better prophet when he wrote in 1879 that 'it is clear that Economics, if it is to be a science at all, must be a mathematical science' and further argued that 'the present chaotic state of Economics arises from the confusing together of several branches of knowledge. Subdivision is the remedy' (Jevons, 1911, pp. 3 and xvii). It was indeed along the lines of a science specialised into many subdivisions and making increasing use of mathematical and quantitative techniques that Economics developed over the ensuing century – so coming to conform more closely to the definition of a science given by Galton.

In the process the distinction between the science and the art of political economy became transmuted into that between positive and normative economics. But this was always a distinction which gave economists considerable trouble, both to make and to observe. Since the time of Cairnes, economists have always been anxious to assert the neutrality of their science as between different policies, and this anxiety ultimately led them to devote considerable and misplaced effort to the attempt to build a value-free welfare economics, in a search for a kind of science of economic policy.

At the time when Keynes wrote his comment about economists and dentists some of these developments were still to come. In 1930 most of his contemporaries in the economics profession were making comparatively little use of the mathematical and statistical techniques available and, indeed, had a fairly limited range of data on which to employ them. Even in the matter of technique, then, they were scarcely on a level with dentists. In matters of policy welfare economics seemed to have no diagnosis or treatment to offer for growing depression and unemployment; but if we accept Professor Stigler's definition of preaching as 'simply a clear and reasoned recommendation (or . . . denunciation) of a policy or form of behaviour' then it seems difficult to deny that after the Great Crash of 1929 economists preached as seldom before, but still achieved no unanimity about the true path to salvation.

It was of course Keynes himself, greatly aided by the opportunities offered by the events of the Second World War, who succeeded in imposing order on this confusion of tongues, as a result of the extraordinarily rapid development of consensus around the *General Theory* framework in the 1940s. The rest of the story is too familiar to need more than the briefest retelling. During the 1950s and 1960s the consensus of views on both macro and microeconomics produced what Samuelson called the 'neo-classical synthesis'; at the same time developments in econometric techniques combined with the availability of increased statistical data and the advent of the digital computer revolutionised the possibilities of model-building and theory testing. The heyday of neutral positive testable economics had arrived,[1] it seemed, and with it had come the possibility that the ranting economic preachers of former days would be replaced by humble competent people diagnosing, dentist-like, where the aches and pains of the economy arose, and prescribing an appropriate course of treatment.

It was not long before this bright prospect faded. In 1971, by a remarkable coincidence, the Presidents of the American Economic Association, the Royal Economic Society, and Section F, all took as their main theme the contrast between the formidable theoretical and technical equipment of mainstream economics and its disappointing performance in the solution of contemporary problems. Much of the sophisticated theory being developed, they contended, was out of touch with reality. Yet 'surely such a comment cannot be made about econometrics: by its very name it is concerned with measurement, so how could it become detached from the facts?' asked Worswick (1972, p. 79), only to go on to give it as his

> impression that the predictive power of econometrics is rather low, certainly very much lower than what one expects in natural sciences, and that progress in the establishment of firmer bases for economic relationships, if it occurs at all, is going at a very slow pace.

More recently, a similar charge against mainstream neoclassical economists has been formulated by Professor Mark Blaug:

They preach the importance of submitting theories to empirical tests, but they rarely live up to their declared methodological canons. Analytical elegance, economy of theoretical means, and the widest possible scope obtained by ever more heroic simplification have been too often prized above predictability and significance for policy questions (Blaug, 1980, p. 259).

So in spite of vast improvements in the available data, and the techniques of working on them, the prospect of establishing economics as a usable and unified hard science seems no nearer to attainment than it was when Keynes sighed for it more than 50 years ago. It was perhaps always something of an illusion; the time when the triumph of positive economics seemed closest was also the time when the emptiness of the concept of a non-normative welfare economics was being most clearly revealed and recognised. And at that same time there were always those who maintained the validity of alternative visions of the economic world – institutionalists like J. K. Galbraith, and Marxists like Paul Sweezy and R. L. Meek, none of whom could be dismissed as negligible thinkers.

As might be expected, with the failure of neoclassical mainstream economics to deliver usable and testable theories relevant to immediate policy problems, we have witnessed in the last 20 years or so, both a revival of interest in these alternative visions, and the emergence of others all claiming the title of 'new political economies', such as the Post-Keynesians.[2] One feature which all these approaches have in common is that they recognise and stress the interdependence and interpenetration of political and economic factors. Consequently most (though not all) of them make no attempt to be 'neutral' but incorporate specific value-judgements into their structure.

We seem, then, to have arrived at a decidedly disorderly state of affairs, calculated to bring the threatening spectre of Galton back into our Section meetings. Some economists, perhaps indeed the majority, do try to ply their trade with humble competence like dentists, although often with less success. Others appear to double the roles of dentist and preacher, while others still devote themselves entirely to preaching. Of all of these it may be said that the texts on which they preach are derived from a wide variety of scriptures. Now it is easy to deplore all this, or to make fun of it, but some aspects of the situation which can be easily overlooked deserve to be emphasised.

First, the analogy between dentistry and applied economics is only superficially valid, and will not bear any very close examination.

Dentists deal with a strictly delimited range of problems affecting the health of individuals; applied economists are concerned with problems which affect society, either as a whole or parts of it. Individuals are usually content to leave the diagnosis and cure of their oral ailments to the trained expert, but they probably have a decided view as to how the economy should be run and, in modern Western societies at least, expect to have the opportunity to influence economic policy even if only by voting for the party whose view corresponds most closely to their own. From this fairly obvious fact two important corollaries follow. One is, that under these conditions the emergence of a consensus about the main lines of economic policy such as existed in the 1950s and 1960s is much more to be wondered at than the emergence of conflicting prescriptions such as are to be found in contention nowadays. The other, not unrelated, corollary, is that the process by which the theories of economists may come to have an influence on policy is now very complex and one which cannot be properly explained or understood in a non-political way (compare Hutchison, 1981, p. 35).

Secondly, and perhaps more fundamentally, it must always be remembered that

> Economics . . . like other social sciences is manifestly different from physical science in that it is a profoundly historical science; its roots lie in the attempt to understand a particular configuration of human (social) institutions . . . economists study a non-constant universe (Kunin and Weaver, 1971, p. 395).

It can scarcely be disputed that Economics has witnessed profound shifts in the configuration of institutions which it studies within the past 25 years or so; let us look at just two of them by way of illustration.

In modern economic thought what Alfred Marshall called 'the measuring-rod of money' has played a central part. Marshall (1890–1961 edn-I, p. 14) stressed that 'the chief motives of business life can be measured in money' and argued that 'it is this definite and exact money measurement of the steadiest motives in business life which has enabled economics far to outrun every other branch of the study of man'. Under the tutelage of Keynes economists learned how to escape from the 'tyranny' of an exogenously determined monetary standard and how to manipulate money in a way which, combined with appropriate fiscal policy, could affect the levels of income and employment in an economy in substantial and beneficial ways. In turn, they succeeded in teaching this lesson to bankers and ministers of finance. In the process money as measuring-rod itself began to alter – which did not seem to matter too much until the attitudes of economic agents towards the measuring-rod also began to change and so to affect some of 'the steadiest motives in business life'.

Economists have long accepted as basic to their subject the idea that resources are scarce in relation to their possible uses, but for almost a century they were sufficiently impressed by the possibilities of substitution and technical change not to be concerned about the possibilities of resource exhaustion. Events in the early 1970s brought that question back on to the economic agenda, although whether it should be at the top or the bottom remains a matter for debate. That this should be so is partly the result of confusing signals from other sciences, which sometimes suggest that we are on the verge of damaging our environment irretrievably through over-rapid use of fossil fuels, sometimes that we are entering an era in which limits to growth will disappear as a result of new technologies producing synthetic materials.

Even this summary, brief, naïve, and incomplete as it is, should be enough to remind us that these recent changes are profound, a veritable shaking of the foundations. It was inevitable that they should lead to revisions in economics involving the questioning of well-established doctrines and attempts to formulate fresh ones. Indeed, the developments of the past 25 years or so have tended to support the position of those who, like myself, have always tended to be sceptical about the view of economics as a 'hard' science, developing independently of political and philosophical influences, in a cumulative fashion primarily as a result of forces internal to the discipline. Twenty-two years ago I wrote, 'There are, in fact, fashions in economic thought and the topics which are in vogue change – sometimes as a result of the pressure of current events, sometimes as a result of internal criticism' (Black, 1963, p. 4). That still seems to me to hold good; the topics in vogue have changed, mainly perhaps as a result of the pressure of events. What is new is the increasing strength and number of alternative schools of thought, reflecting the reaction against positive economics and towards political economy. Progress in technique there has certainly been, and it is noteworthy that technique is increasingly becoming the common property of the various schools. So for the foreseeable future it seems likely that we shall continue to have a number of competing research programmes in economics or, to put it in another way, a variety of preachers expounding their view of the world and the way to mend it.

It is just this state of affairs which gives special significance to the study of the history of ideas in economics today. In the 1950s and 1960s, when the 'neo-classical synthesis' found its widest acceptance, the growth of model-building and econometric testing seemed to imply

the positivistic and/or naturalistic view that since no *logical* distinction exists between the methodologies of the physical and social sciences, economics is a cumulatively progressive science in the same way as, say, physics. By way of analogy then, an economist need not devote his time to outworn theories of the past any more than his counterparts in the physical sciences (Tarascio, 1971, p. 421).

Consequently, as George Stigler suggested (1969, p. 218), 'the young economist will increasingly share the view of the more advanced formal sciences that the history of the discipline is best left to those underendowed for full professional work at the modern level'. Confronted with comments like this it is not to be wondered at that historians of economic thought tended to develop an inferiority complex. They found it hard to refute the view that whatever interest their subject might have in itself, it had little to contribute to the continuing development of economics, and were consequently inclined to concentrate on treating the history of economic analysis on 'absolutist' lines, supporting the view of economics as a cumulatively progressing science.

If that view is abandoned in favour of the idea of economics as comprising a series of co-existing research programmes, attempts to interpret and evaluate these research programmes must make considerable use of the history of economic thought, for most of them are based on revival or reinterpretation of past ideas. Indeed one of the most remarkable features of Economics as a discipline seems to me to be the extent to which it develops by the reinterpretation of concepts and constructs derived from past authors. Of all the research programmes which exist in our field, and are, as modern jargon has it, 'ongoing', the Keynesian is perhaps the only one which does not find its origin in works already written on the day when Henry Sidgwick gave his Presidential Address to this Section one hundred years ago – and even that is questionable. The neoclassical writers of today pay homage to Walras, the monetarists to Hume, the old and the new Left and the post-Keynesians to Ricardo and to Marx.

The implications of this for current economic theories and the history of economic analysis are evident and significant. In an interesting recent article Filippo Cesarano has argued that what he terms the 'path of scientific development' (PSD) takes different shapes in different fields, and even subfields, of knowledge, and certainly does not always have 'a non-decreasing monotonic time-function' (Cesarano, 1983, p. 70). If, as he contends, Economics is a field in which the PSD does not have such a form,

> then the role of the history of economic analysis should be manifest. It is a role which is relevant to the modern theories. The study of past authors may disclose constructs, and links between constructs which, though forgotten, may be important for current research (Cesarano, 1983, p. 77).

A similar point of view has been presented in different terms by Kenneth Boulding who has suggested that 'whether economists who are not primarily historians . . . need to pay attention . . . to any writers of the past depends on one's estimate of the extent to which the evolutionary potential of these past authors has been realised or exhausted' (Boulding, 1971, p. 230). A notable instance of this is to be found in the case of Ricardo. Thirty-five years ago most historians of thought would probably have conceded that one historic figure whose writings their colleagues working in economic theory need spend no time on was Ricardo. Yet the work of Piero Sraffa, first in his definitive edition of Ricardo's *Works and Correspondence* and later in the *Production of Commodities by Means of Commodities*, was to change all this. Whether one accepts or rejects Sraffa's system, the modern economist has to reckon with this, a system squarely founded on Ricardian ideas.

So it can be shown that the history of economic analysis has a contribution to make to the understanding and development of contemporary economic theory. Perhaps that may enhance its standing in the eyes of economic theorists, but the public at large may be forgiven if they are not greatly moved by this. The whole issue may take on a rather different appearance, however, if we widen the focus of our attention from economic analysis to economic doctrine.

In the world of today the interpenetration of political and economic affairs is so all-pervasive that virtually every citizen, whatever the country of his residence, is bound to be affected in some way by the economic policies which its government pursues, and consequently to take some interest in the economic doctrines on which those policies are ostensibly or actually based. Some policies may simply be dictated by hard necessity, but wherever governments have some freedom of manoeuvre they generally also have a rationale for their policy decisions; equally generally that rationale is based on some economic doctrine. Perhaps no quotation from Keynes is more often repeated than that which contains the words:

> the ideas of economists and political philosophers, both when they are right and when they are wrong, are more powerful than is commonly understood. Indeed the world is ruled by little else. Practical men, who believe themselves to be quite exempt from any intellectual influences, are usually the slaves of some defunct economist (Keynes, 1936, p. 383).

This splendid sweeping generalisation, so typical of Keynes, carries as much conviction today as it did 50 years ago. It may have been possible in the 1960s to envisage 'the end of ideology' (Bell, 1962), but today ideology has made a come-back and much of it derives from economist-preachers.

The point I wish to stress here has recently been well put by Professor William Breit:

> economists like artisans, musicians, and scientists, are engaged in the enterprise of making sense of what William James called 'that bloomin', buzzin' confusion' that comes to our senses from the reality we observe. Our minds impose order on this sensory data . . . Although it is not yet understood how order is imposed on sensory data, it is imposed in vastly different ways by different theorists. There is therefore a great variety of world versions. To a great extent we see what we want to see; or what we are prepared to see; or what skilful artists and theorists have made us see (Breit, 1984, p. 20).

What the skilful theorists in Economics make us see is their view of the world. A concrete economic world there certainly is, whose phenomena can be observed and measured and are better measured and recorded than they were 50 years ago. But what can be objectively perceived can still be very variously interpreted. To some economic observers the world appears as a set of interlocking markets, a mechanical system with considerable self-righting properties provided only that it is given the right setting and carefully lubricated. To others the same world appears as a system of alienation and exploitation designed for the purpose of extracting surplus for the benefit of the ruling class. To other again it appears as a world mixing monopoly and competition, plagued by market failure and unstable investment, requiring constant tinkering to keep it functioning.

The influence which these ideas have on public policy may not be as great as Keynes made it out to be, but it is undeniably very substantial. Many present-day governments are openly and firmly committed to policies based on economic doctrines, of which Marxism and monetarism are only the most obvious examples.

Now these doctrines have long and deep historical roots. If we accept Mark Blaug's definition of a monetarist as 'someone who believes in the quantity theory of money' (Blaug, 1985, p. 690) then the origins of monetarist doctrine can be traced back into the seventeenth century if not further. Marxism seems almost modern by comparison, if one traces its origins no farther than Hegel's philosophy and Ricardo's economics. At all events, it seems safe to say that the doctrines which economists preach are usually based on scriptures which go back into the nineteenth century at least.

There is nothing necessarily wrong in that – so long as both the preachers and their audiences have at least some acquaintance with the older writings and their context. On this point a comment made by Lord Robbins seems to me to retain its validity:

> I do not think that, even in the purely analytical field, our knowledge is so far advanced as to justify us in writing off as superseded the propositions of all but our immediate contemporaries; and, in the applied field, I do not think that we can hope to understand the problems and policies of our own day if we do not know the problems and policies out of which they grew. I suspect that damage has been done, not merely to historical and speculative culture, but also to our practical insight by this indifference to our intellectual past – this provincialism in time – which has become so characteristic of our particular branch of social studies (Robbins, 1952, pp. 1–2).

Now this brings up the important question of the transference of ideas in time and space – a question on which we have had a number of interesting and valuable studies in recent years, but on which much more work still requires to be done.[3] Perhaps my analogy, by now well-worn, of dentists and preachers may prove useful here again in sorting out some basic points.

Preachers have few, if any, problems with time and space, for it is clear to them that the scriptures from which they work contain perennial truths – articles of faith and moral imperatives which must be accepted and obeyed by all who seek to attain that state which the preacher commends to them as right. Dentists are at the opposite end of the scale – very much bound and conditioned by time and surrounding circumstances. They will normally apply the most up-to-date techniques of treatment, taking it as axiomatic that these are in advance of anything which has been used in the past. Yet before using the treatment in any particular case they will be careful to enquire whether there is anything in the condition of the patient – a possibility of haemophilia, for example – which might make the use of it undesirable or inappropriate.

The application of economic doctrine to economic policy lies awkwardly between these two positions. On the one hand the economist, unlike the dentist, cannot assume that the newest doctrine is necessarily the most complete and effective. On the other he cannot, or at least should not, derive imperatives or certainties from the doctrines of the past. In matters of political economy we are rarely, if ever, dealing with propositions which can be treated as valid irrespective of time or place. Hence, it seems to me, two dangers arise – the one, to which Lord Robbins drew attention, results from ignorance of the problems and policies which past generations have had to cope with and evolve. This can lead to the making of recommendations without due reference to previous experience and the lessons which can be learned from them. Another, perhaps more prevalent in these ideological days, arises not from plain ignorance of the past and its thinkers, but from a limited acquaintance with the works of such thinkers. This then leads some economist-preachers confidently to present very selective interpretations of such works, which may then be further simplified by their followers into a kind of crude fundamentalism.

In consequence the vital question whether a doctrine developed in one time and place is properly applicable to another time and place may not be posed and examined as it should be. It has been frequently and forcefully pointed out by economists like Seers (1963) and Georgescu-Roegen (1960) that there are serious dangers in attempting to base economic policy for developing countries on theories of market economies which assume 'an autonomous and flexible socio-economic structure, in which each human being responds individually to the material incentives offered, and which is subject to no formidable exogenous strains' (Seers, 1963, p. 83).

Twenty and more years later it is difficult to believe that these warnings have had the effect which they should, but developed economies are not without similar problems. The conception of the economy on which policy ideas are based seems at times to lag seriously behind the facts of economic life – for example, in areas such as automation, environmental pollution, or corporate structures.

In the formulation of economic policy at any level, then, it is arguable that a knowledge of the history of economic thought and its links with past policy can be a valuable corrective to provincialism in time and space and serve to reduce the risk of repeating past mistakes which that involves.

If we accept, as I think we must, that Economics is not, and is unlikely to become, a unified hard science, then it follows that a knowledge of the history of its development and an ability to use that knowledge critically is nothing less than an essential pre-requisite for putting such a science to use. So I must end, I am afraid, by dissenting from both the high authorities whom I quoted at the outset. Economists, in my view, are never likely to get themselves thought of as on a level with dentists, however competent they may become as technicians. In so far as they undertake to influence policy, they must be preachers as well and, whatever Professor Stigler may say, a great many of them seem to me to have done a great deal of preaching and be unlikely to give up the habit. In consequence, like most preachers they run the risk of leading their followers into dogmatic fundamentalism. Perhaps the most useful function the historian of ideas can perform is that of the scholarly agnostic acquainted with a wide variety of scriptures, prepared to draw attention to misreadings and misunderstandings of them and to add that there is a less familiar comment of Keynes which might have application to matters of political economy – 'no one has a gospel'.[4]

NOTES

1. Compare, for example, the confident statement of Popperian methodology in Chapter 1 of the first edition (1963) of R. G. Lipsey's *Introduction to Positive Economics*.
2. For an attempt to document this phenomenon see Black, 1983.

3. See, for example, Goodwin and Holley, 1968; Spengler, 1970; Winch, 1969.
4. 'All the political parties alike have their origins in past ideas and not in new ideas . . . It is not necessary to debate the subtleties of what justifies a man in promoting his gospel by force; for no one has a gospel' (Keynes, 1926–1972 edn, p. 67).

REFERENCES

Bell, D. F. *The End of Ideology* (New York: The Free Press, 1962).

Black, R. D. Collison *Economic Fashions*, an Inaugural Lecture delivered before The Queen's University of Belfast, 4 December 1963 (Belfast: The Queen's University, 1963).

Black, R. D. Collison 'The Present Position and Prospects of Political Economy', in A. W. Coats (ed.), *Methodological Controversy in Economics: Historical Essays in Honor of T. W. Hutchison* (Greenwich, Conn.: JAI Press, 1983) pp. 55–70.

Blaug, M. *The Methodology of Economics* (Cambridge: Cambridge University Press, 1980).

Blaug, M. *Economic Theory in Retrospect*, 4th edn (Cambridge: Cambridge University Press, 1985).

Boulding, K. E. 'After Samuelson, who needs Adam Smith?', *History of Political Economy*, vol. 3, no. 2 (Fall, 1971) pp. 225–37.

Breit, W. 'Galbraith and Friedman: two versions of economic reality', *Journal of Post-Keynesian Economics*, vol. VII, no. 1 (Fall, 1984) pp. 18–29.

Browning, P. *Economic Images* (London: Longman, 1983).

Cesarano, F. 'On the role of the history of economic analysis', *History of Political Economy*, vol. 15, no. 1 (Spring, 1983) pp. 63–82.

Galton, F. 'Considerations Adverse to the Maintenance of Section F', *Journal of the Royal Statistical Society*, vol. XL (September, 1877) pp. 468–72.

Georgescu-Roegen, N. 'Economic Theory and Agrarian Economics', *Oxford Economic Papers*, vol. 12, no. 1 (February, 1960) pp. 1–6.

Goodwin, C. D. W. and I. B. Holley (eds), *The Transfer of Ideas: Historical Essays* (Durham, North Carolina: Duke University Press, 1968).

Hutchison, T. W. *The Politics and Philosophy of Economics* (Oxford: Blackwell, 1981).

Ingram, J. K. 'The Present Position and Prospects of Political Economy', Presidential Address to Section F of the British Association, 1878, reprinted in R. L. Smyth (ed.), *Essays in Economic Method* (London: Duckworth, 1962).

Jevons, W. S. *The Theory of Political Economy*, 4th edn (London: Macmillan, 1911).

Keynes, J. M. 'Trotsky on England' (March 1926) in *Essays in Biography, Collected Writings*, vol. X (London: Macmillan, 1972) pp. 63–7.

Keynes, J. M. 'Economic Possibilities for our Grandchildren' (1930) in *Essays in Persuasion, Collected Writings*, vol. IX (London: Macmillan, 1972) pp. 321–32.

Keynes, J. M. *The General Theory of Employment Interest and Money* (London: Macmillan, 1936).

Kunin, L. and F. S. Weaver, 'On the Structure of Scientific Revolutions in Economics', *History of Political Economy*, vol. 3, no. 2 (Fall, 1971) pp. 391–7.

Lipsey, R. G. *An Introduction to Positive Economics*, 1st edn (London: Weidenfeld & Nicolson, 1963).

Marshall, A. *Principles of Economics* (London: Macmillan, 1890; 9th (variorum) edn, 1961).

Mill, J. S. 'On the Definition of Political Economy', *Essays on Some Unsettled Questions of Political Economy* (London: J. W. Parker, 1844).

Ricardo, D. in P. Sraffa (ed.) *The Works and Correspondence of David Ricardo*, vols I–X (Cambridge: Cambridge University Press, 1951–5).

Robbins, L. C. *The Theory of Economic Policy in English Classical Political Economy* (London: Macmillan, 1952).

Seers, D. 'The Limitations of the Special Case', *Bulletin of the Oxford Institute of Economics and Statistics*, vol. 25, no. 2 (May, 1963) pp. 77–98.

Spengler, J. J. 'Notes on the International Transmission of Economic Ideas', *History of Political Economy*, vol. II, no. 1 (Spring, 1970) pp. 133–51.

Sraffa, P. *Production of Commodities by Means of Commodities: Prelude to a Critique of Economic Theory* (Cambridge: Cambridge University Press, 1960).

Stigler, G. J. 'Has Economics a Useful Past?', *History of Political Economy*, vol. 1, no. 2 (Fall, 1969) pp. 217–30.

Stigler, G. J. *The Economist as Preacher* (Oxford: 1982).

Tarascio, V. J. 'Some Recent Developments in the History of Economic Thought in the United States', *History of Political Economy*, vol. 3, no. 2 (Fall, 1971) pp. 419–31.

Winch, D. N. *Economics and Policy* (London: Hodder & Stoughton, 1969).

Worswick, G. D. N. 'Is Progress in Economic Science Possible?', *Economic Journal*, vol. 82, no. 325 (March, 1972) pp. 73–86.

2 Adam Smith: Then and Now

ANDREW SKINNER

PART I: ANALYSIS[1]

I

During the course of the 1976 celebrations in Glasgow, R. D. C. Black drew attention to the changing interests of economists, and the way in which these had affected our view of Adam Smith. Professor Black referred to a fresh perspective on the relationship between ethics and economics, noting that: 'Some of this represents a very valuable effort to set Smith's work properly into the context of eighteenth century ideas, events and institutions: . . . some of it can also be seen as symptomatic of another shift in viewpoint' (Black, 1976, p. 62).

This judgement is amply confirmed by Wood's massive *Adam Smith: Critical Assessments* (1983) and further illustrated by Gee's recent review (1985) of this work.

The relationships which exist between the different parts of Smith's system have recently been brought out by Anspach (1972), Billet (1976), W. F. Campbell (1967), Lindgren (1973), Recktenwald (1978) and Samuels (1976), to name but a few. Representative figures of an older generation would have to include Morrow (1927), Viner (1927) and Macfie (1967b). To these must be added scholars who have developed certain aspects of Smith's work within the framework of his wider purposes, most notably Haakonssen's exploration of the relationship between Smith's ethics and the theory of jurisprudence (Haakonssen, 1981) and Winch's work on his politics (Winch, 1978). Others have reminded us that there is a 'civic humanist' dimension in Smith's language; a theme which is a major feature of a recent volume, edited by Hont and Ignatieff (1983).

This paper is also and in part a contribution to the 'interdisciplinary' approach to Smith and is based upon the conviction that we cannot otherwise fully understand Smith's intentions. To be more specific, it is the purpose of this paper to review some of the interrelationships which exist between the different parts of Smith's system of moral science before going on to consider their relevance for his treatment of public policy and to assess Smith's standing as an advocate of economic liberalism.[2] In so doing it will be convenient to follow the order of Smith's lecture course as a true guide to his intentions.

We have long been aware that when Smith went to Glasgow University in 1751 as Professor of Logic, he took with him a course on rhetoric which reflected his belief that;

> The best method of explaining and illustrating the various powers of the human mind, the most useful part of metaphysics, arises from an examination of the several ways of communicating our thoughts by speech, and from an attention to the principles of those literary compositions which contribute to persuasion or entertainment (Stewart, I. 16).[3]

When Smith moved to the Chair of Moral Philosophy in 1752, he continued to give these lectures; lectures which now emerge as showing a concern with the principles of human nature, and with all forms of discourse, including the scientific.[4] This interesting extension of the theory of communication provides an intriguing link with Smith's essay on Astronomy, with particular reference to his concern with 'subjectivity' in science.[5]

At the same time, we know from John Millar that in addressing the teaching of moral philosophy, the main business of the Chair, Smith developed a series of subjects in a certain order; namely, natural theology, ethics, jurisprudence, and economics. Millar was to inform Dugald Stewart that the substance of the lectures on ethics was embodied in the *Theory of Moral Sentiments* (1759) and to confirm that:

> In the last part of his lectures, he examined those political regulations which are founded, not upon the principle of *justice*, but that of *expediency*, and which are calculated to increase the riches, the power and the prosperity of a State. . . . What he delivered on these subjects contained the substance of the work he afterwards published under the title of An Inquiry into the Nature and Causes of the Wealth of Nations (Stewart, I. 20).

Smith himself announced his intention further to develop his published work in the concluding sentences of the first edition of TMS, and reminded his readers in the advertisement to the sixth edition of 1790 that he still hoped to add to TMS and WN a published account of 'the general principles of law and government, and of the different revolutions which they had undergone in different ages and periods of society'. The discovery, in 1895, of LJ (B) by Edwin Cannan, made it possible to gain some understanding of the shape and dimensions of the keystone of the system; an opportunity which was dramatically improved by the publication of LJ (A) in 1978.[6]

II

Smith's ethical lectures addressed two questions: first, wherein does virtue consist, and secondly, 'by what means does it come to pass' that the mind prefers one tenor of conduct to another (TMS, VII. i. 2). In concentrating primarily on the latter issue, Smith produced a concise argument which can be reduced to the form of a model, and which was designed to show how men erect barriers against their own passions – thus contributing to explain the observed phenomenon of social order.[7]

Briefly stated, Smith contended that 'How selfish soever man may be supposed, there are evidently some principles in his nature, which interest him in the fortune of others' (TMS, I. i. 1. 1). If selfish, man is also endowed with 'fellow feeling' and it is this, added to a capacity for acts of imaginative sympathy, that permits the spectator to form a judgement as to the propriety of an action or expression of feeling generated by one or more persons. Smith went on to note that we can 'enter into' the situation of another person only to a limited degree, and therefore that a person seeking to attract the approval of the spectator can only do so by 'lowering his passion to that pitch' which will be understood by him. It was Smith's contention that: 'Nature when she formed man for society, endowed him with an original desire to please, and an original aversion to offend his brethren' (TMS, III. 2. 6).

Yet important as this general disposition may be as a source of control, Smith also drew attention to the fact that it was unlikely to be sufficient. Two reasons were advanced.

To begin with, Smith argued that the spectator must be well informed if judgement is to be accurate, recognising that our knowledge is likely to be imperfect with regard to the motives which prompt an action taken by another person. Smith solved this problem by developing the argument that we judge our own conduct by supposing 'ourselves the spectators of our own behaviour'; that is, by considering what the reaction of a supposed or ideal spectator would be to our conduct in full knowledge of the motives which lie behind it. Smith concluded that while man in his capacity of the actual spectator of the conduct of others may form a judgement of it, in respect of his own, reference must be made to a higher tribunal, namely that of the man within the breast, the great judge and arbiter of our conduct, in short, to conscience.[8]

The second problem arises from the fact that we may fail to be impartial, even where the necessary information is available; a problem which gains added point from the fact that man is presented by Smith as an active, self-regarding being. Smith often develops this theme within the context of broadly 'economic' aspirations and of his key assumption that we seek to act in ways which will attract the approval of our fellows. As he noted, this does not stop with questions of propriety or of morality: 'the advantages . . . we propose by that great purpose of human life which we call bettering our condition' are to be 'observed, to be attended to, to be taken notice of with sympathy, complacency, and approbation' (TMS, I. iii. 2. 1). But, as Smith put it: 'When we are about to act, the eagerness of passion will seldom allow us to consider what we are doing, with the candour of an indifferent person' (TMS, III. 4. 3), while even after the event, 'It is so disagreeable to think ill of ourselves, that we often purposely turn away our view from those circumstances which might render that judgement unfavourable' (TMS, III. 4. 4).

Smith's solution to the practical problem thus raised was simple, but important. He suggested that our capacity to form judgements in particular cases permits us to formulate general rules of behaviour which will serve as yardsticks against which we can judge our own actions and at all times: 'It is thus that the general rules of morality are formed. They are ultimately founded upon experience of what, in particular instances, our moral faculties, our natural sense of merit and propriety, approve, or disapprove of' (TMS, III. 4. 8).

Given that general rules may be formulated in the way described, Smith went on to argue that men would be disposed to obey them because they wish to be *praiseworthy*; a disposition which 'is still further enhanced by an opinion which is first impressed by nature, and afterwards confirmed by reasoning and philosophy, that those important rules of morality are the commands and laws of the Deity, who will finally reward the obedient, and punish the transgressors of their duty' (TMS, III. 5. 3). Although it is in this way, and for these reasons, that men impose on themselves some degree of control over their passions, Smith was clear that the basic pre-condition of social order was a system of law embodying current conceptions of justice, and backed by a form of government or magistracy: 'Without this precaution, civil society would become a scene of bloodshed and disorder' (TMS, VII. iv. 36).

III

The spectator is also central to the jurisprudence, which formed the next section of Smith's course. In the context of the discussion of acquired rights, for example, it is observed that such claims may be defended if recognised by the *spectator* as establishing a reasonable expectation. In a similar vein Smith argued that the *spectator* approves of punishment for actions which have, and were intended to have, hurtful consequences (TMS, II. i. 4. 4).

The argument which illustrates the way in which we judge on *particular* occasions is also important in the sense that it explains the origin, and something of the nature, of *general* rules of conduct, including those of justice. This suggests that Smith adopted an empiricist (as distinct from a rationalist) approach to ethical questions, which implies that general rules of behaviour must be related to the experience of what is thought, on particular occasions, to be appropriate. This in turn raises the possibility that since experience may vary, then so too will the content of general rules – a position which is explored to a limited extent in the *Theory of Moral Sentiments* where Smith considers the influence of custom and fashion on moral judgement (TMS, V).

The theme was continued in the lectures on jurisprudence where Smith considered the relationship between environment and law. As John Millar recalled when commenting on the third part of Smith's lecture course: 'Upon this subject he followed the plan that seems to be suggested by Montesquieu' (Stewart, I. 19).

Millar's association of Montesquieu with economic forces, and with the dynamic processes of change through time, may be somewhat overdrawn, but is, as he suggested, very much a feature of Smith's thought. It was in this connection that he made use of four types of economic organisation, or modes of earning subsistence, the now famous stages of 'hunting, pasturage, farming, and commerce' (LJ (B), p. 149). These stages are deployed in the discussion of private law where the lecturer addressed man's rights as a member of a family and as an individual. But it is also significant that Smith should have deployed the 'theory' of economic stages in the discussion of public jurisprudence where he was concerned with the broader questions of constitutional structures; with the origins and changing shape of government.

The 'stadial' thesis which was first deployed by Smith in the *Lectures* is now peculiarly and quite properly associated with the work of the late Ronald Meek, who successfully identified the relationship between the mode of subsistence and the patterns of authority and subordination associated with it.[9] In WN the first two stages, of hunting and pasture, constitute a notable feature of the treatment of defence and justice, while the remaining stages of agriculture and commerce dominate the analysis of Book III, where the purpose is to trace the origins of the 'present establishments' of Europe, starting from the collapse of the Roman Empire in the West.

In the context of WN, the main thrust of the argument is designed to explain the origin of the feudal form of government and the emergence of the stage of commerce, wherein the main forms of activity (agriculture and manufacture) are fully interdependent and where all goods and services command a price. While the same points are made in the lectures, the constitutional dimension is there more marked in the sense that Smith was also concerned to explain a gradual shift in the balance of power which, at least in the peculiar circumstances of England, had led to the House of Commons assuming a position of some dominance.[10] In England especially, Smith argued, liberty was secured by 'an assembly of the representatives of the people, who claim the sole right of imposing taxes' (WN, IV. vii. b. 51), further supported by a judiciary which was independent of the executive power (WN, V. i. b. 25), and confirmed by a standing army 'placed under the command of those who have the greatest interest in the support of the civil authority' (WN, V. i. a. 41). While Smith was not unaware of the dangers of the political process, of standing armies and of manipulation of the civil list, he believed that the system of security which was established in England had been finally set in place by the Revolution of 1688 (WN, IV. v. b. 43).[11] He clearly approved of a situation which had so materially contributed to the 'progress of England towards wealth and improvement' (WN, II. iii. 36). These major themes of Smith's lectures were to find another, and still more complete, expression in the work of his most distinguished pupil, John Millar, whose *Historical View of the English Government* was first published in 1786.

IV

While the ethical and historical aspects of Smith's course are important in their own right, the material so far reveiwed may also help to establish at least one set of linkages with the economic analysis. The stage of commerce, already addressed in the treatment of jurisprudence, helps to explain the structure of the modern economy and the emergence of a situation where 'Every man . . . lives by exchanging, or becomes in some measure a merchant' (WN, I. iv. 1). If Smith gave prominence to the role of self-interest in this context and in this area of activity, his hearers would be aware that the drive to better our condition had a social reference; that 'it is chiefly from this regard to the sentiments of mankind, that we pursue riches and avoid poverty' (TMS, I. iii. 2. 1). Later in the book the position was further clarified when Smith stated that we tend to approve the *means*, as well as the *ends*, of ambition. 'Hence . . . that eminent esteem with which all men naturally regard a steady perseverance in the practice of frugality, industry and application'; an esteem which is alone capable of sustaining such conduct, since in the normal course of events the 'pleasure which we are to enjoy ten years hence interests us so little in comparison with that which we may enjoy today' (TMS, IV. 2. 8).

In the same vein, the lectures on public jurisprudence help to specify the nature of the required system of positive law and the form of government or magistracy needed to administer it. In sum, the ethical and jurisprudential arguments provided the premises for what was to follow.

At a purely analytical level, the *order* of subjects followed that already established by Francis Hutcheson but with one very important difference: in Smith's hands the economic analysis properly so-called is formally separated from the discussion of jurisprudential issues and treated as a subject in its own right.[12] But Smith did follow the precedent established by his old professor, in proceeding from the discussion of the division of labour to the associated problems of exchange, money, and the determinants of price. The latter area is amongst the most notable of Smith's early contributions to theory, and developed in terms of the distinction between market and natural prices before the lecturer went on to demonstrate a clear grasp of the general interdependence of economic phenomena.

But the analysis has its deficiencies; arguably less sophisticated than the work done by Sir James Steuart in the late 1750s, Smith's account is also innocent of a distinction between factors of production and categories of return, including capital and profit.[13] Nor does the analysis feature what would now be described as a macroeconomic model.

Since we know the state of Smith's knowledge in 1763–4 when he left Glasgow, it is possible to gauge quite accurately the debt which he owed to the physiocrats, and especially to Quesnai and Turgot. When Smith arrived in Paris in 1766 for a stay of some ten months, terminated by the sad death of one of his charges, Hew Scott, he met leading members of the Physiocratic School at the very height of their influence. In 1766 Quesnai was at work on the *Analyse*, a development of the earlier *Tableau Economique*, while Turgot was developing the work which became the *Reflections on the Formation and Distribution of Riches* – said to have been written for the benefit of two overseas students (from China).[14] Given Smith's knowledge of economics and his own appreciation of systematic argument, this contact must have been one of the most important and exciting of his life. Whatever may be made of this conjecture, it is undoubtedly true that the analytic structure of the WN represented an enormous advance as compared to the lectures; a step removed from the essentially pre-physiocratic structure of Sir James Steuart's *Principles* despite the latter's publication date of 1767.

The familiar tale need not detain us; it is sufficient to be reminded that in the WN the theory of price and allocation was developed in terms of a model which made due allowance for distinct factors of production (land, labour, capital) and for the appropriate forms of return (rent, wages, profit). This point, now so obvious, struck Smith as novel and permitted him to develop an analysis of the allocative mechanism which ran in terms of interrelated adjustments in both factor and commodity markets. The resulting version of general equilibrium also allowed Smith to move from the discussion of 'micro' to that of 'macro' economic issues, and to develop a model of the 'circular flow' which relies heavily on the distinction between fixed and circulating capital.

But these terms, which were applied to the activities of individual undertakers, were transformed in their meaning by their application to society at large. Working in terms of period analysis, Smith in effect represented the working of the economic process as a series of activities and transactions which linked the main socioeconomic groups (proprietors, undertakers, and wage labour). In Smith's terms, current purchases in effect withdrew consumption and investment goods from the circulating capital of society, which were in turn replaced by virtue of current productive activity.

Looked at from one point of view, the analysis taken as a whole provides one of the most dramatic examples of the doctrine of 'unintended social outcomes', or the working of the 'invisible hand'. The individual undertaker, seeking the most efficient allocation of resources contributes to over-all economic efficiency; the merchant's reaction to price signals helps to ensure that the allocation of resources accurately reflects the structure of consumer preferences; the drive to better our condition contributes to economic growth. Looked at from another perspective, the work can be seen to have resulted in a great conceptual system linking together logically separate, yet interrelated, problems such as price, allocation, distribution, macro-statics and macro-dynamics; points which are neatly brought out by, for example, Richardson (1975) and Lowe (1975).[15]

But the argument is also buttressed by a series of judgements as to *probable* patterns of behaviour and *actual* trends of events. It was Smith's firm opinion, for example, that, in a situation where there was tolerable security, 'The sole use of money is to circulate consumable goods. By means of it, provisions, materials, and finished work, are bought and sold, and distributed to their proper consumers' (WN, II. iii. 23). In the same way he contended that the savings generated during any (annual) period would always be matched by investment (WN, II, iii. 18); a key assumption of the classical system. In the case of Great Britain, Smith also pointed out that real wages had progressively increased during the eighteenth century, and that high wages were to be approved of as a contribution to productivity (WN, I. viii. 44). He concluded, in a famous passage:

> The natural effort of every individual to better his own condition, when suffered to exert itself with freedom and security, is so powerful a principle, that it is alone, and without any assistance, not only capable of carrying on the society to wealth and prosperity, but of surmounting a hundred impertinent obstructions with which the folly of human laws too often incumbers its operations; though the effect of these obstructions is always more or less either to encroach

upon its freedom, or to diminish its security. In Great Britain industry is perfectly secure; and though it is far from being perfectly free, it is as free or freer than in any other part of Europe (WN, IV. v. b. 43).

As Dugald Stewart has reminded us, that claim for economic liberty which is so eloquently stated in the *Wealth of Nations* (IV. ix. 51) dates back to Smith's early days in Edinburgh (Stewart, IV. 25), between 1748 and 1751.

PART II: POLICY

I

Smith's prescriptions, with regard to economic policy, followed directly on the analysis just considered in the sense that he called on governments to minimise their 'impertinent' obstructions to the pursuits of individuals. In particular he recommended that the statutes of apprenticeship, and the privileges of corporations, should be repealed on the ground that they adversely affect the working of the allocative mechanism: 'The statute of apprenticeship obstructs the free circulation of labour from one employment to another, even in the same place. The exclusive privileges of corporations obstruct it from one place to another, even in the same employment' (WN, I. x. c. 42). In the same chapter Smith pointed to the barriers to the deployment of labour generated by the Poor Laws and the Laws of Settlement (WN, IV. ii. 42).

He also objected to positions of privilege, such as monopoly powers, which he regarded as creatures of the civil law. The institution was again represented as impolitic and unjust: unjust in that a position of monopoly is a position of unfair advantage, and impolitic in that the prices at which goods so controlled are 'upon every occasion the highest which can be got' (WN, I. vii. 27). In this context we may usefully distinguish Smith's objection to monopoly in general from his criticism of one manifestation of it; namely, the mercantile system, described as the 'modern system' of policy, best understood 'in our own country and in our own times' (WN, IV. 2). Once again, Smith objected to a policy of constraint in noting that such a policy was liable to 'that general objection which may be made to all the different expedients of the mercantile system; the objection of forcing some part of the industry of the country into a channel less advantageous than that in which it would run of its own accord' (WN, IV. v. a. 24).

On the other hand, Smith was prepared to justify a wide range of policies, all of which have been carefully catalogued by Viner in his justifiably famous article on 'Adam Smith and Laisser Faire' (1927). Smith was prepared to justify the use of stamps on plate and linen as the most effectual guarantee of quality (WN, I. x. c. 13), the compulsory regulation of mortgages (WN, V. ii. h. 17), the legal enforcement of contracts (WN, I. ix. 16) and government control of the coinage. In addition, he defended the granting of temporary monopolies to mercantile groups, to the inventors of new machines, and, not surprisingly, to the authors of new books (WN, V. i. e. 30).

Three broad areas of intervention are of particular interest however, in the sense that they involve issues of general principle. First, Smith advised governments that where they were faced with taxes imposed by their competitors, retaliation could be in order especially if such an action had the effect of ensuring the 'repeal of the high duties or prohibitions complained of. The recovery of a great foreign market will generally more than compensate the transitory inconvenience of paying dearer during a short time for some sorts of goods' (WN, IV. ii. 39). Secondly, Smith advocated the use of taxation, not as a means of raising revenue, but as a means of controlling certain activities, and of compensating for what would now be known as a defective telescopic faculty. In the name of the public interest, Smith supported taxes on the retail sale of liquor in order to discourage the multiplication of alehouses (WN, V. ii. g. 4) and differential rates on ale and spirits in order to reduce the sale of the latter (WN, V. ii. k. 50). To take another example, he advocated taxes on those proprietors who demanded rents in kind, and on those leases which prescribe a certain form of cultivation. In the same vein, we find Smith advocating that the practice of selling a future revenue for the sake of ready money should be discouraged on the ground that it reduced the working capital of the tenant and at the same time transferred a capital sum to those who would use it for the purposes of consumption (WN, V. ii. c. 12).

Smith was also well aware that the modern version of the 'circular flow' depended on paper money and on credit; in effect a system of 'dual circulation' involving a complex of transactions linking producers and merchants, and dealers and consumers (WN, II. ii. 88) It is in this context that Smith advocated control over the rate of interest, set in such a way as to ensure that 'sober people are universally preferred, as borrowers, to prodigals and projectors' (WN, II. iv. 15).[16] He was also willing to regulate the small note issue in the interest of a stable banking system. To those who objected to this proposal, he replied that the interests of the community required it, and concluded that 'the obligation of building party walls, in order to prevent the communication of fire, is a violation of natural liberty, exactly of the same kind (as) the regulations of the banking trade which are here proposed' (WN, II. ii. 94). Although Smith's monetary analysis is not regarded as amongst the strongest of his contributions, it should be remembered that the witness of the collapse of the Ayr Bank was acutely aware of the problems generated by a sophisticated credit structure and that it was in this context that Smith articulated a very general principle, namely, that 'those exertions of the natural liberty of a few individuals, which might endanger the security of the whole society, are, and ought to be, restrained by the laws of all governments; of the most free, as well as of the most despotical' (WN, II. ii. 94).

Finally, emphasis should be given to Smith's contention that a major responsibility of government must be the provision of certain public works and institutions for facilitating the commerce of the society which were 'of such a nature, that the profit could never repay the expence to any individual or small number of individuals, and which it, therefore, cannot be expected that any individual or small number of individuals should erect or maintain' (WN, V. i. c. 1). The examples of public works which Smith provided include such items as roads, bridges, canals and harbours – all thoroughly in keeping with the conditions of the time and with Smith's emphasis on the importance of transport as a contribution to the effective operation of the market and to the process of economic growth. But although the list is short by modern standards, the discussion of what may be called the 'principles of provision' is of interest for two main reasons. First, Smith suggested that public works or services should be provided where the market fails to do so; secondly, he insisted that attention should be given to the requirements of equity and efficiency.

With regard to equity, Smith argued that works such as highways, bridges and canals should be paid for by those who use them and in proportion to the wear and tear occasioned – an expression of his general principle that he who benefits should pay. He also defended direct payment on the grounds of efficiency. Only by this means, he argued, would it be possible to ensure that services are provided where there is a recognisable need (WN, V. i. d. 6). As Nathan Rosenberg pointed out in a classic article, Smith also gave a great deal of attention to the argument that institutional arrangements be 'so structured as to engage the motives and interests of those concerned' (1960, W, ii. p. 114). Smith tirelessly emphasised the point that in every trade and profession 'the exertion of the greater part of those who exercise it, is always in proportion to the necessity they are under of making that exertion' (WN, V. i. f. 4) – teachers, judges, professors, and civil servants alike. In sum, the role of the Visible Hand was scarcely neglected: and more was to come.

II

So far we have treated the linkage between the parts of Smith's course in a particular way; that is, by looking forward from the ethics and the jurisprudence to the economic analysis, and thus to the policy prescriptions which have just been considered. But there is also a sense in which it is useful to look back to the ethics and the jurisprudence from the vantage point supplied by the *Wealth of Nations*. Two examples may be used to illustrate this important subject, both of which contribute to confirm that the component parts of Smith's system should be taken as a whole.

With regard to the ethics, the most important aspect is surely to be found in Smith's concern with what is now rather loosely known as the 'alienation' problem.[17]

It will be recalled that for Smith moral judgement depends on our capacity for acts of imaginative sympathy, and that such acts can therefore only take place within the context of some social group (TMS, III. 1. 3). However, Smith also observed that the mechanism of the impartial spectator might well break down in the context of the modern economy, due in part to the size of some of the manufacturing units and of the cities which housed them.

Smith observed that in the actual circumstances of modern society, the poor man could find himself in a situation where the 'mirror' of society (TMS, III. 1. 3) was ineffective. As Smith noted, the 'man of rank and fortune is by his station the distinguished member of a great society, who attend to every part of his conduct, and who thereby oblige him to attend to every part himself . . . He dare not do any thing which would disgrace or discredit him in it, and he is obliged to a very strict observation of that species of morals, whether liberal or austere, which the general consent of this society prescribes to persons of his rank and fortune'. But, Smith went on, the 'man of low condition', while 'his conduct may be attended to' so long as he is a member of a country village, 'as soon as he comes into a great city, he is sunk in obscurity and darkness. His conduct is observed and attended to by nobody, and he is therefore very likely to neglect it himself, and to abandon himself to every sort of low profligacy and vice' (WN, V. i. g. 12).

If the problems of solitude and isolation consequent on the growth of cities explain Smith's first group of points, a related trend in the shape of the division of labour helps to account for the second. It will be recalled that in discussing the division of labour Smith had emphasised that the undertaker or entrepreneur would naturally endeavour 'both to make among his workmen the most proper distribution of employment, and to furnish them with the best machines which he can either invent or afford to purchase' (WN, II. Intro. 4). While the object is gain to the employer, there is inevitably a gain to society at large in the shape of improved productivity. But, Smith also noted that this important source of economic benefit (which is emphasised to an extraordinary degree in the *Wealth of Nations*) could also involve social costs. Or, as Smith put it in one of the most famous passages from the *Wealth of Nations*:

> In the progress of the division of labour, the employment of the far greater part of those who live by labour, that is, of the great body of the people, comes to be confined to a few very simple operations; frequently to one or two. But the understandings of the greater part of men are necessarily formed by their ordinary employments. The man whose whole life is spent in performing a few simple operations, of which the effects too are, perhaps, always the same, or very nearly the same, has no occasion to exert his understanding, or to exercise his invention in finding out expedients for removing difficulties which never occur. He naturally loses, therefore, the habit of such exertion, and generally becomes as stupid and ignorant as it is possible for a human creature to become (WN, V. i. f. 50).

Smith also drew attention to the decline of martial spirit, consequent on the fourth economic stage, noting that the person thus affected:

> is as much mutilated and deformed in his mind, as another is in his body, who is either deprived of some of its most essential members, or has lost the use of them. He is obviously the more wretched and miserable of the two; because happiness and misery, which reside

altogether in the mind, must necessarily depend more upon the
healthful or unhealthful, the mutilated or entire state of the mind,
than upon that of the body (WN, V. i. f. 60).

Issues such as these are obviously important in any discussion of
welfare and clearly bear directly on man's capacity for moral
judgement. Equally, these areas of concern were to be associated with
some important policy prescriptions. It was in this connection that
Smith recommended the *imposition* of 'some sort of probation, even in
the higher and more difficult sciences, to be undergone by every
person before he was permitted to exercise any liberal profession, or
before he could be received as a candidate for any honourable office of
trust or profit' (WN, V. i. g. 14). In the same vein he defended some
sort of military education, and the view that the poorer classes be
taught the 'most essential parts of education: to read, write, and
account' together with the 'elementary parts of geometry and mechan-
icks' (WN, V. i. f. 54, 55). Indeed, he suggested that:

> The publick can impose upon almost the whole body of the people
> the necessity of acquiring those most essential parts of education, by
> obliging every man to undergo an examination or probation in them
> before he can obtain the freedom in any corporation, or be allowed
> to set up any trade either in a village or town corporate (WN, V. i. f.
> 57).

Smith was also prepared to encourage liberty 'to all those who for their
own interest would attempt, without scandal or indecency, to amuse
and divert the people by painting, poetry, musick, dancing; by all sorts
of dramatic representations . . .' (WN, V. i. g. 15).

III

The historical dimension of Smith's work also affects the treatment of
policy, noting as he did that in every society subject to a process of
transition, 'Laws frequently continue in force long after the circumstances, which first gave occasion to them, and which could alone
render them reasonable, are no more' (WN, III. ii. 4). In such cases
Smith suggested that arrangements which were once appropriate but
are no longer so should be removed, citing as examples the laws of
succession and entail.

In a similar way, the treatment of justice and defence, both central services to be organised by the government, are clearly related to the discussion of the stages of history, an important part of the argument in the latter case being that a gradual change in the economic and social structure had necessitated the formal provision of an army (WN, V. i. a, b).

But perhaps the most striking and interesting features emerge when it is recalled that for Smith the fourth economic stage could be seen to be associated with a particular form of social and political structure which influences the *outline of government* and the context within which it must function. It may be recalled in this connection that Smith associated the fourth economic stage with the advent of freedom in the 'present sense of the term'; that is, with the elimination of the relation of direct dependence which had been a characteristic of the feudal agrarian period. Politically, the significant and associated development appeared to be the diffusion of power consequent on the emergence of new forms of wealth which, *at least in the peculiar circumstances of England*, had been reflected in the increased significance of the House of Commons.

Smith recognised that in this context government was a complex instrument; that the pursuit of office was itself a 'dazzling object of ambition': a competitive game with as its object the attainment of 'the great prizes which sometimes come from the wheel of the great state lottery of British politicks' (WN, IV. vii. c. 75).

Yet for Smith, the most important point was that the same economic forces which had served to elevate the House of Commons to a superior degree of influence had also served to make it an important focal point for sectional interests – a development which could seriously affect the legislation which was passed and thus affect that extensive view of the common good which ought ideally to direct the activities of Parliament.

It is recognised in the *Wealth of Nations* that the landed, moneyed, manufacturing, and mercantile groups all constitute special interests which could impinge on the working of government. Smith referred frequently to their 'clamorous importunity', and went so far as to suggest that the power possessed by employers generally could seriously disadvantage other classes in the society.[18] As he put it, 'Whenever the legislature attempts to regulate the differences between masters and their workmen, its counsellors are always the masters. When the regulation, therefore, is in favour of the workmen, it is always just and equitable; but it is sometimes otherwise when in

favour of the masters' (WN, I. x. c. 61; compare I. viii. 12, 13). Smith
thus insisted that any legislative proposals emanating from this class:

> ought always to be listened to with great precaution, and ought
> never to be adopted till after having been long and carefully
> examined, not only with the most scrupulous, but with the most
> suspicious attention. It comes from an order of men, whose interest
> is never exactly the same with that of the publick, who have
> generally an interest to deceive and even to oppress the publick, and
> who accordingly have, upon many occasions, both deceived and
> oppressed it (WN, I. i. xi. p. 10).

If governments were often prodigal, corrupt and inefficient, it is also
interesting to note how often Smith referred to the constraints
presented by the 'confirmed habits and prejudices' of the people, and
to the necessity of adjusting legislation to what 'the interests,
prejudices, and temper of the times would admit of' (WN, IV. v. b. 40,
53; V. i. g. 8). Smith returned to this point in Part VI of TMS, in a
passage added in the last year of his life (VI. ii. 2. 16), perhaps in
recognition of the fact that governments on the English model are
particularly sensitive to public opinion (Compare WN, IV. vii. c. 66).

Government failure, it would seem, is likely to be as acute a problem
as the failure of the market (see West, 1976) – and it may be noted that
there is no thesis of 'natural harmony' in the sphere of Smith's political
analysis.

CONCLUSION

It is hardly surprising that we should be tempted to regard Smith
primarily as an economist. The *Wealth of Nations* did, after all, provide
the basis of classical economics in the form of a coherent, all-
embracing account of complex phenomena. As Viner has pointed out,
the source of Smith's originality lies in his 'detailed and elaborate
application to the wilderness of economic phenomena of the unifying
concept of a co-ordinated and mutually interdependent system of
cause and effect relationships which philosophers and theologians had
already applied to the world in general' (1927, W, i. p. 143).

It was this aspect of the *Wealth of Nations* which led Smith's
biographer, Dugald Stewart, to comment on its beautiful progression
of ideas. and to draw a parallel between it and the mathematical and

physical sciences (Stewart, IV. 22). In the words of another contemporary (and trenchant critic), Smith's completed work could be regarded as an 'Institute of the Principia *of those laws of motion*, by which the operations of the community are directed and regulated, and by which they should be examined'.[19] The analogy with Newton is particularly apt, especially in view of Smith's admiring assessment in the concluding sections of the *Astronomy*, and in the *Lectures on Rhetoric* (LRBL, ii. 133–4).

Smith did make extensive use of mechanistic *analogies*, notably in the *Theory of Moral Sentiments* and may be seen to have employed a scientific *model* in developing the equilibrium theory of price and allocation – once described by Schumpeter as 'by far the best piece of economic theory turned out by A. Smith' (Schumpeter, 1954, p. 189). But the work of a man who, like Marshall after him, was so interested in the processes of change can hardly be said to have been dominated by the technique just described. Rather Smith admired Newton as a philosopher who had brought order to the apparent chaos of unrelated appearances. This was also Smith's aim:

Systems in many respects resemble machines. A machine is a little system, created to perform, as well as to connect together, in reality, those different movements and effects which the artist has occasion for. A system is an imaginary machine invented to connect together in the fancy those different movements and effects which are already in reality performed (*Astronomy*, IV. 19).

But Smith, the supreme impartial spectator, was also deeply interested in the (constant) principles of human nature. He was well aware of the 'beauty of a systematical arrangement of different observations connected by a few common principles' (WN, V. i. f. 25) and elsewhere likened the pleasure to be derived from a great system of thought to that acquired from listening to a 'well composed concerto of instrumental music' (*Imitative Arts*, II. 30). At the same time, he was acutely aware of the tyranny of theory and of analogy (*Astronomy*, IV. 35) and of the ease with which 'the learned give up the evidence of their senses to preserve the coherence of the ideas of their imagination' (ibid.). Schumpeter, often so grudging in his appraisal of Smith, was surely correct in saying that no one 'can have an adequate idea of Smith's intellectual stature who does not know' the *Essays on Philosophical Subjects*. He added, somewhat spoiling the effect, 'I also venture to say that, were it not for the undeniable fact, nobody would credit the author of the *Wealth of Nations* with the power to write them' (Schumpeter, 1954, p. 182).

But this is at the level of theory; of no less importance were Smith's policy prescriptions and his restatement of an older claim, namely, that individuals should be freed from the impertinent obstructions too often placed in their way by outmoded institutions and by the folly of governments.

The celebration to mark the fiftieth anniversary of the book showed wide and continuing acceptance of the doctrines of free trade, while it is also salutary to recall that the Political Economy Club was founded in 1821 'to support its principles'. In 1876, at a dinner held by the Club to mark the centenary of the *Wealth of Nations* one speaker identified free trade as the most important consequence of the work done by 'this simple Glasgow professor'. It was also predicted that 'there will be what may be called a large negative development of Political Economy tending to produce an important beneficial effect; and that is, such a development of Political Economy as will reduce the functions of government within a smaller and smaller compass'. It is hardly surprising that a contemporary leader in the *Times* could claim that 'the time is not yet distant when the supremacy of Adam Smith's teaching shall surpass his largest hopes'.[20]

Nor is Professor Stigler's famous claim, uttered on the occasion of the 1976 celebrations, lightly to be dismissed: 'Adam Smith is alive and well and living in Chicago' (compare Winch, 1978, 1985).

It could be argued that Smith's critique of the mercantile system can only be fully understood against the background of his own *theory* of rhetoric; as a remarkable essay in persuasion explicitly designed to influence the government of his and later days.[21] Few have been able to resist the splendid oratory of Smith's critique of intervention or the flourish with which he enjoined the sovereign to discharge himself from a duty:

in the attempting to perform which he must always be exposed to innumerable delusions, and for the proper performance of which no human wisdom or knowledge could ever be sufficient; the duty of superintending the industry of private people, and of directing it towards the employments most suitable to the interest of the society (WN, IV. ix. 51).

But three broad points may be made by way of qualification to the impression thus left. To begin with, there can be no argument with

Viner's contention that 'Smith in general believed that there was, to say the least, a strong presumption against government intervention' – or that this judgement was directly related to Smith's knowledge of *contemporary British experience*. Viner also reminded his auditors during the course of the Chicago conference of 1926 that:

> Adam Smith was not a doctrinaire advocate of laisser-faire. He saw a wide and elastic range of activity for government, and he was prepared to extend it even further if government, by improving its standard of competence, honesty, and public spirit, showed itself entitled to wider responsibilities (1927, W, i. p. 164).

Indeed Professor Macfie once remarked, on reviewing Viner's list of specific policies garnered from the *Wealth of Nations*, that 'they add up to suggest a formidable state autocracy; a socialist spread of controls that would make some modern socialist's eyes pop' (1967a, W, i. p. 348). Alec Macfie was indulging his dry humour – while making a point that finds a more serious echo in Eric Roll's judgement that Smith and Keynes 'would find much common ground in respect of the broad principles that should guide the management of the economy' (Roll, 1976, W, ii. p. 154).

Such judgements reflect the care with which earlier commentators actually read the text; they reflect a knowledge of the *agenda* which Smith established, and more importantly, of the general principles (reviewed in Part II above) which he employed in establishing that *agenda*. It is these principles which we must confront before claiming Smith as a writer whose views on the role of the state are still strictly relevant given the conditions which now obtain. As Seligman reminded readers of the 1910 edition of the *Wealth of Nations*, 'Adam Smith's doctrine of natural law in economics created, especially in the hands of his followers, a more or less rigid and absolute economic system. Recent investigation has called attention to the changing conditions of time and place, and has emphasised the principles of relativity rather than of absolutism' (Seligman, 1910, p. xv). Smith's own work was marked by an extreme relativity in perspective – dominant features both of the treatment of scientific knowledge in the *Astronomy*, and of his analysis of rules of behaviour in TMS.

Secondly, it could be argued that if the business of claim and counterclaim with respect to Smith's authority can never be clear cut, there is one general problem which Smith isolated and which raises a question of whose universal relevance there can be little doubt.

Without giving the matter undue prominence, it would be agreed that market failure helps to justify Smith's prescriptions, whether we are considering the regulation of the rate of interest, of the banking trade, the provision of canals, education, state-supported entertainment, or public health (WN, V. i. f. 60).

Now it will be noted that when Smith speaks of market failure, he generally refers to failure to provide important *services*, as distinct from *opportunities* for investment or employment. He was well aware that the economy was a system in movement involving risk and uncertainty and that crises of commercial confidence could not be discounted. But Smith's views on economic adjustment were long run; certainly much longer-run than those adumbrated by his great 'rival in fame', Sir James Steuart. They were also set against a background of economic growth in *Britain*. In contrast, Sir James Steuart had a wealth of experience of conditions on the Continent, largely as a result of exile, and was, I believe, profoundly influenced by cameralist (as distinct from mercantilist) literature. As Schumpeter once said of von Justi (1717–71),

He was much more concerned than A. Smith with the practical problems of government action in the short-run vicissitudes of his time and country . . . His laisser faire policy was a laisser faire plus watchfulness, his private enterprise economy a machine that was logically automatic but exposed the breakdowns and hitches which his government was to stand ready to mend . . . his vision of economic policy might look like laisser faire with the nonsense left out (Schumpeter, 1954, p. 172).

While there may still be misguided souls who would reject this assessment, as applied to Steuart, there can be no doubt that if Steuart and Smith adopted different perspectives on the economic process, they could have agreed on at least *one* proposition: namely that governments must intervene in the event of market failure, simply because there is no alternative agency. The problem which remains to perplex us, is exactly that which exercised our eighteenth century predecessors and over which they differed: it is the problem of *how* and with what degree of confidence, we can identify just where and when markets (or governments) *have* failed, and then of deciding what should or should not be done.

The final point relates back to the structure of Smith's broader system of thought. While the modern reader has to make a considerable effort to understand Smith's intentions, students of his course in Glasgow, and perhaps contemporary readers of his works, would quite readily perceive that the different parts were important of themselves and also that they display a certain pattern of inter-dependence. As we have seen, the ethical argument indicates the manner in which general rules of conduct emerge, and postulates the need for a system of force-backed law, appropriately administered. The treatment of jurisprudence showed the manner in which government emerged and developed through time, while throwing some light on the actual content of rules of behaviour.

It would also be evident to Smith's students that the treatment of *economics* was based upon psychological judgements (such as the desire for status) which are only explained in the ethics, and that this branch of Smith's argument takes as given the particular socioeconomic structure which is appropriate to the fourth economic stage; that of commerce. This kind of perspective can only be attained if we examine the logical progression of ideas as outlined in the lectures on ethics, jurisprudence, and economics as they unfolded in the order in which they are known to have been delivered. Equally, the analysis of the *Wealth of Nations*, and especially the treatment of public policy, is transformed in its meaning when seen not merely as a development of the earlier treatment of economics, but also in terms of the appropriate ethical and constitutional background: a background which helps to expose something of the moral, political, and historical dimensions of the book.

Such themes look back towards the 'civic humanist' dimension of which we took note at the outset[22] and forward to modern concerns with the working of the political process and the revision of the liberal creed. If Smith is a liberal, the style is perhaps that of Green who was concerned with the distinction between negative and positive freedom – and the role of the state in ensuring the latter condition.[23] If he is a socialist, as Alec Macfie once dared humorously to claim, surely he was a Fabian.

But even if we leave aside the question of which label applies best to Adam Smith, proponents of different political philosophies might do well to bear in mind one of his more celebrated warnings:

The man of system . . . is apt to be very wise in his own conceit; and is often so enamoured with the supposed beauty of his own ideal plan of government, that he cannot suffer the smallest deviation from it. He seems to imagine that he can arrange the different members of a great society with as much ease as the hand arranges the different pieces upon a chess-board. He does not consider that the pieces upon the chess-board have no other principle of motion besides that which the hand impresses upon them; but that, in the great chess-board of human society, every single piece has a principle of motion of its own, altogether different from that which the legislature might chuse to impress upon it. If those two principles coincide and act in the same direction, the game of human society will go on easily and harmoniously, and is very likely to be happy and successful. If they are opposite or different, the game will go on miserably, and the society must be at all times in the highest degree of disorder (TMS, VI. ii. 2. 17).

REFERENCES

References to Wood (1983) give date of article on first publication, followed by the reference 'W', volume and page number. But no attempt is made here to make exhaustive reference to such an extensive and valuable collection. References to Smith's works employ the usages of the Glasgow edition, that is,

WN = *The Wealth of Nations*; TMS = *Theory of Moral Sentiments*; Astronomy = 'The History of Astronomy', from *Essays on Philosophical Subjects* (EPS); Stewart = Dugald Stewart, 'Account of the Life and Writings of Adam Smith'; LJ (A) = *Lectures on Jurisprudence*, Report dated 1762–63; LJ (B) = *Lectures on Jurisprudence*, Report dated 1766; LRBL = *Lectures on Rhetoric and Belles Lettres*; Corr. = *Correspondence of Adam Smith*; EAS = *Essays on Adam Smith*, ed. A. S. Skinner and T. Wilson (1975).

In the Glasgow edition, WN was edited by R. H. Campbell, A. S. Skinner, and W. B. Todd (1976); TMS, by D. D. Raphael and A. L. Macfie (1976); Corr., by E. C. Mossner and I. S. Ross (1977); EPS, by W. P. D. Wightman (1980); LJ (A) and LJ (B) by R. L. Meek, D. D. Raphael, and P. G. Stein (1978), and LRBL, by J. C. Bryce (1983). Oxford University Press.

References to Corr. give letter number and date.

References to LJ and LRBL give volume and page number from the MS.

All other references provide section, chapter, and paragraph number in order to facilitate the use of different editions.

For example:

Astronomy, II. 4 = History of Astronomy, Section II, para. 4

Stewart, I. 12 = Dugald Stewart 'Account', Section I, para. 12

TMS, I. i. 5. 5 = TMS, Part I, section i, chapter 5, para. 5

WN, V. i. f. 26 = WN, Book V, chapter i, section 6, para. 26.

NOTES

1. I am indebted to R. D. C. Black, Sir Alec Cairncross, D. D. Raphael, Thomas Wilson and Donald Winch for a number of helpful comments.
2. The present writer's views on the interrelationships are set out in Skinner (1979); and on the role of the state see Skinner (1974, 1979, ch. 9, and 1984).
3. LRBL was discovered by Lothian in 1958 and edited by him in 1963.
4. For comment, see Howell (1969).
5. For a review of some of the relevant literature, see Skinner (1979), chapter 2.
6. LJ (A) was also discovered by Lothian in 1958, but first appeared in published form 20 years later.
7. For comment, see T. D. Campbell (1971).
8. The editors of TMS have drawn attention to the fact that Smith gave progressively more emphasis to the role of conscience.
9. See especially Meek (1967, 1976 and 1977).
10. Curiously, the order of subjects changes between LJ (A) and LJ (B). In the former case, the treatment of public law follows that of private law: in LJ (B), given in Smith's last session, the order is reversed.
11. See Reisman (1976). The political dimension in this discussion is addressed by Winch (1978) and by Forbes (1975); the link with economic development by Billet (1975).
12. This point is brought out by Enzo Pesciarelli, of the University of Ancona, in a forthcoming article in the *Scottish Journal of Political Economy*. Hutcheson's economics are commented on by W. R. Scott (1900) and W. L. Taylor (1965).
13. Sir James Steuart's *Principles of Political Economy* was published in 1767 although the first two books were completed, in Germany, by 1759 (see Skinner, 1966).
14. Quesnai's works cited in the text are translated in Meek (1962) Turgot's *Reflections* are translated in Meek (1973).
15. The present writer's views on the organisation of the 'system' are set out in Skinner (1979), chapter 7.
16. It was of course this argument, which Smith did not change in later editions, which led to Bentham's letter XIII in the *Defence of Usury* (1787). The relevant materials have been collected by the editors of Corr. in Appendix C.
17. A representative example of this literature is the article by West (1975) (see also Winch, 1978, chapter 5).
18. This theme has been developed by Samuels (1973).
19. Thomas Pownall (1776), former Governor of Massachusetts. Pownall's *Letter* appears in Corr., Appendix A.
20. This paragraph is drawn from Black (1976) pp. 47–51.
21. The present writer's views on this aspect of Smith's work are set out in Skinner (1979), chapter 8.
22. This approach is particularly associated with the work of John Pocock (1972) (compare his contribution in Hont and Ignatieff, 1983, and John Robertson, 1983).

23. In a lecture on 'Liberal Legislation and Freedom of Contract' delivered in 1880, T. H. Green introduced a distinction between negative and positive freedom. Negative freedom is defined as freedom from restraint, and positive freedom as 'a power or capacity of doing or enjoying something worth doing or enjoying'. Green argued, as Smith may be seen to do, that the latter state may require the attention of government (Green, 1906 in *Works of Thomas Green*, vol. 3, pp. 370–71). The whole lecture still repays scrutiny.

AUTHORITIES

Anspach, R. 'The Implications of the *Theory of Moral Sentiments* for Adam Smith's Economic Thought' (first published in the *History of Political Economy*, vol. 4 (1972); *Wood*, vol. 1 (1983) pp. 438–58).

Billet, L. 'Political Order and Economic Development: Reflections on Adam Smith's "Wealth of Nations"', *Political Studies*, vol. 23 (1975) pp. 430–41.

Billet, L. 'The Just Economy: The Moral Basis of the *Wealth of Nations*' (first published in *Review of Social Economy*, vol. 34 (1976); *Wood*, vol. 2 (1983) pp. 205–20).

Black, R. D. C. 'Smith's Contribution in Historical Perspective', in T. Wilson and A. Skinner (eds) *The Market and the State: Essays in Honour of Adam Smith* (Oxford: Oxford University Press, 1976) pp. 42–63.

Campbell, T. D. *Adam Smith's Science of Morals* (Oxford: Oxford University Press, 1971).

Campbell, W. F. 'Adam Smith's Theory of Justice, Prudence, and Beneficence' (first published in *American Economic Review*, vol. 57 (1967); *Wood*, vol. 1 (1983) pp. 351–6).

Forbes, D. 'Sceptical Whiggism, Commerce and Liberty', *Essays on Adam Smith* (1975) pp. 179–201.

Gee, A. 'Adam Smith: Critical Assessments', *Scottish Journal of Political Economy*, vol. 32 (1985) pp. 209–18.

Green, T. H. in R. L. Nettleship (ed.), *Works of Thomas Green*, 3 vols (London: Longman, 1906).

Haakonssen, K. *The Science of a Legislator: The Natural Jurisprudence of David Hume and Adam Smith* (Cambridge: Cambridge University Press, 1981).

Hont, I. and Ignatieff, M. *Wealth and Virtue: The Shaping of Political Economy in the Scottish Enlightenment* (Cambridge: Cambridge University Press, 1983).

Howell, W. S. 'Adam Smith's Lectures on Rhetoric: An Historical Assessment', *Speech Monographs*, vol. 36 (1969) pp. 393–418, and *Essays on Adam Smith* (1969), pp. 11–43.

Lindgren, J. R. *The Social Philosophy of Adam Smith* (The Hague: Martinus Nijhoff, 1973).

Lowe, A. 'Adam Smith's System of Equilibrium Growth', *Essays on Adam Smith* (1975) pp. 415–25.

Macfie, A. L. 'The Moral Justification of Free Enterprise. A Lay Sermon on an Adam Smith Text' (first published in *Scottish Journal of Political Economy*, vol. 14 (1967a); *Wood*, vol. 1 (1983) pp. 342–50.

Macfie, A. L. *The Individual in Society* (London: Allen & Unwin, 1967b).

Meek, R. L. *The Economics of Physiocracy: Essays and Translations* (London: Allen & Unwin, 1962).

Meek, R. L. *Economics and Ideology and Other Essays: Studies in the Development of Economic Thought* (London: Chapman Hall, 1967).

Meek, R. L. *Turgot on Progress, Sociology and Economics* (Cambridge: Cambridge University Press, 1973).

Meek, R. L. *Social Science and the Ignoble Savage* (Cambridge: Cambridge University Press, 1976).

Meek, R. L. *Smith, Marx and After* (London: Chapman Hall, 1977).

Morrow, G. 'Adam Smith: Moralist and Philospher' (first published in *Journal of Political Economy*, vol. 35 (1927); *Wood*, vol. 1 (1983), pp. 168–81).

Pocock, J. 'Virtue and Commerce in the Eighteenth Century', *Journal of Interdisciplinary History*, vol. 3, (1972), pp. 119–34.

Recktenwald, H. 'An Adam Smith Renaissance anno 1976? The Bicentenary Output – A reappraisal of his Scholarship' (first published in *Journal of Economic Literature*, vol. 16 (1978); *Wood* vol. 4 (1983) pp. 249–77).

Reisman, D. *Adam Smith's Sociological Economics* (London: Croom Helm, 1976).

Richardson, G. B., 'Adam Smith on Competition and Increasing Returns', *Essays on Adam Smith* (1975) pp. 350–60.

Robertson, J. 'Scottish Political Economy Beyond the Civic Tradition: Government and Economic Development in the *Wealth of Nations*', *History of Political Thought*, vol. 4 (1983) pp. 451–82.

Roll, E. '*The Wealth of Nations 1776–1976*' (first published in *Lloyds Bank Review*, 119 (1976): *Wood*, vol. 2 (1983) pp. 146–55.

Rosenberg, N 'Some Institutional Aspects of the *Wealth of Nations*' (first published in *Journal of Political Economy*, vol. 18 (1960); *Wood*, vol. 2 (1983) pp. 105–20.

Samuels, W. 'Adam Smith and the Economy as a System of Power' (first published in *Review of Social Economy*, vol. 31 (1973); *Wood*, vol. 1 (1983) pp. 489–507).

Samuels, W. 'The Political Economy of Adam Smith' (first published in *Ethics*, vol. 87 (1976); *Wood*, vol. 1 (1983) pp. 698–714).

Schumpeter, J. A. *History of Economic Analysis* (London: Allen & Unwin, 1954).

Scott, W. R. *Francis Hutcheson* (Cambridge: Cambridge University Press, 1900).

Seligman, E. R. A. (ed.) *Wealth of Nations* (London: Dent, 1910).

Skinner, A. S (ed.), *Sir James Steuart: Principles of Political Economy* (Edinburgh: Edinburgh University Press and Chicago: Oliver and Boyd, 1966).

Skinner, A. S. 'Adam Smith and the Role of the State' (Glasgow: Glasgow University Press, 1974).

Skinner, A. S. *A System of Social Science: Papers Relating to Adam Smith* (Oxford: Oxford University Press, 1979).

Skinner, A. S. 'Adam Smith: Ein System der Sozialwissenschaft', in F. Kaufmann, and H. Krusselberg (eds), *Market, Staat und Solidaritat bei Adam Smith*, (Frankfurt: Campus Verlag, 1984).

Taylor, W. L. *Francis Hutchison and David Hume as Precursors of Adam Smith* (North Carolina: Duke University Press, 1965).

Viner, J. 'Adam Smith and Laisser-Faire' (first published in *Journal of Political Economy*, vol. 35 (1927); *Wood*, vol. 1 (1983) pp. 143–67.

West, E. G. 'Adam Smith and Alienation. Wealth Increases, Men Decay?' in *Essays on Adam Smith* (1975) pp. 540–52.

West, E. G. 'Adam Smith's Economics of Politics' (first published in *History of Political Economy*, vol. 8 (1976); *Wood*, vol. 1 (1983) pp. 581–600).

Winch, D. *Adam Smith's Politics. An Essay in Historiographic Revision* (Cambridge: Cambridge University Press, 1978).

Winch, D. 'Economic Liberalism as Ideology: The Appleby Version', *Economic History Review*, vol. 38 (1985) pp. 287–97.

Wood, J. C. *Adam Smith, Critical Assessments*, 4 vols (London: Croom Helm, 1983).

3 Sir James Steuart's Corporate State

WALTER ELTIS

It is well known that Smith and Hume have had great influence on conservative economic policy in the twentieth century. Hume argued that the balance of payments was self-correcting so that governments could ignore the international implications of their policies, and that money was neutral in the long run so that monetary expansion offered no long-term benefits. Smith showed that the demand for labour depended on the capital stock and its effectiveness which would be maximised if capital was always allowed to earn the highest possible return. This required that the allocation of capital be in no way interfered with by government regulation and control, and that all investment decisions be taken by those who actually stood to benefit. It followed that workers' living standards would be maximised if capitalists were left entirely free to invest in whatever they regarded as the most profitable ways, while the role of government was restricted to the creation of an environment where capitalist property rights were guaranteed. Government investments would reduce living standards because they would yield less than private investments since those who took the decisions would have no inducement to get them right. All interference with trade would make workers poorer because the effectiveness of the capital stock would be reduced. Government consumption would be still more damaging because it would actually reduce the capital stock and not merely its effectiveness. The connection between these propositions and twentieth-century conservative economic policy is patent.

Eighteenth-century economics left a wholly different legacy which is less well known. An eighteenth-century Scottish aristocrat, Sir James Steuart, went into exile in 1745 (as a prospective Minister if the Stuarts had triumphed)[1] where he absorbed a good deal of the interventionism which prevailed in Europe, and published a 1200 page treatise, *An Inquiry into the Principles of Political Oeconomy*, in 1767 after his return from the continent.[2] This offered his countrymen heavy taxation, an unlimited public debt, monetary expansion to reduce interest rates to 2 per cent, import controls, export subsidies, government-managed corporations, and the Agricultural Policy which the EEC went on to adopt 200 years later. Still more astonishingly he described as, 'the most perfect plan of political oeconomy . . . anywhere to be met with' (218), one where there was no private property, no imports, no foreign travel, and no private consumption beyond the barest necessities. The potential effectiveness of such a society where the entire non-agricultural population was available for war was such that if any European nation adopted it, 'every other nation' would be obliged 'to adopt, as far as possible, a similar conduct, from a principle of self-preservation'. (227)

In the period of Keynesian ascendancy, Steuart's economics was preferred to Smith's by admirers of his cheap money and full employment policies,[3] and a distinguished Indian planner welcomed his collectivism and justification for unlimited intervention,[4] but soviet economists have yet to follow up the admiration for Steuart which Marx repeatedly expressed.[5]

An Inquiry into the Principles of Political Oeconomy was referred to by Smith in 1772 in a well-known letter to William Pulteney: 'Without once mentioning it [Steuart's book], I flatter myself, that every false principle in it, will meet with a clear and distinct confutation in mine'.[6] Smith succeeded so well that Steuart remarked shortly before his death that a book of equal length about his dog would have excited as much interest as the treatise on political economy which occupied 18 years of his life.[7]

As with most economists who merit attention, Steuart's conclusions, including his twentieth-century policy proposals, follow straightforwardly from his premises. The present restatement will start with an account of Steuart's assumptions and how these led him to conclude that a nation would suffer a variety of economic maladjustments leading to inevitable economic decline, in the absence of very detailed interventions by an enlightened *statesman*. The actual policies Steuart put forward to enable a nation to develop fully its physical and human resources and so prevent the economic decline which would otherwise be inevitable, will be the subject of the second part of the paper. Finally something will be said about Smith's reasons for regarding these policies as utterly misconceived. It will become evident that the sharply different policy implications of these two major eighteenth-century economic treatises have echoes, and indeed, considerably more than echoes, in the economic debates of the 1980s.

SIR JAMES STEUART'S ASSUMPTIONS AND HOW THEY LED HIM TO CONCLUDE THAT ONLY AN ENLIGHTENED STATESMAN COULD PREVENT SEVERE ECONOMIC MALADJUSTMENT AND DECLINE

Steuart divided the people of a country into two classes, 'The first is that of the farmers who produce the subsistence, and who are necessarily employed in this branch of business; the other I shall call *free hands*; because their occupation being to procure themselves subsistence out of the superfluity of the farmers, and by a labour adapted to the wants of the society, may vary according to these wants, and these again according to the spirit of the times'.(43)

Steuart anticipated Malthus in linking population closely to the growth of agricultural output. The non-agricultural population which depends on the surplus that farmers produce for the consumption of 'free hands' will rely on powers of coercion in a society where slavery prevails, but most of Steuart's book is concerned with market economies, and here the amount that farmers produce in excess of their own needs will depend on the range of manufactured goods which can be offered in exchange for their surplus food, and since these will be more extensively available in a monetised than a barter economy, agricultural productivity and therefore the size of the agricultural surplus will also vary with the degree of monetisation:

> When once this imaginary wealth (money) becomes well introduced into a country, luxury will very naturally follow; and when money becomes the object of our wants, mankind become industrious, in turning their labour towards every object which may engage the rich to part with it; and thus the inhabitants of any country may increase in numbers, until the ground refuses farther nourishment. (45)

Steuart was convinced like Malthus that the level of agricultural productivity and output would vary sharply with the effective demand of other classes for food. If the demand for food falls for any reason:

The laziest part of the farmers, disgusted with a labour which produces a plenty superfluous to themselves, which they cannot dispose of for any equivalent, will give over working, and return to their ancient simplicity. The more laborious will not furnish the food to the necessitous for nothing . . . Thus by the diminution of labour, a part of the country, proportional to the quantity of food which the farmers formerly found superfluous, will again become uncultivated.

Here then will be found a country, the population of which must stop for want of food; and which, by the supposition, is abundantly able to produce more. Experience every where shews the possible existence of such a case, since no country in Europe is cultivated to the utmost: and that there are many still, where cultivation, and consequently multiplication, is at a stop. (41–2)

Agriculture and industry therefore have to grow together. Industrial growth provides the incentives for farmers to produce the surpluses which industry's free hands require for their subsistence.[8] 'agriculture, when encouraged for the sake of multiplying inhabitants, must keep pace with the progress of industry; or else an outlet must be provided for all superfluity'. (41)

The free hands whom the agricultural surplus supports (who amounted to approximately half the population in the Britain of 1767 according to Steuart (54–5)) may produce manufactures for home consumption or for export, provide personal services for the wealthy, or be employed by the state in the armed forces, or else to produce public works or services, The 'wants of society' and the 'spirit of the times' will determine which of these predominate.

Steuart believed a historical sequence which is often found is that the development of agriculture is first associated with a reciprocal growth in manufacturing. As industry develops, costs are low initially because surplus labour can be drawn cheaply from the land ('The desertion of the hands employed in a trifling agriculture' (183)) while industrialists have not yet become accustomed to high personal incomes which will in due course be 'consolidated' into manufacturing prices. Industry will then be internationally competitive, and there will be a fruitful period in which the free hands are predominantly employed in industry to produce luxuries for home consumption and for export. This will produce a comfortable period in which there is parallel growth in industry and agriculture, but industrial expansion contains the seeds of subsequent decline.

First, the relative price of food will rise and raise wages in a Ricardian manner:[9]

> Now the augmentation of food is relative to the soil, and as long as this can be brought to produce, at an expence proportioned to the value of the returns, agriculture without any doubt, will go forward in every country of industry. But as soon as the progress of agriculture demands an additional expence, which the natural return, at the stated prices of subsistence, will not defray, agriculture comes to a stop, and so would numbers, did not the consequences of industry push them forward, in spite of small difficulties. The industrious then, I say, continue to multiply, and the consequence is, that food becomes scarce, and that the inhabitants enter into competition for it.
>
> This is no contingent consequence, it is an infallible one; because food is an article of the first necessity, and here the provision is supposed to fall short of demand. This raises the profits of those who have food ready to sell; and as the balance upon this article must remain overturned for some time . . . these profits will be consolidated with the price, and give encouragement to a more expensive improvement of the soil . . .
>
> This augmentation on the value of subsistence must necessarily raise the price of all work . . . (197)

The consequent rise in wages and the prices of manufactures will weaken industrial competitiveness, reduce exports of manufactures and increase imports.

At the same time as industry advances, any high profits and wages which are earned over any considerable period will tend to be consolidated into the income levels that producers come to expect, and a subsequent weakening of demand will not reduce their incomes to the former level. Moreover, as industry advances, all kinds of barriers to competition will develop, and manufacturers will acquire peculiar privileges which enable them to sustain prices at high levels. According to Steuart, monopoly and monopsony are widespread, and departures from perfect competition will be greater, the more mature a country's industry, so in time any successful country will become increasingly vulnerable to international competition.

Finally export markets will inevitably weaken and competition from imports increase as foreign industry develops as it must.

when the inhabitants themselves foolishly enter into competition with strangers for their own commodities; and when a statesman looks coolly on, with his arms across, or takes it into his head, that it is not his business to interpose, the prices of the dexterous workman will rise above the amount of the mismanagement, loss, and reasonable profits, of the new beginners; and when this comes to be the case, trade will decay where it flourished most, and take root in a new soil. (205)

As soon as foreign manufacturers begin to outcompete domestic producers, a country will find it increasingly difficult to employ its free hands in industry.

Trade having subsisted long in the nation we are now to keep in our eye, I shall suppose that, through length of time, her neighbours have learned to supply one article of their own and other people's wants cheaper than she can do. What is to be done? Nobody will buy from her, when they can be supplied from another quarter at a less price. I say, what is to be done? For if there be no check put upon trade, and if the statesman do not interpose with the greatest care, it is certain, that merchants will import the produce, and even the manufactures of rival nations; the inhabitants will buy them preferably to their own; the wealth of the nation will be exported; and her industrious manufacturers will be brought to starve. (284)

The lost jobs due to increasing import penetration present considerable problems for a society in Steuart's analysis because the economy's 'free hands', approximately half the labour force, will necessarily have to find work outside agriculture, but he does not believe that there is a satisfactory mechanism to clear the labour market at an acceptable wage. He believes that attention should be continually focused on the relationship between *demand* and *work* in an economy:

when we say that the balance between work and demand is to be sustained in equilibrio, as far as possible, we mean that the quantity supplied should be in proportion to the quantity *demanded*, that is, *wanted*. While the balance stands justly poised, prices are found in the adequate proportion of the real expence of making the goods, with a small addition for profit to the manufacturer and merchant. (189)

If demand falls while work (or potential supply) remains unchanged, 'reasonable profits will be diminished', and perhaps workmen will be obliged to sell 'below prime cost' with the result that 'workmen fall into distress, and that industry suffers a discouragement'. If on the contrary demand exceeds work, 'the manufacturers are enriched for a little time, by a rise of profits', 'but as soon as these profits become *consolidated* with the intrinsic value, they will cease to have the advantage of profits, and, becoming in a manner necessary to the existence of the goods, will cease to be considered as advantageous'. The continual tendency for import penetration to rise will reduce demand in relation to work with the result that manufacturers will be 'forced to starve' (192–4).

A further result of increased imports is that any consequent balance of payments deficit will lead to a continual drain of the precious metals, and therefore a loss of part of the money supply:

> if . . . a nation . . . be found to consume not only the whole work of the inhabitants, but part of that of other countries, it must have a balance of trade against it, equivalent to the amount of foreign consumption; and this must be paid for in specie, or in an annual interest, to the diminution of the former capital. Let this trade continue long enough, they will not only come at the end of their metals, but they may render themselves virtually tributary to other nations, by paying to them annually a part of the income of their lands, as the interest due upon the accumulated balances of many years' unfavourable trade. (359)

Steuart rejects Hume's argument that a loss of specie will produce self-correcting adjustments in relative prices.

A loss of specie will continue indefinitely in a country which is spending more than its national income so that it not only suffers adverse trade but also a continual need to sell real assets to foreigners and to borrow internationally:

> [Mr Hume] is led from his principles to believe, that there is no such thing as a wrong balance of trade against a nation, but on the contrary thinks that the nature of money resembles that of a fluid, which tends every where to a level . . . [N]othing is so easy, or more common than a right or a wrong balance of trade; and I observe, that what we mean by a balance, is not the bringing the fluid to a level, but either the accumulating or raising it in some countries, by the

means of national industry and frugality, which is a right balance; or the depressing it in others, by national luxury and dissipation which is a wrong one. Thus the general doctrine of the *level* can only take place, on the supposition that all countries are equally frugal and industrious . . . (1767 i.515–16)

Steuart also objects to Hume's assumption that prices will rise smoothly in countries which gain specie and fall in those which lose gold and silver, because an increased supply of the precious metals may stagnate in countries with surpluses, where, because of all the imperfections in competition, 'prices remain regulated as before, by the complicated operations of demand and competition'. (363)[10] If a gold inflow does not raise prices:

What then will become of the additional quantity of coin, or paper-money? . . . if upon the increase of riches it be found that the state of demand remains without any variation, then *the additional coin* will probably be locked up, or converted into plate; because they who have it, not being inspired with a desire of increasing their consumption, and far less with the generous sentiment of giving their money away, their riches will remain without producing more effect than if they had remained in the mine . . . Let the specie of a country, therefore, be augmented or diminished, in ever so great a proportion, commodities will still rise and fall according to the principles of demand and competition . . . Let the quantity of coin be ever so much increased, it is the desire of spending it alone which will raise prices. (344–5)

A drain of money in countries with deficits is liable to produce irreversible adverse effects if there is an accompanying decline in the degree of monetisation, which is so important to the creation of incentives to prcduce. If a country with a trade deficit is also borrowing internationally, or selling assets to foreigners, because its aggregate expenditure exceeds its domestic production, which can all too easily occur in a country with declining real incomes, then, as in the case of Ireland (where the improvidence of heirs is supposedly shifting property rights to England):

so soon as . . . demand . . . comes to fail, for want of money, or industry, in Ireland, to purchase it, what remains on hand will be sent over to England in kind; or, by the way of trade, be made to circulate with other nations (in beef, butter, tallow, &c.) who will give silver and gold for it, to the proprietors of the Irish lands. By such a diminution of demand in the country, for the fruits of the earth, the depopulation of Ireland is implied; because they who consumed them formerly, consume them no more; that is to say, they are dead, or have left the country. (371)

Thus adverse specie flows as a result of lack of demand for domestic produce, may lead to demonetisation and depopulation.

Steuart was deeply concerned that a country which threw its frontiers open to international competition, could easily arrive at a situation where its manufactures were overpriced, with the result that it had a chronic tendency to raise its imports and to export less. At the same time the monopolistic and restrictive practices which emerged while its industry was internationally viable would prevent prices from falling to a competitive level, for in so many states, 'domestic luxury, taxes, and the high price of living, have put out of a capacity to support a competition with strangers' (1767 i.505). If foreigners are nevertheless permitted to sell manufactures freely to an increasingly fickle population which often prefers foreign goods merely because they are foreign, domestic industry will provide employment for diminishing numbers of 'free hands'. There will then be an inevitable excess of 'work' or potential output over 'demand' resulting in inevitable unemployment and starvation for industrial workers. The failure of domestic manufacturing will moreover reduce demand for surplus food from the farmers, for there will be insufficient demand from 'free hands' to buy up the agricultural surplus. The continuing loss of the domestic money supply which accompanies these adverse trends will compound the decline in both industry and agriculture, which, Steuart believed, had often occurred in the past as once prosperous states fell:

If . . . there be found too many hands for the demand, work will fall too low for workmen to be able to live; or, if there be too few, work will rise, and manufactures will not be exported.

For want of this just balance, no trading state has ever been of long duration, after arriving at a certain height of prosperity. We perceive in history the rise, progress, grandeur, and decline of Sydon, Tyre, Carthage, Alexandria, and Venice, not to come nearer home. (195)

But this decline in great manufacturing nations is avoidable because:

When a nation, which has long dealt and enriched herself by a reciprocal commerce in manufactures with other nations, finds the balance of trade turn against her, it is her interest to put a total stop to it, and to remain as she is, rather than to persist habitually in a practice, which, by a change of circumstances, must have effects very opposite to those advantages which it produced formerly. Such a stop may be brought about by the means of duties and prohibitions, which a statesman can lay on importations, so soon as he perceives that they begin to preponderate with respect to the *exportations* of his own country. (1767 i.504)

The further stages of historical development of a nation therefore depend on the decisions of statesmen, and the second part of this paper will be concerned with Steuart's detailed theory of state intervention.

SIR JAMES STEUART'S THEORY OF ECONOMIC POLICY

Steuart was very optimistic about the motivation of statesmen and their desire to further economic welfare. Like Smith, he believed that self-interest is the ruling principle which governs humanity, and 'From this principle, men are engaged to act in a thousand different ways, and every action draws after it certain necessary consequences'; but self-interest will not similarly influence the conduct of a statesman,[11] 'Self-interest, when considered with regard to him, is public spirit; and it can only be called self-interest, when it is applied to those who are to be governed by it.' (142) Steuart's statesman desires nothing less than to plan the functioning of the whole economy in order to advance the good of all:

When the statesman knows the extent and quality of the territory of his country, so as to be able to estimate what numbers it may feed; he may lay down his plan of political oeconomy, and chalk out a distribution of inhabitants, as if the number were already compleat. It will depend upon his judgement alone, and upon the combination of circumstances, foreign and domestic, to distribute, and to employ the classes, at every period during this execution, in the best manner . . . (384)

Steuart's statesman requires vast knowledge in order to plan the economy successfully:

There is no governing a state in perfection, and consequently no executing the plan for a right distribution of the inhabitants, without exactly knowing their situation as to numbers, their employment, the gains upon every species of industry, the numbers produced from each class. (70)

The more perfect and more extended any statesman's knowledge is of the circumstances and situation of every individual in the state he governs, the more he has it in his power to do them good or harm. I always suppose his inclinations to be virtuous and benevolent. (333)

Steuart's statesman becomes indispensable as soon as a country's industry begins to become less competitive in relation to foreign producers, because that is the point from which employment, output and population will continually fall if the statesman 'looks coolly on, with his arms across, or takes it into his head, that it is not his business to interpose'. What should the statesman then do to preserve industry at its peak? His desire above all is to sustain the nation's capital at this maximum level.

The first object of the care of a statesman, who governs a nation, which is upon the point of losing her foreign trade, without any prospect or probability of recovering it, is to preserve the wealth she has already acquired. No motive ought to engage him to sacrifice this wealth, the safety alone of the whole society excepted, when suddenly threatened by foreign enemies. The gratification of particular people's habitual desires, although the wealth they possess may enable them, without the smallest hurt to their private fortunes, to consume the productions of other nations; the motive of preventing hoards; that of promoting a brisk circulation within the country; the advantages to be made by merchants, who may enrich themselves by carrying on a trade disadvantageous to the nation; to say all in one word, even the supporting of the same number of inhabitants, ought not to engage his consent to the diminution of national wealth. (293)

Since it is a loss of trade competitiveness that is threatening the wealth of the nation, the statesman's immediate desire will be to restrict imports and encourage exports so as to attempt to overcome the increasing competitive advantages of other nations. The statesman will need to have extremely detailed knowledge if he is to restrict imports to the best effect:

> He must first examine minutely every use to which the merchandize imported is put: if a part is re-exported with profit, this profit must be deducted from the balance of loss incurred by the consumption of the remainder. If it be consumed upon the account of other branches of industry, which are thereby advanced, the balance of loss may still be more than compensated. If it be a mean of supporting a correspondence with a neighbouring nation, otherwise advantageous, the loss resulting from it may be submitted to, in a certain degree. But if upon examining the whole chain of consequences, he find the nation's wealth not at all increased, nor her trade encouraged, in proportion to the damage at first incurred by the importation; I believe he may decide such a branch of trade to be hurtful; and therefore that it ought to be cut off, in the most prudent manner . . . (293)

The declining competitiveness of exports can be counteracted in a variety of ways. Most directly, exports can be subsidised. '[P]ublic money must be made to operate upon the price of *the surplus* of industry only so as to make it exportable, even in cases where the national prices upon home consumption have got up beyond the proper standard'. (235) An example of a proposal to subsidise exports is:

> Let me suppose a nation which is accustomed to export to the value of a million of sterling of fish every year, to be undersold in this article by another which has found a fishery on its own coasts, so abundant as to enable it to undersell the first by 20 *per cent*. In this case, let the statesman buy up all the fish of his subjects, and undersell his competitors at every foreign market, at the loss to himself of perhaps £250,000. What is the consequence? That the million he paid for the fish remains at home, and that £750,000 comes in from abroad for the prices of them. How is the £250,000 to be made up? By a general imposition upon all the inhabitants. This returns into the public coffers, and all stands as it was. If this expedient be not followed, what will be the consequence? That those employed in the fishery will starve; that the fish taken will either remain upon hand, or be sold by the proprietors at a great

loss; they will be undone, and the nation for the future will lose the acquisition of £750,000 a year. (256–7)

If the decline in exports is the result of an inevitable Ricardian rise in food and raw material prices as the country develops, then the statesman may use public money to counteract the adverse effects on competitiveness of these fundamental developments:

When the progress of industry has augmented numbers, and made subsistence scarce, he must estimate to what height it is expedient that the price of subsistence should rise. If he finds, that, in order to encourage the breaking up of new lands, the price of it must rise too high and stand high too long, to preserve the intrinsic value of goods at the same standard as formerly; then he must assist agriculture with his purse, in order that exportation may not be discouraged. This will have the effect of increasing subsistence, according to the true proportion of the augmentation required, without raising the price of it too high. (200)

If it is a consolidation of previous inflated incomes that has made export prices unduly high, new export producers can be set up in green field sites uncontaminated with consolidation:

All methods . . . should be fallen upon to supply manufacturers with new hands; and lest the contagion of example should get the better of all precautions, the seat of manufacturers might be changed; especially when they are found in great and populous cities, where living is dear: in this case, others should be erected in the provinces where living is cheap. The state must encourage these new undertakings; numbers of children must be taken in, in order to be bred early to industry and frugality . . . (251)

Steuart also supports a state role in the day-to-day management of industrial companies:

in the infancy of such undertakings . . . the want of experience frequently occasions considerable losses; and while this continues to be the case, no complaints are heard against such associations. Few pretend to rival their undertaking, and it becomes at first more commonly the object of raillery than of jealousy. During this period, the statesman should lay the foundation of his authority; he ought to spare no pains nor encouragement to support the undertaking; he ought to inquire into the capacity of those at the head of it; order their projects to be laid before him; and when he finds them reasonable, and well planned, he ought to take unforeseen losses upon himself: he is working for the public, not for the company; and the more care and expence he is at in setting the undertaking on foot, the more he has a right to direct the prosecution of it towards the general good. This kind of assistance given, entitles him to the inspection of their books; and from this, more than any thing, he will come to an exact knowledge of every circumstance relating to their trade. (391)

It will already be evident that Steuart's interventionism is not confined to industry, because fisheries are also receiving support, and the statesman's purse has been opened to agricultural improvement. In 1759, before his return from exile, he wrote a paper which was only published in 1805 in which he proposed 'a Policy of Grain' in 'the Common Markets of England'. In this he proposed that the government should be prepared to buy up all the grain that farmers were prepared to produce at 'the minimum price expedient for the farmers', sell all that could be sold at 'the maximum price expedient for the wage-earners', and store any excess in state granaries. This proposal for the Common Markets of England in grain which he wrote for his countrymen from Tübingen has, of course, become the extremely controversial policy of grain of the European Common Market.

The detailed interventions in industry and agriculture which have been set out, were avoidable while industrial and agricultural growth were compatible with international competitiveness, but they become increasingly necessary as soon as foreign industry threatens to undermine the employment of the country's 'free hands'. Actual intervention in industry would of course be unnecessary if there was blanket protection against all imports. But a consequence of this would be that domestic monopoly incomes would grow and the home production of an extensive range of luxury consumer goods for the landlords and the recipients of consolidated monopoly incomes would occupy the free hands who formerly produced for international markets. But a shift into luxury production where domestic producers have no need to fear foreign competition has several disadvantages:

The consequences of *excessive luxury, moral and physical*, as well as the dissipation of private fortunes, may render both the statesman, and those whom he employs, negligent in their duty, unfit to discharge it, rapacious and corrupt. (267)

The growth of domestic luxury production will tend to encourage the formation of large private fortunes. The need to compete internationally acted as a constraint in the former period, but there is now no limit to the extent to which prices can be raised. This will lead to great personal inequalities; and the growth of private fortunes which will tend to dominate money markets also threatens the power and prestige of the state. Here there are remedies:

> The statesman looks about with amazement; he, who was wont to consider himself the first man in the society in every respect, perceives himself eclipsed by the lustre of private wealth, which avoids his grasp when he attempts to seize it. This makes his government more complex and more difficult to be carried on; he must now avail himself of art and address as well as of power and authority. By the help of cajoling and intrigues, he gets a little into debt; this lays a foundation for public credit, which, growing by degrees, and in its progress assuming many new forms, becomes from the most tender beginnings, a most formidable monster, striking terror into those who cherished it in its infancy. Upon this, as upon a triumphant war-horse, the statesman gets a-stride, he then appears formidable anew; his head turns giddy; he is cloaked with the dust he has raised; and at the moment he is ready to fall, he finds, to his utter astonishment and surprise, a strong monied interest, of his own creating, which, instead of swallowing him up as he apprehended, flies to his support. Through this he gets the better of all opposition . . . (181–2)

Steuart saw great potential advantages from the establishment of state controlled banks and issues of government bonds to create paper assets, and he believed that these would simultaneously raise the money supply and reduce interest rates. He argued that John Law's Mississippi scheme could have been successful in France with only a few minor modifications in the manner in which it was set up and administered; and that this would have established a long-term rate of interest of 2 per cent in France (557–63).

As well as asserting his authority via the market for public debt, a statesman also has the power to tax, which offers to governments the most powerful means to influence the economy and society:

By taxes a statesman is enriched, and by means of his wealth, he is enabled to keep his subjects in awe, and to preserve his dignity and consideration.

By the distribution of taxes, and maner of levying them, the power is thrown into such hands as the spirit of the constitution requires it should be found in. (304)

[T]he intention of taxes as I understand them, is to advance only the public good, by throwing a part of the wealth of the rich into the hands of the industrious poor . . . (334)

In addition to furthering income redistribution and social improvement, large sums of public money are needed to finance Steuart's policies to sustain the competitiveness of industry, so tax revenues will become increasingly necessary as foreign industry advances:

[T]axes become necessary; in order, with the amount of them, to correct the bad effects of luxury, by giving larger premiums to support exportation. And in proportion as a statesman's endeavours to support by these means the trade of his country becomes ineffectual, from the growing taste of dissipation in his subjects, the utility of an opulent exchequer will be more and more discovered; as he will be thereby enabled both to support his own authority against the influence of a great load of riches thrown into domestic circulation, and to defend his luxurious and wealthy subjects from the effects of the jealousy of those nations which enriched them. (336–7)

Another use of taxes, after the extinction of foreign trade, is to assist circulation, by performing, as it were, the function of the heart of a child, when at its birth that of the mother can be of no farther use to it. The public treasure, by receiving from the amount of taxes, a continual flux of money, may throw it out into the most proper channels, and thereby keep that industry alive, which formerly flourished, and depended upon the prosperity of foreign commerce only.

In proportion, therefore, as a statesman perceives the rivers of wealth . . ., which were in brisk circulation with all the world, begin to flow abroad more slowly, and to form stagnations, which break out into domestic circulation, he ought to set a plan of taxation on foot, as a fund for premiums to indemnify exportation for the loss it must sustain from the rise of prices, occasioned by luxury; and also for securing the state itself, against the influence of domestic riches, as well as for recompensing those who are employed in its service. (337–8)

The need for high taxation in order to finance Steuart's industrial policies is underlined by the need to pay high salaries to administer them. As the role of government increases, it needs to attract a proportion of those with high ability to execute the vast array of tasks which Steuart has in mind, and top people (which meant aristocrats to Steuart who had lived more in France than in Smith's Edinburgh and Glasgow) need to be well paid:

> Is it not very natural, that he who is employed by the state should receive an equivalent proportioned to the value of his services? Is it to be supposed, that a person born in a high rank, who, from this circumstance alone, acquires an advantage in most nations, hardly to be made up by any acquired abilities, will dedicate his time and his attendance for the remuneration which might satisfy an inferior? The talents of great men deserve reward as much as those of the lowest among the industrious; and the state is with reason made to pay for every service she receives. (337)

Steuart also needed high taxation in order to finance his full employment policies, and these have attracted much favourable twentieth-century attention:[12]

> The nation's wealth must be kept entire, and made to circulate, so as to provide subsistence and employment for every body. (1767 i.506)
>
> The more money becomes necessary for carrying on consumption, the more it is easy to levy taxes; the use of which is to advance the public good, by drawing from the rich, a fund sufficient to employ both the *deserving*, and the *poor*, in the service of the state . . . (1767 i.512–3)

If there is insufficient demand for labour:

> When home-demand does not fill up the void, of which we have spoken, a vicious competition takes place among those that work for a physical-necessary; the price of their labour falls below the general standard of subsistence . . .

> A statesman therefore, at the head of a luxurious people, must endeavour to keep his balance [between 'work' and 'demand'] even; and if a subversion is necessary, it is far better it should happen by the preponderancy of the scale of demand. Here is my reason for preferring this alternative.
>
> All subversions are bad, and are attended with bad consequences. If the scale of work preponderates, the industrious will starve, their subsistence will be exported; the nation gains by the balance, but appears in a manner to sell her inhabitants. If the scale of demand preponderates, luxury must increase, but the poor are fed at the expence of the rich, and the national stock of wealth stands as it was. (1767 i.506–7)

The poor should be employed above all on public works to carry through major investments in the social infrastructure:

> If a thousand pounds are bestowed upon making a fire-work, a number of people are thereby employed, and gain a temporary livelihood. If the same sum is bestowed for making a canal for watering the fields of a province, a like number of people may reap the same benefit, and hitherto accounts stand even; but the fire-work played off, what remains, but the smoke and stink of the powder? Whereas the consequence of the canal is a perpetual fertility to a formerly barren soil. (1767 i.519)

> I say that whoever can transform the most consumable commodities of a country into the most durable and most beneficial works, makes a high improvement. If therefore meat and drink, which are of all things the most consumable, can be turned into harbours, high roads, canals, and public buildings, is not the improvement inexpressible? This is the power of every statesman to accomplish, who has subsistence at his disposal; and beyond the power of all those who have it not. (383)

As policies which require public expenditure are pushed further, rates of taxation and borrowing will have a continual tendency to increase, and Steuart believed that taxation should rise continually as competitiveness declines and the government has to create a demand for labour to fill the gap left by declining foreign sales. He was convinced that higher taxation would have a clear tendency to raise effective demand, since the state definitely spends what might only be partly spent if left in private hands:

[T]axes promote industry; not in consequence of their being raised upon individuals, but in consequence of their being expended by the state; that is, by increasing demand and circulation . . .

Every application of public money implies a want in the state; and every want supplied, implies an encouragement given to industry. In proportion, therefore, as taxes draw money into circulation, which otherwise would not have entered into it at that time, they encourage industry; not by taking the money from individuals, but by throwing it into the hands of the state, which spends it; and which thereby throws it directly into the hands of the industrious, or of the luxurious who employ them.

It is no objection to this representation of the matter, that the persons from whom the money is taken, would have spent it as well as the state. The answer is, that it might be so, or not; whereas when the state gets it, it will be spent undoubtedly. (725–6)

If the demand-side effects of higher taxation are favourable as Steuart and present-day Keynesians insist for precisely these reasons, what of the supply-side effects which are now so often believed to be unfavourable? Steuart differed from almost all his successors in that he believed that higher taxation would actually have *favourable effects upon supply*.

When in any country the work of manufacturers, who live luxuriously, and who can afford to be idle some days of the week, finds a ready market; this circumstance alone proves beyond all dispute, that subsistence in that country is not too dear, at least in proportion to the market prices of goods at home; and if taxes on consumption have, in fact raised the prices of necessaries, beyond the former standard, this rise, cannot, in fact, discourage industry: it may discourage idleness; and idleness will not be totally rooted out, until people be forced, in one way or other, to give up both superfluity and days of recreation. (691)

When the hands employed are not diligent, the best expedient is to raise the price of their subsistence, by taxing it. By this you never will raise their wages, until the market can afford to give a better price for their work. (695)

Since higher taxation will thus have favourable effects upon both *demand* and *supply*,[13] there really are no problems in raising it whenever this is necessary for the financing of social, or industrial, or full employment policies. Steuart's attitude to private incomes has twentieth-century echoes:

> [M]y original plan, . . . was to keep constantly in view those virtuous statesmen who think of nothing but the good of their subjects. Taxes and impositions in their hands, are the wealth of the father of the family; who therewith feeds, clothes, provides for, and defends every one within his house. (703)

> If the money raised be more beneficially employed by the state, than it would have been by those who have contributed it, then I say the public has gained, in consequence of the burden laid upon individuals; consequently the statesman has done his duty, both in imposing the taxes, and in rightly expending them. (709)

With economic activity increasingly concentrated in public hands where normal market incentives do not apply. there are clear risks of abuse which Steuart recognised, and he recommended penalties for economic sabotage which have been widely applied in the twentieth century; though not quite his insistence that the appropriate method of execution for the abuse of public money was drawing and quartering (the eighteenth-century penalty for high treason) and not mere hanging (the penalty for highway robbery):

> [I]f there be a crime called high treason, which is punished with greater severity than highway robbery, and assassination, I should be apt (where I a statesman) to put at the head of this bloody list, every attempt to defeat the application of public money, for the purposes here mentioned . . . If severe punishment can . . . put a stop to frauds, I believe it will be thought very well applied. (257)

Steuart was of course far ahead of his time in his eulogies of high taxation, and in the emphasis he placed on the public sector. He recognised this, but because he was confident that his argument was logically correct, he believed a time would surely come when his propositions would also be politically acceptable:

> In treating of taxes, I frequently look no farther than my pen, when I raise my head and look about, I find the politics of my closet very different from those of the century in which I live. I agree that the

difference is striking; but still reason is reason, and there is no impossibility in the supposition of its becoming practice. (1767 i.514)

Steuart's attitude to public debt is equally modern, but here it is Latin America that has gone furthest in the directions he advocated. He reasoned that there is no limit to the heights that domestically held public debt can reach. He first posed the question:

If the interest paid upon the national debt of England, for example, be found constantly to increase upon every new war, the consequence will be, that more money must be raised on the subject for the payment of it. The question then comes to be. First, How far may debts extend? Secondly, How far may taxes be carried? And Thirdly, What will be the consequence, supposing the one and the other carried to the greatest height possible? (645)

Steuart's answer is that, 'debts may be increased to the full proportion of all that can be raised for the payment of the interest', and the land-tax, for instance:

may be carried to the full value of all the real estate of England. The notion of actually imposing 20 shillings in the pound upon the real value of all the land-rents of England, appears to us perfectly ridiculous. I admit it to be so; and could I have discovered any argument by which I could have limited the rising of the land-tax to any precise number of shillings under twenty, I should have stated this as the maximum rather than the other. (646)

But the upper limit to government debt is not even the level where the interest upon it equals the revenue of a 100 per cent land-tax plus all the other taxes which can be levied. '[T]he state will then be in possession of all that can be raised on the land, on the consumption, industry and trade of the country; in short, of all that can be called income, which it will administer for the public creditors.' (646) In effect, the property rights of all former property owners will then have been transferred to the state, since their wealth no longer yields a net of tax income, but there will then be a new set of property owners, the holders of public debt, or gilt-edged stock. The government can go on to finance still further borrowing by taxing their income at 100 per cent, and so an, *ad infinitum*:

If no check be put to the augmentation of public debts, if they be allowed constantly to accumulate, and if the spirit of a nation can patiently submit to the natural consequences of such a plan, it must end in this, that all property, that is income, will be swallowed up by taxes; and these will be transferred to the creditors, the state retaining the administration of the revenue.

The state, in that case, will always consider those who enjoy the national income as the body of proprietors. This income will continue the same, and the real proprietors will pay the taxes imposed; which may be mortgaged again to a new set of men, who will retain the denomination of creditors; until by swallowing up the former, they slip into their places, and become the body of proprietors in their turn, and thus perpetuate the circle. (1767 ii.633–4)

Such reasoning appeared strange to Steuart's contemporaries, but the analytical device he is using which is extremely familiar today is the limiting case. He says, 'Do not be put off from raising taxes when this appears correct in the short term, for there is no theory which says that a land-tax, for instance, cannot be raised to 100 per cent; and Britain (levying just four shillings in the pound) is far short of that. Do not be put off from borrowing for fear of the size of the public debt, because immeasurably greater debt is conceivable'. Finally, to explain his praise for a wholly collectivist and egalitarian society which has been remarked on,[14] do not fear to restrict freedom of choice in consumption by restricting imports and taxing the better off heavily in order to reduce their luxury consumption, because a society which pushed such trends immeasurably further would still be agreeable to live in, and militarily formidable to boot. In each of these examples, Steuart is careful to point out that they are chimerical. Thus, the scheme of taxing property owners at 100 per cent in order to finance massive government borrowing, and then going on to tax the holders of gilt-edged shares in order to provide the interest to finance still more borrowing is 'destitute of all probability; because of the infinite variety of circumstances which may frustrate such a scheme'. (647) As for the egalitarian collectivist society where none consume imports or luxuries, this has been, 'introduced purposely to serve as an illustration of general principles, and as a relaxation to the mind, like a farce between the acts of a serious opera'. (227) Steuart's solid and substantial argument is the detailed case he consistently develops for the establishment of what is nowadays called 'a corporate state', where the interests of both capitalists and workers as producers are paramount. His fundamental approach to economy and society is summarised in the passage below:

Cities and corporations may be considered as nations, where luxury and taxes have rendered living so expensive, that goods cannot be furnished but at a high rate. If labour, therefore, of all kinds, were permitted to be brought from the provinces, or from the country, to supply the demand of the capital and smaller corporations, what would become of tradesmen and manufacturers who have their residence there? If these, on the other hand, were to remove beyond the liberties of such corporations, what would become of the public revenue, collected in these little states, as I call them?

By the establishment of corporations, a statesman is enabled to raise high impositions upon all sorts of consumption; and notwithstanding these have the necessary consequence of increasing the price of labour, yet by other regulations . . . the bad consequences thereby resulting to foreign trade may be avoided, and every article of exportation be prevented from rising above the proper standard for making it vendible, in spite of all foreign competition . . .

Cities having obtained the privilege of incorporation, began, in consequence of the powers vested in their magistrates, to levy taxes: and finding the inconveniences resulting from external competition (foreign trade), they erected the different classes of their industrious into confraternities, or corporations of a lower denomination, with power to prevent the importation of work from their fellow tradesmen not of the society . . . Nobody ever advanced, that the industry carried on in *towns*, where living is dear, ought to suffer a competition with that of the *country*, where living is cheap . . . (286–7)

Steuart himself underlines the importance of this example of a social contract between rulers who tax, and unionised citizens whose livelihood they then protect from competition, when he summarise this chapter:

I shew how [incorporated cities] may be considered as so many states, which domestic luxury, taxes, and the high price of living, have put out of a capacity to support a competition with strangers (that is with the open country) which here represents the rest of the world. I show the reasonableness of such exclusive privileges, in favour of those who share the burthens peculiar to the community, in so far only as regards the supply of their own consumption; and I point out, by what methods any discouragements to industry may be prevented, as often as that industry has for its object the supplying the wants of those who are not included in the corporation.

From the long and constant practice of raising *taxes* within incorporated cities, I conclude, that *taxes* are a very natural consequence of luxury, and of the loss of foreign trade; and as Princes have taken the hint from the cities, to extend them universally, it is no wonder to see foreign trade put an end to, in consequence of such injudicious extensions. (1767 i.504–5)

Steuart thus perceived a parallel between a country which is no longer competitive in trade and therefore incapable of providing employment for its 'free hands', and a mature city state, and he proposed that the remedies for the problems of the mature nation were precisely those that successful city states had discovered in their efforts to sustain an adequate standard of living for all within their corporations. The full range of Steuart's policy proposals is explicable in this context,[15] and also the extensive support for very similar policies in the twentieth century by those who see the problems of their countries in similar terms.

It is thus central to the analysis of the Cambridge Economic Policy Group that British industry ceased to be internationally competitive in the 1970s, for reasons which echo several of Steuart's, and the consequent damage to employment to which they attach the same overriding importance can only be averted by import controls and positive job-creating industrial policies which resemble those that Steuart specifically outlined. At the same time, like Steuart, they foresee little damage from higher taxation, heavier government borrowing and a narrower range of availability of 'luxury' consumer goods.[16] Similar analyses have naturally emerged elsewhere.

Smith considered this analysis entirely mistaken in 1776. This paper will conclude with a summary of why he objected so strongly to Steuart's interventionist policies. The reasons for his opposition to Steuart's corporatist approach naturally have much in common with the arguments used today by those who oppose moves towards a corporate state in the Britain of the 1980s.

WHY ADAM SMITH BELIEVED THAT SIR JAMES STEUART'S POLITICAL OECONOMY WAS MISTAKEN

There are several obvious reasons why Smith believed strongly that Steuart's analysis was misconceived. First and most fundamentally, his view of the knowledge, skill and motivation of statesmen was entirely different. The contrast between Steuart's omniscient and benevolently intentioned statesmen, and those to be found in *The Wealth of Nations* below[17] could hardly be greater:

> The stateman, who should attempt to direct private people in what manner they ought to employ their capitals, would not only load himself with a most unnecessary attention, but assume an authority which could safely be trusted, not only to no single person, but to no council or senate whatever, and which would nowhere be so dangerous as in the hands of a man who had folly and presumption enough to fancy himself fit to exercise it. (456)

> What is the species of domestick industry which his capital can employ, and of which the produce is likely to be of the greatest value, every individual, it is evident, can, in his local situation, judge much better than any statesman or lawgiver can do for him. (456)

As well as lacking the knowledge of entrepreneurs, Smith also believed that statesmen were by nature extravagant, and prone to maladministration:

> The uniform, constant, and uninterrupted effort of every man to better his condition, the principle from which publick and national, as well as private opulence is originally derived, is frequently powerful enough to maintin the natural progress of things towards improvement, in spite both of the extravagance of government, and of the greatest errors of administration. (343)

The eighteenth-century readers of Smith and Steuart who actually determined which would be taken seriously, recognised Smith's statesmen, but not Steuart's Utopian supermen (who re-emerged only in the detailed blueprints for 'the economics of control' which followed 'the Keynesian revolution').[18] There is one point where some of the statesmen whom Steuart must actually have encountered surface, when he writes,

> In my inquiries. I have constantly in my eye, how man *may* be governed, and never how *he is* governed. How a righteous and intelligent statesman may restrain the liberty of individuals, in order to promote the common good; never how an ignorant and unrighteous statesman may destroy public liberty, for the sake of individuals. (708)

It is precisely because Smith described how man *is* governed, while Steuart merely sought to show how he *may be* governed that his analysis carried extra conviction to his contemporaries. And today there is an equal difference between those who believe governments have sufficient information to execute complex interventionist policies in order to maximise social welfare functions over immense (and sometimes infinite) time horizons, and those who believe that in practice politicians will often be concerned with little more than the parochial interests of their own party over a period little longer than the memory of an electorate. These 'realists' are as unready as Smith to expect benefits from government control over the minutiae of economic life.

An equally far-reaching objection to Steuart stemmed for Smith's belief that economies were sufficiently self-correcting in the short term to avoid many of the ills that Steuart predicted. In particular, in *The Wealth of Nations* the demand for labour always depends on the capital stock, and this will be used most effectively if it is allowed to earn as much profit as possible for those who own it. The prosperity of workers which Smith and Steuart both desired depended on continual growth in the stock of capital, and Smith analysed the conditions which can be expected to contribute to accumulation with great care. It has been widely pointed out that potential supply in Steuart's economy, 'work' as he calls it, is merely the available labour force.[19] Smith's perception that 'stock' influences the demand for labour is lacking. Even if many of Steuart's full employment policies actually raised demand in the short term, they would undoubtedly reduce the rate of capital accumulation afterwards, and therefore reduce the demand for labour in the medium term. Smith did not refer to the possibility of unused capital even in the short term, but even if the short run is conceded to Steuart, the lack of a concept of 'stock' means that he fails to provide an analysis of the progression of the demand for labour, and of how the growth of government expenditure may inhibit this, and of how private saving will generally increase it. Today there is equal disagreement between those like Steuart who focus on the correction of immediate demand deficiencies at whatever cost, and those like Smith who believe that the trend demand for labour must react favourably if the appropriate conditions for long-term private sector capital accumulation can be established.

Finally, because he believed that private capitalists would always be able to find profitable openings for the physical capital at their disposal, Smith had no need for the paraphernalia of the corporate state:

> The general industry of the society never can exceed what the capital of the society can employ. As the number of workmen that can be kept in employment by any particular person must bear a certain proportion to his capital, so the number of those that can be continually employed by all the members of a great society, must bear a certain proportion to the whole capital of that society, and never can exceed that proportion. No regulation of commerce can increase the quantity of industry in any society beyond what its capital can maintain. It can only divert a part of it into a direction into which it might not otherwise have gone . . . (453)

If foreign competitors provided some goods more cheaply than home producers, Smith's industrialists can be expected to switch their capital to the production of alternative products. An eighteenth-century capital stock consisted largely of food and raw materials which could be used to produce a variety of final products. If one of these became uncompetitive, production could switch to others at a trivial cost in comparison with the twentieth-century penalty for having to switch capital out of textiles, a car, or an aircraft industry, because these are losing out to foreigners. Smith believed that competition would always steer the capital stock into the directions which would maximise returns. Steuart believed that the extent of domestic competition was extremely limited, and that the superior knowledge of the statesman would generally enable him to out-think the market, and that the powers of government to limit competition would in any case ensure that whatever the statesman produced was sold. Smith believed that such departures from the competitive process would misdirect investment, and reduce the aggregate returns a nation derived from its physical capital. Today there are equally those who wish to set up a corporate state behind tariff walls, and others who believe that maximum competition will ensure that the best use is made of a country's productive resources.

A vital difficulty which economies encounter today that never occurred to Smith is that a country's general price or cost level may be stuck above those of competitors. Smith readily accepted Hume's argument that gold losses by such a country would reduce its domestic costs and prices to a level where domestic markets cleared. Today's market economists are perfectly ready to echo Smith and Hume, but Steuart's rejection of Hume's argument because many domestic costs and prices are fixed independently of the money supply, and because a country can lose gold cumulatively like Ireland and never find equilibrium, also finds eloquent and persuasive support. It is difficult to believe that eighteenth-century economies had sufficient wage and price rigidities to defeat Hume's argument, but in the Britain of 1985 Steuart's belief that a country's wage or price structure can get so far out of line that its industries cannot remain sufficiently competitive to sustain full employment is accepted by many ranging from the Cambridge Economic Policy Group to the Chancellor of the Exchequer.

NOTES

1. The best accounts of Sir James Steuart's life are to be found in Skinner (1966) and Chamley (1965).
2. References and quotations will, wherever possible, be to the Scottish Economic Society's 1966 edition, edited by Andrew Skinner, and page references will be to this edition, unless a passage is only to be found in the original edition in which case a page reference will be preceded by 1767. The publishers of the 1966 edition unfortunately insisted on the omission of approximately one-quarter of Steuart's text.
3. See, in particular, Sen (1957), Stettner (1945), and Vickers (1959) and (1970).
4. See Sen (1957), 'Steuart's historical and evolutionist approach, his views on the economic structure, his conception of labour as a social category, his theory of perpetual crisis facing the exchange economy, his analysis of inner contradictions as transforming one economic stage into another, his treatment of Spartan communism and general anti-individualist bias had undoubtedly a profound influence on Marx' (pp. 187–8).
5. There are, for instance, 13 references to Steuart in the first volume of *Capital*, 'Sir James Steuart, a writer altogether remarkable for his quick eye for the characteristic social distinctions between different modes of production' (p. 314); and 'Sir James Steuart is the economist who has handled this subject [population] best. How little his book, which appeared ten years before *The Wealth of Nations*, is known, even at the present time, may be judged from the fact that admires of Malthus do not even know that the first edition of the latter's work on population

contains, except in the purely declamatory part, very little but extracts from Steuart, and in a less degree, from Wallace and Townsend' (p. 333).

6. See, Smith, *Correspondence*, p. 164. Skinner (1981) in his magisterial article written to commemorate the bicentenary of Steuart's death, discounts the evident contempt for Steuart's economics that this letter conveys: 'it will be noted that remarks such as these are not overtly hostile or even hypercritical, and that Smith's reply to Pulteney cannot be fully assessed until the latter's opinion is known' (p. 39).

7. See Skinner (1966), p. lv, and Steuart (1767) vol. 2, p. 646

8. See Eagly (1961) for an account of the importance of incentives and aspirations in Steuart.

9. Hollander (1973) has drawn attention to the presence of agricultural diminishing returns in Steuart.

10. The relationship between Steuart's monetary theory and the quantity theory is discussed in detail in Skinner (1967), and Skinner also explains (1981) the importance for Steuart's interventionist approach to economic policy of his rejection of Hume's self-correcting specie flow propositions.

11. Skinner (1962) provides a valuable account of the relationship of Steuart's politics to his economics.

12. See especially, Vickers (1959) and (1970), Meek (1967), Schumpeter (1954), Hutchison (1978) and Stettner (1945).

13. It is not easy to reconcile Steuart's argument here that higher taxation may have *favourable* effects on the supply produced by, for instance, farmers, with the propositions referred to above (pp. 45–6) that the availability of a greater variety of manufactures in exchange for food will often persuade them to produce more. Brian Loasby drew my attention to this contradiction, which may be a by-product of Steuart's evident desire to set out a strong case for high taxation.

14. Anderson and Tollison (1984) suggest that Steuart seriously desired the establishment of an egalitarian collectivist society of this kind, without referring to the context in which he outlines his account of this society. Their doubts about the uncritical praise for Steuart's interventionism in the secondary literature are similar to those in the present article.

15. Skinner (1966) has suggested that Steuart 'appeared too often in the guise of a "political matron"' (p. lxxxii). This is certainly a plausible interpretation of his attitude to policy, but it is also possible that he was systematically setting out the case for the establishment of 'a corporate state' rather than outlining a series of piecemeal remedies for every difficulty.

16. See the successive issues of the *Cambridge Economic Policy Review* which this group published from 1975 to 1981, after which they apparently lost hope of influencing policy in Britain, for the publication of the *Review* ceased.

17. Page references are to the Glasgow Edition of *The Wealth of Nations*, edited by R. H. Campbell and A. S. Skinner.

18. Sen (1957) has suggested that, 'It would not be any great exaggeration to say that A. P. Lerner's chapter on functional finance seems almost a paraphrase of Steuart' (p. 122).

19. See, for instance, Meek (1967) and Akhtar (1978 and 1979). In 1979

Akhtar wrote 'The most serious flaw in his treatment is that it completely neglected the subject of capital accumulation, and the role of capital in the production process' (p. 301). Perelman (1983) has shown that there are valuable accounts of primitive accumulation in Steuart.

REFERENCES

Akhtar, M. A. 'Steuart on Growth', *Scottish Journal of Political Economy*, 25 (1978) pp. 57–74.

Akhtar, M. A. 'An Analytical Outline of Sir James Steuart's Macroeconomic Model', *Oxford Economic Papers*, 31 (1979) pp. 283–302.

Anderson, G. M. and R. B. Tollison 'Sir James Steuart as the Apotheosis of Mercantilism and His Relation to Adam Smith', *Southern Economic Journal*, 51 (1984) pp. 456–68.

Cambridge Economic Policy Group *Cambridge Economic Policy Review* (Farnborough: Gower, 1975–81).

Chamley, P. *Documents Relatifs à Sir James Steuart* (Paris: Dalloz, 1965).

Eagly, R. V. 'Sir James Steuart and the Aspiration Effect', *Economica*, 28 (1961) pp. 53–81.

Hollander, S. *The Economics of Adam Smith* (Toronto: Toronto University Press, 1973).

Hume, D. *Political Discourses* (Edinburgh: 1752).

Hutchison, T. W. *On Revolutions and Progress in Economic Knowledge* (Cambridge: Cambridge University Press, 1978).

Lerner, A. P. *The Economics of Control* (New York: Macmillan, 1944).

Malthus, T. R. *An Essay on the Principle of Population as it Affects the Future Improvement of Society* (London: 1798).

Marx, K. (1867) *Capital* (Moscow: Progress Publishers for Lawrence & Wishart, 1974, reprint).

Meek, R. L. *Economics and Ideology and Other Essays* (London: Chapman and Hall, 1967).

Perelman, M. 'Classical Political Economy and Primitive Accumulation: The Case of Smith and Steuart', *History of Political Economy*, 15 (1983) pp. 451–94.

Ricardo, D. *On the Principles of Political Economy and Taxation* (London: 1817).

Schumpeter, J. A. *History of Economic Analysis* (New York: Oxford University Press, 1954).

Sen, S. R. *The Economics of Sir James Steuart* (London: Bell, 1957).

Skinner, A. S 'Sir James Steuart: Economics and Politics', *Scottish Journal of Political Economy*, 9 (1962) pp. 275–90.

Skinner, A. S. 'Biographical Sketch', and 'Analytical Introduction', in the Scottish Economic Society's edition of Sir James Steuart, *Principles of Political Oeconomy* (Edinburgh: Oliver & Boyd, 1966).

Skinner, A. S. 'Money and Prices: A Critique of the Quantity Theory', *Scottish Journal of Political Economy*, 14 (1967) pp. 275–90.

Skinner, A. S. 'Sir James Steuart: Author of a System', *Scottish Journal of Political Economy*, 28 (1981) pp. 20–42.

Smith, A. (1776) *An Inquiry into the Nature and Causes of the Wealth of Nations*. Republished as R. H. Campbell and A. S. Skinner (eds) *The Glasgow Edition of the Works and Correspondence of Adam Smith*, II (Oxford: Oxford University Press, 1976).

Smith, A. *The Correspondence of Adam Smith*, E. C. Mossner and I. S. Ross (eds) *The Glasgow Edition of the Works and Correspondence of Adam Smith*, VI (Oxford: Oxford University Press, 1977).

Stettner, W. F. 'Sir James Steuart on the Public Debt', *Quarterly Journal of Economics*, 59 (1945) pp. 451–76.

Steuart, Sir James (1759) *A Dissertation on the Policy of Grain, with a view to a Plan for preventing scarcity or exorbitant prices in the Common Markets of England* in Sir James Steuart (ed.) *Works, Political, Metaphysical and Chronological* (1805).

Steuart, Sir James *An Inquiry into the Principles of Political Oeconomy: being an Essay on the Science of Domestic Policy in Free Nations*, 2 vols (London: 1767). Reprinted (abbreviated) for the Scottish Economic Society in 2 vols, A. Skinner (ed.) (Edinburgh: Oliver & Boyd, 1966).

Steuart, Sir James (ed.) *Works, Political, Metaphysical and Chronological*, 6 vols (London: 1805).

Vickers, D. *Studies in the Theory of Money 1690–1776* (Philadelphia: Chilton, 1959).

Vickers, D. 'The Works, Political, Philosophical and Metaphysical of Sir James Steuart: A Review Article', *Journal of Economic Literature*, 7 (1970) pp. 1190–5.

4 Jeremy Bentham's Democratic Despotism

PEDRO SCHWARTZ

I have not, I never had, nor ever shall have any horror, sentimental or anarchical of the hand of government. I leave it to Adam Smith, and the champions of the rights of man, (for confusion of ideas will jumble the best subjects and the worst citizens upon the same ground) to talk of invasions of natural liberty, and to give as a special argument against this or that law, an argument the effect of which would be to put a negative upon all laws (Jeremy Bentham *Defence of a Maximum*).

The object of this paper is to discuss whether the concept of democracy which appears in the writings of Jeremy Bentham (1748–1832) is one which takes liberty as very much a secondary aim in the good society and inadvertently gives a recipe for a social organisation where virtue is despotically imposed.

In 1981, Dr James published an article titled 'Public Interest and the Majority Rule in Bentham's Democratic Theory', where a thesis similar to the one I wish to defend was first brought to my notice.[1] James argued there that 'the logic of Bentham's democratic system actually points to an increase in the influence of sectional interests, caused by the creation of new opportunities for their promotion'.

This was so, James proceeded, because:

upon conversion to the cause of democratic reform, Bentham did not essentially modify his established theory of law and sovereignty. The legislative competence of the representative assembly was to be no less absolute than that of the oligarchy which ruled under the unreformed constitution (p. 51).

The present paper expands James's argument in two ways: it adds new reasons for holding that Bentham inadvertently[2] created a despotic system; and it expands the basis of proof by going in some detail into the institutions proposed in the recently re-edited Volume 1 of Bentham's *Constitutional Code* (the form *CC* is used in references in this paper).

The paper will be organised in the following way. In Section 1, a justification will be presented for introducing this topic into a volume on the importance of the history of economic thought for the understanding of society. Jeremy Bentham's theory of democracy, relevant to many of the more recent interests of the economics profession, is an exercise in the relations between ethical principles and economic systems, and gives rise to intriguing thoughts about the influence of utilitarian ideas on the twentieth-century welfare state.

In Section 2, a brief sketch of the evolution of Bentham's doctrine on the Constitution of a democracy is presented, and the predominant attention given to his *Constitutional Code* in this paper is justified.

In Section 3 the actual institutions of a democracy in Bentham's *Constitutional Code* are summarised, and his proposals for the organisation of bureaucracy recalled.

In Section 4 the thesis of this paper will be restated in full. Special insistence will be laid on the belief that Bentham did not harbour animadversion against liberty, but that the unwanted consequences of his system would make for a regulated society where social control was the paramount object.

Section 5 deals with two central ideas of Bentham's political philosophy: his concept of law as will, and his principle of utility or efficiency. In contrast, the rule of law and the nurturing of novelty and creative destruction are presented as alternative principles of social organisation.

Section 6 concludes the paper by reviewing the arguments for and against the assertion that Bentham's political philosophy was, without his wishing it so, a doctrine of democratic despotism.

1. WHY THIS PAPER

Three reasons induce me to discuss the topic of Jeremy Bentham and democracy: that the study of political systems has come into the purlieu of the economist; that with the challenge of the contractarians against the utilitarians the relations between ethical principles and the economic organisation of society is seen as crucial again; and that the importance of ideas in the evolution of social reality is being taken more seriously than ever.

Firstly then, economists in the last 15 years have taken to studying the political market with the same tools that they have applied for more than 200 years to the economic market. The new discipline is called 'Public Choice', in contrast to Private Choices that can be expressed by quoting a price in money.

Since Professors Black, Buchanan, and Tullock re-started work on the economics of politics,[3] many theorems, some of them invented a long time ago, have become established.

Jeremy Bentham was in fact one of the first to use some of these ideas for his political analysis. For example, the whole of Public Choice is based on the assumption that men are self-regarding: this is the starting point that allows predictions to be made about man's political behaviour, later to be tested by observation. Bentham states this assumption very clearly, from early years to later texts. He said it in 1780.[4] He stated it in Volume 1 of the *Constitutional Code*, which he published in 1830:

> In all human minds, in howsoever widely different proportions, –
> *self-regard*, and *sympathy* for others or say *extra-regard* have been
> placed . . . But, in self-regard even sympathy has its root: and if in
> the general tenour of human conduct, self-regard were not prevalent
> over sympathy, – even over sympathy of all others put together, – no
> such species as the human could have existence (*CC*, vol. I (VI. 31.
> A–8) p. 119).

This shows also that Bentham, or for that matter modern economists, leave a role for Smithian sympathy. Other-regarding sympathy, however, is a very scarce commodity and well designed institutions based on the spring of self-interest multiply the effects of such sympathy as men feel in their breasts. As Bentham puts it somewhat obscurely:

> To give increase to the influence of sympathy at the expense of that
> self-regard, and of sympathy for the greater number at the expense
> of sympathy for the lesser number, – is the constant and arduous
> task, as of every moralist, so of every legislator who deserves to be
> so. But, in regard to sympathy, the less the proportion of it [it] is, the
> natural and actual existence of which he assumes as and for the the

basis of his arrangements, the greater will be the success of whatever endeavour he uses to give increase to it (*CC*, Vol. I (VI.31.A10)).

Another idea of Public Choice which Bentham foresaw is the so-called 'agency problem'. By this, economists mean that a person deputed may not faithfully carry out the orders of his principal, but rather appropriate some of the gains to himself.[5] This happens in politics constantly and can be made to be greater or less with different institutional arrangements. Bentham was obsessed by this question and made its prevention one of the linchpins of his design for a democratic society. In his chapter on the Legislature, Chapter VI of his *Constitutional Code*, he inserted a Section 31, called 'Securities for Appropriate Aptitude,' which he started thus:

Art. 1. The assemblage of securities, here proposed with reference to the highest department, the Legislature, forms the commencement of an all-pervading system of the like securities, covering the whole field of the Official establishment, and applying to all public functionaries in every department and subdepartment . . . Art. 2. For this purpose, . . . confidence (it cannot be denied) may with truth be said to be minimized: *distrust* and *suspicion* maximized (*CC*, Vol. I (VI.31.A1-2) pp. 117–18).

Bentham did not foresee some of the theorems of Public Choice and they were of crucial importance for the feasibility of his democratic system. One was the theory of the 'median voter',[6] according to which in a democracy the policies put into effect by elected representatives would be those of interest to the median voter. This is one of the reasons why the political system is less efficient than the economic and must only be resorted to for the supply of public goods: in the economic market, results are usually the consequence of unanimous votes (each weighted by the wealth of the person casting it, and if goods are divisible), so that minority tastes are satisfied; while in the political market, the choices of the median voter rule over those of everyone else.

Similarly, Bentham seemed to have no idea of the cost of information in politics and the fact that the 'rational voter' will be with difficulty prevailed upon to go to the polling station or to find out what the programmes of the different candidates have to offer, let alone participate actively in meetings or voluntary work. The whole democratic system proposed by Bentham is based on a theory of costless political action and costless search for information by the citizen.

Also overlooked by Bentham was a theorem proposed by his contemporary Condorcet[7] about the paradox of voting, later elaborated by Duncan Black[8] in his work on unstable results in committee votes, and by Professor Arrow[9] more generally in his famous 'impossibility theorem': any system, a majority system, as for Condorcet, or a system of unanimous 'Pareto' choices, as for Arrow, is subject to absurd results in some limiting cases. That is why political systems can never be pure and must have an admixture of fail-safe 'checks and balances' against their getting into a loop.

Secondly, many present-day authors believe that philosophical first principles are crucial for the formulation of theories of society.

For a long time it seemed as if utilitarianism had become the only possible philosophical basis of political economy: not only were individuals presumed to be ever maximising utility over given resources, but utility was thought to be comparable as between individuals and summable into a general utility for the whole of society. Even after Pareto devised a method of determining improvements in social welfare that was not dependent on comparing and summing the utilities of different individuals,[10] the practice of speaking in Benthamite terms continued, and the net total welfare gained by realising projects was calculated by the cost-benefit method (after individual utilities were supposed to have been revealed by the 'willingness to pay' of each person affected).[11] However, a return to the theory of the social contract in the last 20 years has signified a radical change in what now cannot be called 'welfare economics', for the concept of collective welfare is seen as inconceivable. Professors Buchanan and Tullock have shown us how it is possible to derive decision rules for a democratic society from the contractarian starting point that in principle all decisions must be taken unanimously: the cost of establishing unanimity for less important decisions makes people accept re-inforced or simple majority rules. This would mean a very different democracy from that which, as we shall see, Bentham designed.[12]

It is Professor Buchanan, too, who has spearheaded the attack against another utilitarian pre-conception: the paradigm of maximisation under constrictions as the model for economic analysis.[13] Rather than present the economic man (I should say 'person') as a housewife choosing goods from the shelves of a supermarket, under the constriction of her monthly allowance, economic human beings should be represented as groups of people at a fair bargaining for mutually beneficial trades: 'the unifying principle becomes *gains from trade*, not maximisation', (p. 229). In this Buchanan is harking back to the Austrian School, or indeed to Adam Smith, the great discoverer of the concept of mutually benefitting trade. The main point that these 'disequilibrium economists' want to make is that the housewife paradigm wrongly assumes that maximum welfare, or rather wealth, must come from everybody reaching the margin of maximum efficiency under the constriction of given resources. But Professor Schultz has shown that an underdeveloped static agrarian economy has usually reached the margin of efficiency, given its low accumulation of human and other capital.[14] A richer and growing economy may be one where constant changes in technology and tastes incite the entrepreneurs to discover where to make a profit by putting together hidden information, knowledge about new methods of production, new systems of organisation, or latent tastes. In this case efficiency is a by-product, and liberty, novelty, discovery, are the engines of wealth creation. Again, a different kind of democracy is posited, one which is not so stable and orderly as Bentham's, but one which is dynamically self-regulating.

Also, the very conception of human nature of the utilitarian is being challenged in recent years. Professor Karl Brunner has drawn a contrast between the 'sociological' man and the resourceful, evaluating, maximising man' (REMM, for short).[15] For Brunner, the man of the *Panopticon* and the *Constitutional Code* would be too similar to a Pavlovian dog, reacting to external stimuli instead of constantly seeking opportunities of modifying his habitat. The kind of treatment for the poor that Bentham wants to mete out to them in his *Panopticon* (as described by C. Bahmueller in his *National Charity Company*) is enough to make them react like the nasty young men of *A Clockwork Orange*.[16] Here too, the concept of a democracy made up of REMMs is very different from a democracy made up of malleable sociological men who are the mere products of their circumstances.

Thirdly, the case of Bentham may be important when taking a view on the vexed question of the influence of ideas on social reality. Were his ideas on democracy influential? Can they in any way be said to have shaped reality?

Bentham had a group of friends and disciples who put his ideas to work after he was dead. When he was in the process of finishing as much as he could of the *Constitutional Code* for its speedy application in an emancipating Greece, he wrote to Leicester Stanhope on 19–21 February 1824 that, though he might die before he finished writing his work, he hoped there would be someone 'capable as well as willing, to put in tolerable order, the mass, not a small one, already got together, though not completed'.[17]

He was right to think so in 1824, and even in 1832, at the time of his death. In 1824, as the editors of the *Constitutional Code*, Rosen and Burns, aptly note, the group was large: James Mill, his friend since General Miranda had introduced them to each other in 1802; John Mill, at the time editing from the MS *The Rationale of Judicial Evidence*; Etienne Dumont, the editor of the *Traités de législation civile et pénale* in 1802, who thus had done, and would still do, sterling work for him; Francis Place, the radical tailor of Charing Cross; John Grote, the historian of Greece; George Bentham, his botanist nephew; Edwin Chadwick, the local government reformer; T. Perronet Thompson, the editor of the *Westminster Review*; and others less well known today, such as Richard Smith, who translated Dumont into English, or his amanuensis Richard Doane, who, in 1843 would edit the *Constitutional Code* for Bowring's edition of the *Works of Jeremy Bentham*: all were ready to broadcast the utilitarian good news, and did so. And even if at the time of his death, Bentham had alienated some of these disciples by the favours he was showering on the generally disliked John Bowring, the general message seeped through and made utilitarianism one of the *idées-force* of British philosophy (legal, political, ethical) for the next 150 years.

About his influence abroad one can be much less positive. True, he was called 'the dead legislator of India' because of the power wielded by James Mill, Macaulay, and John Stuart Mill at the East India Company. But in many cases, it is my belief that his ideas were either misunderstood or used as a convenient armoury of weapons for local wars. Dr John Dinwiddy has given a well-balanced summary of the diffusion of Bentham's ideas in the world at large while he was still alive: they were broadcast through the reading of Dumont's edition in France, Italy, and the Iberian world; through the work of James Mill and Macaulay in India; through the efforts of Edward Livingstone in Louisiana; through the ideological and political struggle of the philosophic radicals in England.[18] The question, however, is not only whether a direct line of descent of ideas can be traced from his work to somebody influential later on, but whether, on top of this, his ideas, whether published or in manuscript, express coherently the world-view of an influential group of people and their ever-widening circle of followers.

The *Constitutional Code* can be considered an important work, though there is evidence that not many people read it: 13 copies were reported sold in 1830 and 1831 by Bentham's publisher;[19] and not many must have read it in the tiny script and two columned pages of the Bowring edition. But the work is such a clear *exposé* of the ideology of the utilitarian democracy that it helps one understand real life developments much better. Great books have a way of working out the logical consequences of diffuse ideologies and also of helping to point out as yet unseen and unexpected developments when they were written. One could say that Bentham was in the *Constitutional Code* the unwitting formulator of the philosophy of the welfare state. His *Code* may contain a working model of a coherently built welfare state and may allow us to reconstruct the reasons why the welfare state has turned out to be a failure.[20]

2.   THE EVOLUTION OF THE CONSTITUTIONAL CODE

The leading ideas of Bentham's social and political thought are present in his writings from the very beginning. They underwent a degree of evolution but their nature did not change. One might distinguish four elements in his thought: (a) the idea that the social contract is a dangerous fiction and that the principle of utility affords a much better explanation of the social bond; (b) that the essence of the law is an act of will or command on the part of the sovereign or his deputies, and that hence the Common Law and Judge-Made Law were pathological developments to be eradicated from society; (c) that political economy was a branch of legislation, or as Professor L. J. Hume says,[21] a part of government business concerned with abundance; (d) that, for the convenience and security of the people, all the laws had better be gathered in a 'Digest of Laws',[22] or, he elaborated, re-written from scratch in a series of Codes forming a *Pannomion*.

These elements form a very distinctive social philosophy and one which many people think less than acceptable. Utilitarianism can be unfair to minorities, and may lead to the idea that some omniscient planner may know the 'social welfare function' and push individuals willy-nilly towards it. The idea of the law as will may lead to the positivistic belief that whatever is in the statute book is just; and also to the belief that the legislator's will can change society without limit. The vision of political economy as a tool of government again blinds one to the fact that the economic laws of society cannot be bent at the sovereign's behest, and that the principal lesson of political economy is the futility of most kinds of government interference, if only because individuals discount it and circumvent it. Finally, the thought that it is possible to clean the slate of society and write all its laws anew is the reverse of what experience shows to be possible.

Bentham's first substantial works, published and unpublished, all start with a criticism of Sir William Blackstone's *Commentaries on the Laws of England*. Blackstone was a believer in natural law and in the perfection of the British Constitution. In *A Fragment on Government*, Bentham's first substantial, though anonymous, publication, almost the first words were to proclaim the principle of utility as a fundamental axiom: *It is the greatest happiness of the greatest number that is the measure of right and wrong,* (*Fragment, CW*, p. 393).

Also in the same work he derides the use of the idea of a social contract by Blackstone, for he 'was in hopes . . . that this chimera had been effectively demolished by Mr HUME'.[23]

In another work which he wrote at that time but did not publish until 1789, *An Introduction to the Principles of Morals and Legislation*, he expanded notably on the principle of utility. It is there that we find the famous phrase:

> Nature has placed mankind under the governance of two sovereign masters, *pain* and *pleasure*. It is for them alone to point out what we ought to do, as well as to determine what we shall do. On the one hand the standard of right and wrong, on the other the chain of causes and effects, are fastened to their throne (*Introduction, CW*, p. 11).

He also gave a clear definition of law as an expression of will: 'Every law, when complete, is either of a *coercive* or *uncoercive* nature. A coercive law is a *command*. An uncoercive, or rather a *dis*coercive, law is the revocation, in whole or in part, of a coercive law' (*Introduction, CW*, p. 302).

And in the preface of this last book he developed an ambitious programme of publication in ten parts, where he was going to set down the principles of legislation in matters of civil law, of penal law, of procedural, of constitutional, and others.[24] So indeed all the themes of his intellectual life were there from the beginning.

There is one important point for the thesis of this paper where he changed his mind when he wrote the *Constitutional Code* in his old age. In *Of Laws in General*, a book which he had substantially finished in 1782, but left unpublished, he has a Chapter II on the 'Source of Law' where he asserted that the law-giver, whose will made law, must be the sovereign: 'First then with respect to its [the law's] *source*. Considered in this point of view, the will of which it is the expression must, as the definition intimates, be the will of the sovereign in *a* state' (*Of Laws*, *CW*, p. 18).

Dr Rosen underlines very justly that in the *Constitutional Code* the people is the sovereign though not the legislator. The single-chambered Parliament is, however, the expressor of the legislative will: 'the Legislature is omnicompetent', Bentham in any case concludes. Now, the change as to who is the sovereign is very expressive of the democratic change which had taken place in Bentham's opinions. All the same, it does not affect the fundamentals of his philosophy of the law, a positivistic philosophy, where law is whatever the sovereign wills and where the rule of utility is an empirical criterion for criticism but not a source of legal obligation.

The constitutional part of his thought gathered importance with the years. He prepared a book of rules for the French Assembly in 1792, and also for the 1810 Spanish Cortes (this he published too late in 1815, when the King of Spain had reasserted his absolute powers). In 1811 he had drafted a press law, or the rudiments of it, for General Miranda on his ill-fated expedition to Venezuela. In 1809–10 he started his series of works on electoral reform, culminating in his *Plan for Parliamentary Reform*, published in 1818. Also in 1818 he was visited by the Argentinian Rivadavia, who was in search of a King for the Rio de la Plata: this is when, I believe, Bentham started to think of a Constitutional Code for those parts of the world. He thereupon began rewriting his French pamphlet on colonial emancipation, which led him from 1821 to 1823, to produce a book called 'Rid Yourselves of Ultramaria,' which he never published because of the demise of the second attempt of the Spanish to establish a liberal regime. In the course of this work, where he discussed the ill effects of a colonial empire on the democratic Constitution of Spain, the *Constitución de Cádiz*, he adumbrated many thoughts useful for his code work.[25]

However, the first direct commission to write a Constitutional Code came in a letter from the Portuguese Cortes in April 1821. As Professors Rosen and Burns relate in their introduction to the recent re-edition of the *Constitutional Code*, Bentham set to work enthusiastically. In 1822 he published a sort of promotional pamphlet in English and Spanish called *Codification Proposal . . . for any nation professing liberal opinions*. He had hopes that the liberals in Spain would also commission from him one of his codes. However, the Portuguese liberal regime ended forcibly in 1822, and the Spanish in 1823.

He then turned to Greece. Through Colonel Leicester Stanhope, whom I mentioned above as one of his disciples, he sent to Greece a large part of the material which he was using to write his *Constitutional Code*. Bentham did not have too many hopes that his Code would be promulgated in Greece: he knew the Greek freedom fighters from the inside, having had occasion to see them operate unscrupulously in the matter of the Greek loan.

However, when the American *criollos* definitely routed the Spaniards at Ayacucho in 1824, Bentham turned his attention once more to Latin America. A Catalan refugee priest, Antoni Puigblanch, had translated his *Codification Proposal* and now he asked him to turn his hand to the Code. A large part of Volume 1 of the *Code*, and the 'Legislator's Inaugural Declaration' (of which more below) made its way into the hands of José Cecilio del Valle, the Central American writer and politician.[26]

Finally, in 1830 Volume 1 of the *Code* was published. Bentham typically promised that he would soon have Volumes 2 and 3 ready. Also, in view of his advanced age he promised he would give in those two future volumes the skeletons of the other parts of his *Pannomion*: these skeletons would all pertain to domestic or municipal law and would summarise the Civil Code, the Penal Code, and the Procedure Code. In fact, he gave some idea of the principles of the Civil Code in the very preface, where he outlined his future work. Furthermore he included a table of contents of the Penal Code in that Volume 1, and worked all through this time on the Procedure Code but died before he had finished it.

Volume 1 of the *Constitutional Code*, edited by Richard Doane, was re-published in Bowring's *The Works of Jeremy Bentham*. There was merit in Doane's editorial labours, for he preceded the said volume with a collection of Bentham texts on the *rationale* of the *Code*, and added the subject-matter of Volume 2 on defence and the several functions of the ministers. This last will allow us to enter in a little more detail into the institutions of Bentham's democracy.

As we can see, Bentham was on the side of the angels. From the time at the turn of the century when he had embraced radical opinions, there was no doubt that he was in favour of liberating people and peoples (especially if they were white[27]). There was a time when Bentham wrote for enlightened despots. After a first flirtation with democratic ideas, the cruelty of the French revolution made him conservative. However, the combined experiences of failure in the *Panopticon* affair and in Scotch law reform, together with the influence of his new friend James Mill, turned him into a radical in the first five years of the nineteenth century. He never looked back.

There is no doubt then that if the democratic system Bentham proposed had despotic implications this would not have been Bentham's wish, quite the contrary. But ideas leave the hands of their creators and have a life of their own.

3.   THE INSTITUTIONS OF THE CONSTITUTIONAL CODE

It is time to describe the main lines of Bentham's republic, to let the reader get a feel for the way the institutions of such a society would hang together. I will do it without references or comments, so that one may judge whether I am caricaturing Bentham when I attribute despotic consequences to his doctrines. The full details may be found in the recently published Volume 1 of the *Constitutional Code*, or in Dr Rosen's Chapter VII on 'The Institutions of Democratic Government'.

The over-all end of political action and institutions was to obtain the greatest sum of happiness in the commonwealth.

This end was attained by pursuing four subordinate aims, which were, in order of decreasing importance, security, subsistence, abundance, and equality.

Note that liberty was not among them, for, in the opinion of Bentham, the goods for which liberty was desired were precisely the four above-mentioned. Liberty was simply redundant as a goal. Security, by guaranteeing the individual the enjoyment of his life and his property, allowed him to do as he wished within his own sphere.

Without a minimum of subsistence, Bentham alleged, there could be no happiness, so that the state should guarantee it, but without loosening the springs of activity which brought about abundance.

Equality could conflict with security, when ill-distributed private property had to be reformed or taxed to foster this fourth subordinate aim. However, security was to prevail over equality, save for the most extreme cases.

The utilitarian commonwealth was to be a republic. Though some of its institutions, especially those giving securities against misrule, or guaranteeing an economical organisation of the administration, could be applicable in a monarchy, Bentham in his later years was as adamant and anti-monarchist as he was a convinced atheist.

The sovereign in his sort of commonwealth was the people. When they voted they became the Constitutive Authority. Hence Bentham wanted to extend the franchise as widely as possible, but he agreed rather unwillingly to exclude females for the sake of feasibility.

The Constitutive Authority expressed itself through one important institution, apart from elections: the Public Opinion Tribunal. This tribunal was the ultimate sanction for authorities disobeying the Constitution. The authorities had to accept being criticised, denounced, traduced in front of that tribunal: 'The military functionary is paid for being shot at. The civil functionary is paid for being spoken and written at' (*CC*, vol. I (V.6.A2)) said Bentham in a memorable line. The freedom of the press and of opinion had to be complete.

The people elected the Supreme Legislature. Constituencies were single-seated. Parliaments lasted for a year. The legislature was omnicompetent. Deputies had to sit every single day except on the seventh day of the week and were paid daily on attendance. Two institutions were of special importance: the 'Legislation Enquiry Judicatory', established to gather facts, statistics, information, with judicial powers to obtain it; and the 'Legislation Penal Judicatory', whose function it was to punish the misbehaviour of deputies, of Prime Ministers, and of Ministers of Justice. The Legislature was not bound by any previous act and could not bind its successors.

One of the securities for appropriate aptitude of the deputies was the Legislator's 'Inaugural Declaration', some of whose headings it may be instructive to spell out. The deputy would promise economy and honesty; equally, declaration of law to all; and more things, among which, 'insincerity and arrogance abjured'.

The Prime Minister was elected by the Legislature for four years and could not be re-elected until there were three or four former Prime Ministers to choose from. His powers were very wide, but he could be 'dislocated', or displaced, by a vote in Parliament.

He appointed the ministers for life, but again could easily dislocate them. Their departments were as follows: Elections, Legislation, Army, Navy, Preventive Service, Interior Communication, Indigence Relief, Education, Domain, Health, Foreign Relations, Trade and Finance.

The functionaries, or civil servants, were also designated for life. They were chosen among the 'List of Locables', who had passed the course of education, and the examinations, which secured their aptitude. (Deputies also had to pass these two hurdles.)

One of the main worries of Bentham was to obviate oppression, of functionaries over other functionaries, and of functionaries over 'non-functionaries', which is what ordinary people were called in the

Constitutional Code. These securities were manifold: some were architectural, such as the carefully designed cubicles in the ministries: they allowed both for secret meetings between the functionary and the non-functionary, and for the public listening in, as a sort of committee of the Public Opinion Tribunal.

Of great importance for Bentham were the arrangements for combining cheapness with efficiency in government. Thus the arrangements he proposed for bettering the vigilance of contracts and stores, for ensuring the attendance of functionaries, and for collecting usable information on the working of the ministries – all indicated a man well versed in the science of bureaucracy. He laid great store by the system of competition in pay, whereby the 'locables' aspiring to a post could bid for it by offering to accept a reduction in their salaries.

Justice was to be prompt, cheap, and based on codified and easily comprehensible law – or rather, the law would be couched in very precise Benthamese, which Bentham thought would be comprehensible.

Such was the 'glasshouse society', the efficient, centralised, socially-controlled, and, above all, happy society that Bentham wanted to build on England's green and pleasant land, and also on foreign parts for the lesser breeds without the law.

It is a moot question whether this would have been a despotic society. It would certainly have been efficient, through the minimisation of expense and the speed of decision of single-seated, centralised authority. There would have been securities for appropriate attitude in all authorities, through a severe system of selection and the relevant incentive structure. The officeholders would certainly have been responsible for their mistakes, watched over as they were by the Public Opinion Tribunal, and dislocable by their superiors or the voters. But would this commonwealth have been as free and unregulated as one could wish?

4.   THE TYRANNY OF THE MAJORITY?

The thesis of this paper may now be restated. As Rosen says in his able defence of our hero, in his *Jeremy Bentham and Representative Democracy*, the important question is whether: 'if . . . [Bentham's] *Code* was actually adopted by a state (together with the whole *Pannomion*) and an economy to complement the codes of law, the result might be quite different from what Bentham intended'.[28]

The thesis of this paper is that Bentham did indeed build a system which would in all probability have resulted in a stifling, hypocritical, and sterilely efficient democracy.

This is not to say that he did not foresee some of the snags of his kind of democracy, indeed of any kind of democracy. The agency problem we have noted; Bentham tried to take all sorts of precautions against it, but it is doubtful that his recipe of granting wide powers to officials, while establishing securities against misrule in the form of publicity and the fear of removal (or 'dislocation', as he called it) would have been sufficient. Without the reduction and limitation of the powers of authorities even at the cost of efficiency in the Administration, there seems to be no stopping the growth of government in modern democracies.

Another question on which he anticipated the kind of worry we feel today about the future of democracy is that of expense. Rosen is right in saying that: 'his belief that the problem of expense is a major constitutional problem is most probably unique in the history of democratic thought'.[29]

This, by the way, is a deadly comment on the history of democratic thought before the coming of Public Choice theory. Bentham put all his ingenuity to work to show 'that democracy can be less expensive than monarchy and aristocracy'.[30]

In his important Chapter II of the *Code*, on 'Ends and Means', Bentham stated the following: 'Art.1. Of this construction, the all-comprehensive object, or end in view, is, from first to last, the greatest happiness of the greatest number . . . Art.2. Means employed, two – aptitude maximized; expense minimized' (*CC*, vol. I (II.A1-2) pp. 18–19). This principle of expense minimised he applied sedulously at every point of the official establishment. He has special hopes of one nostrum: his 'pecuniary competition system', whereby, as I have said, the candidates who had proved themselves fitted for a given place by means of a competitive examination, then bid to have that place at a lower than posted salary. Bentham thus expected to reduce personnel expenses drastically.

Despite the fact that he had coined the expression 'sinister interests' to signify coalitions of people seeking to extract rents from the majority of the population, he thought that such occurrences were avoidable in a democracy. He put his confidence in two institutions: the Public Opinion Tribunal, and the possibility to 'dislocate' deputies, the Prime Minister, the ministers, judges, local headmen, *et al.*, ultimately by popular vote. About the Public Opinion Tribunal he had these words to say: 'To the pernicious exercise of the power of the government it is the only check; to the beneficial, an indispensable supplement. Able rulers lead it; prudent rulers lead or follow it; foolish rulers disregard it'.

And here comes the important point: the Public Opinion Tribunal cannot really go wrong.

> Even at the present stage in the career of civilization, its dictates coincide, on most points, with those of the *greatest happiness principle*; on some, however, it still deviates from them: but as its deviations have all along been less and less numerous, and less wide, sooner or later they will cease to be discernible (*CC*, vol. I (V.4. A4) p. 36).

This is an excessively sanguine view of the identification of public opinion with the Rousseaunian general will. From the history of tariffs and regulations we know that the individual gain expected by rent-seekers is much larger than the per capita loss of general welfare which their activities cost, when distributed among the whole of the population. Not until national income is seriously held down by the web of Lilliputian threads laid down by the rent-seekers, does the population at large start reacting.

As for the 'dislocation' of peccant legislators or administrators, the mechanism would work if only the snag just alluded to did not lay in wait – corrupt officials will only be dismissed by popular vote when the majority can be bothered to overrule the profiting minorities.

On the other points that one must take into account to know whether a political system can become despotic, Bentham showed no sensibility.

It is to be expected that he would not agree with those who say that it is impossible to compare utilities as between differing individuals. But the whole point of a free society is that one does not decide what makes people happy. As soon as one starts summing happiness over individuals one is ready to fall into the temptation of telling people what is good for them.

Neither did Bentham gauge the importance of the idea of mutually beneficial bargains, formulated by Adam Smith. In his mind, unless interests coincided perfectly, there had to be collective intervention to maximise the welfare of society. Rosen has quoted a most interesting passage from some unpublished papers containing the justification or *rationale* for popular sovereignty. According to Rosen, the argument is in two parts: Firstly, each person desires his own happiness and endeavours to secure this at the expense of that of everyone else. But as each man tries to achieve this end, he runs into the opposition of everyone, and his own endeavours are without success.[31]

Now Bentham's texts could not be clearer: there are only two kinds of interests, coincidental and incompatible. Thus Bentham:

> In the language of interest, each has a particular interest; all have a common interest: what is by all believed to be the common interest of all, is endeav[our]ed to be promoted by all. [E]ach particular interest is opposed by those and those only, by whom it is regarded as adverse to their own.[32]

Not only does Bentham seem to forget, on the plane of fact, his own idea of 'sinister interests' and the possibility of coalitions, but also, on the plane of value, there is this idea, which recurs in the *Constitutional Code*, that unless there is perfect coincidence, the interest of some must be sacrificed to that of the majority. In the Legislator's Inaugural Declaration, which every deputy had to pronounce when elected, one may find the following passage:

> I recognize, as the *all-comprehensive*, and only right and proper end of Government, the greatest happiness of the greatest number of the members of the community: all without exception, in so far as possible: of the greatest number, on every occasion on which the nature of the case renders it impossible by rendering it a matter of necessity, to make sacrifice of a portion of the happiness of a few, to the greater happiness of the rest (*CC*, I (VI.2) p. 136).[33]

The idea that, precisely because they have different utility schedules or different initial resources, both bargainers can profit from their contraposition, from *voluntarily* sacrificing a portion of their happiness for their own gain, is quite alien to Bentham. Such voluntary bargains form the great majority of agreements reached in a society and they need not be imposed by the legislators or the government.

All these mistakes of principle lead Bentham to give excuses for state intervention. Despite his more than Smithian stance in his *Defence of Usury*, Bentham was no defender of *laissez-faire*. Let me quote the famous phrases in *Defence of a Maximum*, where he likens *laissez-faire* to letting a boat sink when it has sprung a leak – and then proceeds to ask for the imposition of a maximum price for corn.

The particles of a mass of fluid, the particles of a mass of water, have a propensity, when left to themselves, to range themselves upon the same level; human creatures have on their part, a propensity to save their own lives: and when water in the search after a level is making its way too fast into a ship, pumps are employed by men to prevail on it to get the better of that propensity, and betake itself to a higher level, and this may serve as an argument in favour of a maximum to any gentleman who finds himself ready to consider it as such.[34]

I can also recall the pamphlets on paper money written by Bentham around the turn of the century and published by W. Stark in Volume 2 of his *Jeremy Bentham's Economic Writings*.[35] All the works contained in that volume propose schemes for the state issuing paper money, for extending the government monopoly from the coinage to the notes, for increasing government revenue, and for displacing private bankers in favour of the government.

This was nothing new, for in 1794 he had published a 'Proposal for a mode of taxation in which the burthen may be alleviated or even ballanced by an indemnity . . . applied in the first instance to the case of bankers'.[36] He there proposed that the government impose a tax on bankers and compensate by granting them a monopoly against newcomers. The monopoly in the financial trade did not matter, thought Bentham.

A banker a trader? no such thing. They buy nothing; they sell nothing. A banker a trader? then so is every individual in the kingdom, who possesses money and lives by lending it and derives income from the interest of it (Stark, I, p. 405).

As with Ricardian land in Madras, a monopoly could be created for bankers and taxed because they had no alternative employ.

It was John Stuart Mill, as Rosen reminds us, who criticised Bentham's political theory for leading to the 'tyranny of the majority'.[35] It is very revealing, therefore, to read in Mill's *Autobiography* why he reneged on pure, doctrinaire Benthamism. What finally triggered his mental breakdown was the discovery that the possible realisation of the utilitarian Utopia left him quite unmoved. Utilitarianism seemed to be all based on social satisfaction.

The question was [said Mill], whether, if the reformers of society and government could succeed in their objects, and every person in the community were free and in a state of physical comfort, the pleasures of life, being no longer kept up by struggle and privation, would cease to be pleasures.[38]

Curiously for a creed based on the pursuit of pleasure, personal happiness had disappeared through a trap. This is underlined by the following reflexion of Mill's:

The other important change which my opinions at this time underwent, was that I, for the first time, gave its proper place, among the prime necessities of human well-being, to the internal culture of the individual (ibid., p. 147).

5.   LAW AND UTILITY

The reason why Bentham's constitutional thought turned out to have despotic consequences is to be found in two points of his social philosophy: his theory of law and his principle of utility.

(a) For the young Bentham the law was the expression of the will of the sovereign. For the older Bentham this cannot be so because the people are the sovereign and they do not make laws. The people are the constitutive authority and set up the Legislature, who make the laws. Says Bentham: 'The sovereignty is in the people. It is reserved by and to them. It is exercised, by the exercise of the Constitutive authority . . . The Constitutive authority is in the whole body of Electors belonging to this state' (*CC*, vol. I (III.A1&5.2.A2).

Despite this important change in the matter of sovereignty (in the direction of democracy), Bentham still clung to his idea that the law is a command: 'In the present Pannomion . . . need has been found for making exclusive application of the term *law* . . . to designate exclusively a species of command' (*CC*, vol. I (IX.4.A31)).

Neither is the next step implied logically in the idea that the law is the will of a properly constituted sovereign authority. It is the idea that there are no limits to this will, because it is of the essence of will to be united by precedent, to be capricious, to be, if I may say so, wilful. This idea reinforces a tradition of the British Constitution: the Queen in Parliament (for Bentham, a unicameral parliament) can do everything except turn a man into a woman, as the saying goes: 'The Supreme Legislature is omnicompetent . . . To its powers there are no limits, it has checks. These checks are applied, by the securities, provided for good conduct on the part of the several members, individually operated upon' (*CC*, I (VI.1.A1)).

About these securities, something was said in Section 3. But here Bentham is taking over the Cromwellian idea that there should be no limit to the powers of the Commons. Professor G. Vedel[39] has noted that in the popular democracies of Eastern Europe the tendency is to have unicameral parliaments, while in the West the tendency is towards bi-cameralism. Perhaps a unitary conception of the happiness of all, as of the interests of the proletariat, make for the same constitutional tendencies.

This legitimation of the will makes Bentham do away with the time-honoured distinction between private and public bills: the first deal with *individual* persons or things, the second with *classes* of persons or things. The title of law is usually reserved for the latter, for the public acts, for they embody the idea of the neutrality of the law as between equals; or to put it is a more metaphysical way, the equality of all before the law, by having the law apply to classes instead of singling out any individual. Bentham substitutes for the classical distinction that of 'transitory and permanent mandates':

> By *transitory*, understand those in the case of which, at the end of a certain length of time . . ., giving *ulterior* execution and effect to the mandate is rendered impossible: as where the mandate having for its sole object the exercise of a certain act, on a certain person or thing, such as exercise has been performed (*CC*, Vol. I (IX.4.A25)).

And Bentham adds what he thinks follows obviously: 'Note however, that in case of necessity, there is nothing to hinder the Legislature from issuing mandates, as above, of the ephemeral kind, as well as those of the naturally permanent kind' (*CC*, vol. I (IX.4.A27)).

Of course, there are 'securities' within the Benthamite system. Parliaments are annual. The deputies by and large are not eligible for re-election. The Prime Minister, the ministers, the administrators, the judges are 'dislocable'. There is total freedom of the press, of information, of opinion, so as to follow the Public Opinion Tribunal to exercise its functions to the full. The legislators have to make a full inaugural declaration, so that the electors can compare their promises with their acts. There is a 'Legislation Penal Judicatory' to try for misconduct, present or past deputies, and present or past Prime Ministers and Ministers of Justice, and so on.

However, Bentham is very much against 'checks and balances'. To give one instance:

> If on any occasion, any ordinance, which to some shall appear repugnant to the principles of this Constitution, shall come to have been enacted by the Legislature, such ordinance is not on that account to be, by any judge, treated or spoken of, as being null and void (*CC*, Vol. I (VI.2.A2)).

This is not to detract from the admiration that Bentham felt for the 'American United States', as the living proof that democracy worked. But he always underlined the democratic side of the American system and attributed no importance to the limits set in it to the democratic or majoritarian principle, by the division of powers into Executive, Legislative, and Judiciary; and by the pre-eminence of the Constitutional text over the decisions of Congress.

Another peculiarity which throws light on Bentham's philosophy of law is the subordinate place he gives the civil law in the *Pannomion*. The civil law is the 'right conferring' part of the law for Bentham, while the penal is the 'wrong repressing'. All is well up to here. But Bentham wants 'from each portion of the *Civil* Code, reference to be made to the correspondent portion of the *Penal* Code'.[40] This is an echo of the idea that the essence of the law is coercion, and that there can be no right if there is no exactly corresponding coercion.

It is true that one of the essential elements of the legal system is the ultimate power of coercion exercised by the Courts and the police. The whole of the law, however, is much larger than what is enforced. The right kind of legal coercion diminishes the total sum of coercion in society. It aims at avoiding social coercion or undue thwarting of personal decisions, taken within the pale of property rights, by other members of society. Much of the law simply establishes the way individuals can best reach mutually beneficial agreements. The best service of the law is to define all that is taken as understood in social relations, either beforehand in the Common Law, or *ex post facto* through judge-made law.

Much of the civil law, therefore, will have no correspondence in the penal law. To express my objection to Bentham's position by a *reductio ad absurdum*, all this would imply saying that the institution of the family would dissolve if adultery were not punished in the penal code. It appears that, for Bentham, individuals have to be permanently controlled by articles of the penal code if they are to respect the rights of others or the full tenor of the agreements they have voluntarily entered into.

Professor Hart's concept of coercion[41] is much more economical than Bentham's: for Hart, coercion comes at the margin for each individual, stopping us from disregarding that part of the property right of others we are just tempted to disregard. But in most things we are law-abiding and contract-respecting, though the margin comes at different points for each of us. As for the content of the greater part of our social actions the penal law has nothing to say.

(b) Bentham's principle of utility makes for two kinds of difficulties in democratic theory: it lends itself to unwarranted assumptions about what is good for others; and it fosters ideas of equality through redistribution.

The seriousness of the problem is revealed by the contradiction between the two parts of the utilitarian dictum: the contradiction between 'the greatest happiness', on the one hand, and 'of the greatest number' on the other.

Bentham realised this contradiction. It is one thing to wish for the greatest sum of happiness in society, allowing for different intensities of enjoyment in different people, and another to say that what counts is the number of people one makes happy. One does not even need to assume that everyone has the same capacity for happiness to give the dictum an egalitarian meaning on the numbers count.

In the *Constitutional Code* as published in 1830, the Legislator's Inaugural Declaration had a passage that Bentham corrected one year after publication. In 1830 it said:

> I recognize, as the . . . end of Government the greatest happiness of the greatest number of the members of the community: of all without exception, in so far as possible: of the greatest number, on every occasion on which the nature of the case renders it impossible . . . (*CC*, vol. I (VII.2)).

The other text appeared in the 1831 revised version of the Inaugural Declaration, and I italicise the relevant parts that Bentham changed.

> I recognize, as the . . . end of government, the greatest happiness of the greatest number of the community in question: the greatest happiness – of all of them, without exception, in so far as possible, on every occasion on which the nature of the case *renders the*

provision of an equal quantity of happiness for everyone of them impossible.[42]

The change is telling: there is no conflict in the apportioning of happiness in the community when everyone has an equal quantity of it. This Benthamite paradise I would consider as the acme of stealthy oppression. This would demand an investigation into the happiness of individuals; or a forced revelation of their preferences, especially of their preferences for public goods; or that someone decide for everyone else.

The other danger lies in the forcible re-distribution of income or wealth and the oppression of minorities. There is a most interesting passage of Bentham's, which shows that the master had his doubts:

> So long as the greatest number – the 1001 – were in the enjoyment of the greatest degree of comfort, the greatest degree of torment might be the lot of the smallest of the two numbers – the 1000! and still . . . the proper object to endeavour of the greatest happiness of the greatest number be actually conformed to – not contravened . . .[43]

This sounds almost like the Dan Usher paradox,[44] which shows the possibility of the exploitation of a minority, when a majority of one keeps all the income. Bentham did not go on explicitly to show the instability of democratic distributive solutions (the 1000 would always bribe one person from the other side), but he did propose barriers against the expropriation game: one was the security of property, the other the 'disappointment prevention principle'.

Security was for Bentham the principal of the four aims of government. He was certainly conscious of the dangers for industry of making inroads into property rights. However, in the Dumont *Traités* of 1802 he allowed texts to be published where he applied (or rather misapplied) the marginal utility principle to examples of forcible transfers of property.[45] This is precisely the kind of abuse to which the greatest happiness principle is open.

The 'disappointment prevention principle' is a thought Bentham had *en passant* in an article in the *Westminster Review*. Rosen is right to emphasise its importance and wonder why Bentham did not develop it further. It afforded a solid base for the notion of vested rights. Bentham, according to Rosen, also distinguished between fixed and floating expectations, when considering the degree of resistance reforms might have to face. All these were attenuations of the pro-redistribution slant of the utilitarian principle, but no guarantee that later ages would respect them.[46]

Professor Usher believes, rightly in my view, that a democracy cannot resist the political distribution of income and calls the non-political distribution method of a society its 'equity'. The distribution of income by the free market would increase the 'equity' or capital of a democracy. In Usher's view

> Government by majority rule, though necessary for the preservation of what we think of as a good society, is unstable and unworkable unless the range of issues to be settled by majority rule is severely circumscribed. In particular, government by majority rule cannot be relied upon to assign citizen's shares of the national income (Usher, 1981, p. 10).

6. CONCLUSIONS

The thesis presented at the beginning of this paper, indeed its very title, proposes that Bentham, though unwittingly, did defend a system of democratic despotism in his *Constitutional Code*.

In this paper I go further than James in his. Not only did the logic of Bentham's system lead to an increase in the influence of sectional interests: that logic led to the establishment of a glasshouse society where regulation was maximised and spontaneity minimised.

The curious thing is that Bentham was methodologically an individualist. He maintained that social institutions were fictions. He thought that the decisions of society had to be in some efficient way the resultant of the choices of its citizens.

He wanted to extend the suffrage to all men above 21 years and would have dearly loved to see it granted to women. He was a stickler for the freedom of the press and gave so much importance to opinion as a security of good government in a democracy that he constituted it into the Public Opinion Tribunal.

In the Benthamite democracy there was to be publicity and accountability: publicity of decisions, deliberations, statistics; accountability of all authorities, save the Constituting one, the people, in whom sovereignty resided.

But the Legislature was to be omnicompetent. It was to be bound by no precedent and could not bind its successors. There was no remedy against its decisions but to 'dislocate' the deputies at the next election (most of them could not be re-elected anyhow). There was the fatigue of yearly elections and the peculiar fact that a yearly Parliament elected a Prime Minister for four years.

The Prime Minister designated the ministers for life. The next Prime Minister could dislocate them, but then he might not. The ministers appointed the functionaries for life, too. They were chosen from a list of people who had undergone special training and had passed the appropriate examination. Everybody was educated and examined for the purpose, even the deputies. The government was represented locally by the 'headman', who were more powerful than a French *maire* or *préfet*, though they were also easily dislocable.

As for the judges, they were there to interpret the law to the letter and apply it according to the will of the legislator. Ideally the law was all set out in the *Pannomion*, but it could be changed every year, according to the changeable yearly majorities in Parliament. No law was above any other, or changeable with more difficulty than another, even the Constitution. The law was the will of the people at any moment, or of the deputies at any moment, for they sat all year round without remission.

And above it all was enthroned the all-comprehensive rule: the greatest happiness of all equally divided, or if the circumstances of the case forbade unanimity, then the happiness of the greatest number. And there was no difficulty in knowing when somebody was happy.

This is not the place to argue for alternative principles to Bentham's on the law or on the criterion of welfare.

However, one need not to be a believer in natural law to reject Bentham's positivism. Professor Hayek (though himself a philosophical utilitarian) has been the principal modern expositor of the need for the Rule of Law if freedom is not to disappear from our societies:[47] since the law cannot be written once and for all,[48] the rule of law must embody established practice of what is reasonable and what the citizen might reasonably expect, so that he is not deceived in his belief that he will be able to make the most of his own choices and his own bargains. The quandary of modern democracies is that the rule of law must be foreseeable and flexible at the same time. In any case, the rule of law cannot hold if all the power is vested in one body or person, however well constituted: the experience of many free nations, from the largest, the US, to the smaller, such as Switzerland, shows that federal checks and balances allow freedom to strike root and prosper.

Equally, the belief that the polity is the result of a constantly renewed, though implicit, social contract may be a sounder view than that the social bond exists to promote the happiness of the individuals. Happiness is a private matter, not a right, whatever the American Constitution may say. Individuals, within a framework of neutral rules, must be free to pursue their own happiness. Our age of religious revivals must make one aware that the happiness of each individual cannot be grasped rationally by anyone else, and especially cannot be confused with merely material well-being.

The rule of law and the neutrality of the social framework constitute the basis for a tacit social contract that may afford a safer grounding for a free commonwealth than that afforded by Benthamite philosophy.

NOTES AND REFERENCES

1. M. James 'Public Interest and the Majority Rule in Bentham's Democratic Theory', *Political Theory*, IX, 1 (February 1981) pp. 49–64.
2. I say inadvertently because, as Dr James noted, Bentham was not open to the charge of 'majoritarianism', that is, he did not propose a commonwealth where the majority could do as it wished (p. 52).
3. See D. C. Mueller, *Public Choice* (Cambridge University Press, 1979) pp. 2–3 and *passim*.
4. 'What motives (independent of such as legislation and religion may chance to furnish) can one man have to consult the happiness of another? by what motives, or, which comes to the same thing, by what obligations can he be bound to obey the dictates of *probity* and *beneficence*? In answer to this, it cannot but be admitted, that the only interests which a man at all times and upon all occasions is sure to find *adequate* motives for consulting, are his own.' *An Introduction to the Principles of Morals and Legislation* in J. H. Burn and H. L. A. Hart (eds), in *The Collected Works of Jeremy Bentham* (*CW*) (London: The Athlone Press, 1970) p. 284.
5. Much of what appears in the *Constitutional Code* was present in a previous text about which I would rather write a separate article, to wit, 'Rid Yourselves of Ultramaria'. This MS, which Bentham put aside in 1823, had something to say about the agency problem, namely 'that of the sweets of government the quantity in the hands of the functionaries of government should be as small as possible, consistently with the exercise of the power of government in a manner contributing to the greatest happiness of the greatest number, and as to the sweets of misgovernment no such sources of mischief should have place' (*UC*, clxxii, 225).

    I owe my knowledge of 'Rid Yourselves' to Dr C. Rodríguez Braun, 'Pensamiento económico y cuestión colonial en el siglo clásico: los casos de Bentham y Marx' (Doctoral Dissertation, Madrid, 1984), and to the transcript of the Bentham MS by Miss Claire Gobbi.
6. This happens if the preferences of all the voters are 'single-peaked' (see Mueller, *Public Choice*, pp. 40–41). See also pp. 99ff. for the predictive consequences of this theorem.

7. M. de Condorcet, *Essai sur l'application de l'annalyse à la probabilité des décisions rendues à la pluralité des voix* (Paris: 1785).

8. D. Black, *The Theory of Committees and Elections* (Cambridge: University Press, 1958).

9. K. J. Arrow, *Social Choice and Individual Values* (New York: Wiley, 1951).

10. V. Pareto, 'Il massimo di utilità per una colletività in sociologia', *Giornale degli Economisti*, 3ª serie 46 (1913) pp. 337–41. Pareto there defines an index V_i, which represents 'Pareto' social optima as seen by each subject i; and another index W, strictly unknowable, which would in theory be a function of the Vs of each individual weighted by appropriate indices. W would represent social welfare as impartially seen by government. The only thing known about W is that it is an increasing function of the V_is: W cannot be a maximum, unless each V_i is at a maximum for given values of the other Vs (see also his *Trattato di sociologia generale* (1916) sections 2131–9).

    Three criticisms can be directed at this conception: (a) most political decisions better the position of some only at the expense of all the rest; (b) people are not indifferent to the progress of others even if they are not themselves set back in their own terms as a result; (c) there is no such thing as an imperial government, in other words, speaking about W is simply a ploy to disguise the utilities of the powerful.

    It would be much simpler to go straight to a contractarian theory of welfare.

11. The limitation of the 'Pareto' criterion have led applied welfare economists to use the Kaldor compensation principle, whereby a change can be effected if it leaves enough benefit in principle to compensate the losers and leave some over. In cost-benefit analysis, this is expressed by saying that beneficiaries would be 'willing to pay' for the change if they were asked to do so. This, however, is nothing but contractarian application of the concept of eminent domain misleadingly dressed in Benthamite garb.

12. J. Buchanan and G. Tullock, *The Calculus of Consent* (Ann Arbor: University of Michigan Press, 1962).

13. J. Buchanan 'A Contractarian Paradigm for Applying Economic Theory', *American Economic Association, Papers and Proceedings*, 65 (May, 1975) pp. 225–30.

14. T. W. Schultz, *Transforming Traditional Agriculture* (New Haven: Yale University Press, 1965), Chapter 3, 'The Allocative Efficiency of Traditional Agriculture'.

15. K. Brunner and W. Meckling, 'The Perception of Man and the Conception of Government' *Journal of Credit, Money and Banking*, IX, 1, (February 1977), pp. 70–85.

16. C. F. Bahmueller, *The National Charity Company: Jeremy Bentham's Silent Revolution* (Berkeley: University of California Press, 1981); Burgess, *A Clockwork Orange* (1962).

17. Stanhope Archive K 121/39, General State Archives, Athens (quoted in the Editorial Introduction by F. Rosen and J. H. Burns to the *Constitutional Code*, Vol. 1, I, *CW*, p. xxvii).

18. J. R. Dinwiddy, 'Bentham and the Early Nineteenth Century', *The*

Bentham Newsletter, VII (June 1984), pp. 15–33.

19. Rosen and Burns, 'Editorial Introduction, *CC*, vol. I, *CW*, p. xiii.

20. I am drawing on Sir Karl Popper's suggestion that people stumble onto logical developments of ideas, developments that are implicit in the original ideas and that will appear in real life if those ideas are applied. In 'Epistemology without a Knowing Subject' (1967), reprinted in his *Objective Knowledge: an evolutionary approach* (Oxford: Clarendon Press, 1972), Popper uses the example of natural numbers throwing up unexpected problems, as Bentham's utilitarian republic suffers from unexpected snags, forerunners of the actual difficulties of the welfare state. Says Popper:

> I agree with Brouwer that the sequence of natural numbers is a human construction. But although we create this sequence, it creates its own autonomous problems in its turn. The distinction between odd and even numbers is not created by us: it is an unintended and unavoidable consequence of our creation. Prime numbers, of course, are similarly unintended autonomous and objective facts; and in their case it is obvious that there are many hard facts here for us to *discover* (p. 118).

21. L. J. Hume, *Bentham and Bureaucracy* (Cambridge: University Press, 1981), pp. 93ff. Bentham was thus much more of a mercantilist in matters of economic policy than Adam Smith.

22. David Lierberman, 'Bentham's Digest', *The Bentham Newsletter* (June 1985), pp. 7–20.

23. *A Fragment on Government*, *CW*, p. 439.

24. *An Introduction to the Principles of Morals and Legislation*, *CW*, p. 6.

25. Bentham, despite his criticisms, liked the 1812 Cádiz Constitution, mainly for its initial declaration in art. 12: 'The object of Government is the happiness of the nation, since the end of every political society is none other than the welfare of the individuals that compose it?'

26. I saw them with the remains of the Valle library in Guatemala City, in the house of Mr and Mrs Asturias. In the preface to Volume 1, Bentham said that he had written the *Code* with the new nations appearing on the American Continent in mind, and later for those of the British Commonwealth.

27. All the utilitarians adopted a paternalistic attitude towards coloured subject races. Bentham himself, in his 1830 'Postscript' to 'Emancipate your Colonies', doubted the ripeness of the Chinese and the Indians for self-government.

28. F. Rosen, *Jeremy Bentham and Representative Democracy* (Oxford: Clarendon Press, 1983), p. 236.

29. Ibid., p. 94.

30. Ibid., p. 92.

31. Rosen quotes this passage on p. 49. The source is *UC*, xxxviii, 217.

32. ibid., p. 50.

33. In 1831 Bentham changed this passage of the 'Inaugural Declaration' to delete the expression 'of the greatest number'. I will comment on this

further on Compare Rosen, *Jeremy Bentham and Representative Democracy*, pp. 201, and 202–3.

34. J. Bentham, 'Defence of a Maximum', in W. Stark (ed.) *Jeremy Bentham's Economic Writings* (London: Allen & Unwin, 1952–4), Vol. 3, p. 258.

35. This volume contains among others the following works, all proposing administrative interventions in the financial markets. 'A Plan for the Augmentation of the Revenue' (MS, 1794); 'A Proposal for the Circulation of a [New] Species of Paper Currency' (MS, 1795–6); 'Abstract or Compressed View of a Tract Intituled Circulating Annuities' (MS, 1800); 'Paper Mischief [of country bankers, Exposed]' (MS, 1800–1).

36. Stark, (ed.) *Jeremy Bentham's Economic Writings* Vol. 1, pp. 377–412.

37. Rosen, *Jeremy Bentham* and *Representative Democracy*, p. 195. Mill says so in his essay on Bentham (1838) – *Essays on Religion and Society, Collected Works*, X: 'Is it . . . the proper condition of man, in all ages and nations, to be under the despotism of Public Opinion?' (p. 107); 'We cannot think that Bentham made the most useful employment which might have been made of his great powers, when, not content with enthroning the majority as sovereign, by means of universal suffrage without king or house of lords, he exhausted all the resources of his ingenuity in devising means for riveting the yoke of public opinion closer and closer round the necks of all public functionaries, and excluding every possibility of the exercise of the slightest or most temporary influence, either by a minority or by the functionary's own notions of right' (p. 108).

38. J. S. Mill, *Autobiography and Literary Essays*, in J. M. Robson and J. Stillinger (eds), *Collected Works of J. S. Mill* (Toronto: University of Toronto Press), Vol. I, p. 149.

39. Georges Vedel, *Les démocraties marxistes* (Paris: 1953).

40. J. Bentham, Preface to the *Constitutional Code*, Vol. I, pp. 4, 6.

41. H. L. A. Hart, *The Concept of Law* (Oxford: Clarendon Press, 1961).

42. Quoted by Rosen, *Jeremy Bentham and Representative Democracy*, pp. 201, 202–3.

43. Ibid., p. 201.

44. Dan Usher *The Economic Prerequisite to Democracy* (Oxford: Blackwell, 1981), Chapter ii.

45. *Traités de législation civile et pénale M. Jeremie Bentham, Jurisconsulte anglois. Publies en françois par Ét. Dumont, de Genève, d'après les manuscrits con-fiés par l'auteur* (Paris, 1802) vol. II, 'Principes du Code Civil', ch. 6, 'Propositions de Pathologie sur lesquelles se fonde le bien de l'Égalité'.

46. Rosen, *Jeremy Bentham and Representative Democracy*, pp. 101ff.

47. For Hayek, should the rule of law be seen 'as an impracticable or even undesirable ideal', individual freedom would in the end disappear. F. von Hayek, *The Constitution of Liberty* (London: Routledge & Kegan Paul, 1960), p. 206. I was reminded of this text by J. A. Dorn, 'Law and Liberty: a comparison of Hayek and Bastiat', *Journal of Libertarian Studies*, V, 4 (Fall, 1981) p. 382. By rule of law, Hayek understands a system of formal guarantees for legal instruments, wider than that of their having been promulgated by the Queen in Parliament. The act must be 'general, equal,

certain, and just' to be a law. By 'just', Hayek means four further qualities: the law should not endanger the spontaneous market order; it should allow individuals to pursue their own interests while not infringing the equal rights of others; it should limit itself to the protection of 'life, liberty, and the possessions of a man'; it should pass the test of universal applicability (pp. 376–7).

48. H. Demsetz, 'Towards a Theory of Property Rights', *American Economic Review*, LVII (May 1967) pp. 347–59, shows that every change in preferences or, in production conditions, modifies what it is worth our whole to appropriate and defend. 'The emergence of new property rights takes place in response to the desires of the interacting persons for adjustment to new benefit – cost opportunities,' (p. 350). Richard Posner, *Economic Analysis of the Law* (Boston: Little, Brown, 1972), sees legal and judical decisions as increasing social efficiency, by adjudications which innovate on rights made obsolete by changes in demand or supply conditions: these decisions tend to attribute new rights directly to the most efficient prospective user, thus short cutting his bargains to buy out the less efficient owners.

5 David Ricardo's Treatment of Wages

TERRY PEACH

To anyone unacquainted with Ricardo-scholarship, it may seem odd
that the writings of a man who died in 1823 should continue to be the
focus for lively and sometimes acrimonious debate. Yet the fact is that
Ricardo's 'legacy' attracts unflagging interest (as a recently published
book on the subject – Caravale (ed.) 1985 – bears witness). How can
this be explained? I suggest that two factors are particularly germane:
interpretative method and the evaluative location of Ricardo within
some 'stream' of economic thought.

Historians of economic thought, perhaps in part because of their
rigorous training as economists, are excessively preoccupied with
finding consistent models. I intend to illustrate, for the case of
Ricardo's treatment of wages, that this may favour the interests of
paper merchants rather than historical enquiry: the textual difficulties
that manifestly exist provide abundant scope for a bewildering array of
neat, sometimes sophisticated, 'Ricardian models', which are
obtained at varying costs of misrepresentation and distortion. As for
Ricardo's 'placement' – does he belong with the 'neoclassicals' or
elsewhere? – and the frequently encountered evaluations which
follow, one may be left with the impression that the purpose of the
exercise is to sanctify beliefs about the present. Even if this intent is
lacking, the mere acceptance of 'Ricardo's place' as a worthy object of
investigation carries with it the danger of a teleological 'grid-reading'
which conveniently 'proves' a thesis by selective emphasis. Again,
interpretations of Ricardo's treatment of wages provide an illuminating study, with commentators believing that 'the position of Ricardo's
whole theoretical construction in one tradition of thought rather than
the other' is at issue (Caravale, 1985, p. 132).[1]

A review of the main interpretative and evaluative strands will follow. They will then be critically explored in an exegesis centring on Ricardo's *Principles of Political Economy and Taxation*, after which I conclude.

I

Until recently, the most common interpretation of Ricardo's treatment of wages in the *Principles* has been the 'subsistence' account. I will term this the 'traditional' interpretation. The idea is that Ricardo equated the 'natural wage' with a 'subsistence' basket of commodities – an analytical *datum* – with 'subsistence' understood in either a narrow physiological sense or as something determined by historical convention. Either way, subsistence wages would be associated with a stationary labouring population.

In principle, 'market wages' – those actually ruling at a given point in time – could be above, below, or equal to, the natural level, but it is mostly affirmed that Ricardo assumed a permanent correspondence between the two rates or treated inequality as a fleeting occurrence. To that extent he allegedly 'short-circuited' the lengthy process whereby, for example, 'high' wages encourage marriage, procreation and reduce infant mortality, with the supply of labour increased at some future time and market wages falling consequentially.[2]

Evaluative reaction to an analysis along these lines has depended on the nature of the 'correct' approach as endorsed by the commentator. 'Neoclassical' writers have found little to applaud.

The stage was set by Jevons. Lumping together Ricardo and his followers, he passed the verdict that their treatment of wages, especially, was 'mazy and preposterous', adding for good measure that they had been 'living in a fool's paradise' (Jevons [1879] 1970, pp. xliv–xlv). The astringency of this judgement reflected Jevons's belief in the vast superiority of his own analysis, but the substantive allegation was that the natural wage is non-existent. The only satisfactory way to proceed is to impute the value of wages from that of the product and certainly not to take it as given (Jevons [1879] 1970, p. 165), a point subsequently amplified by Schumpeter:

Production in the economic sense of the term is nothing but a combination, by purchase, of requisite and scarce services. In this process, each of the requisite and scarce services secures a price, and the determination of these prices is all that distribution or income formation fundamentally consists in. Thus the process effects, in one and the same series of steps, production in the economic sense and, through the evaluation of productive services incident to production, also distribution or the formation of incomes.

He continued his peroration:

Ricardo failed to see the explanatory principle offered by the valuation aspect. This failure . . . proves better than does anything else that [his] work constitutes in fact a detour and falls out of the historical line of ['neoclassical'] economists' endeavours (Schumpeter, 1954, pp. 567–8).

Ricardo, then, had grievously erred in not treating wages in the same way as all other prices: analytically endogenous and competitively determined. In short, he had separated the theories of value and distribution.

Marx saw things differently. In his own work, the adoption of a given value for labour-power served the purpose of exposing profit to be the surplus-value or unpaid labour of a dispossessed working class.[3] It therefore comes as no surprise to find him praising Ricardo for treating wages as a given bundle of 'means of subsistence', even though he allegedly failed to take the next step of revealing the 'true' origin of profit (Marx, 1969, pp. 400–6).

The subsistence treatment of wages has also received support from writers who see themselves as lineal descendents of Ricardo and whose twentieth-century mentor was Sraffa. A brief explanation is called for.

Sraffa's *Production of Commodities by Means of Commodities: Prelude to a Critique of Economic Theory* (1960) was perceived by some as a 'magnificent rehabilitation' of the 'Ricardian' and, more generally, the 'classical' approach to the study of economic phenomena. The family resemblance supposedly includes, among other things, the postulation of a prior concrete magnitude – the social product – limiting the extent of class incomes, and the exogenous specification of a distributive variable. Such an approach is purported to have significant advantages over its 'mainstream' rival which include, *inter alia*: the 'Ricardian virtue' of considering simple causal relationships in preference to general interrelationships, a method best suited to a subject so complex as economics;[4] and, by taking a distributive variable as given rather than simultaneously determined with all other prices, the advantage of including historical/sociological/class considerations in the discussion of distribution (see Garegnani, 1984, for a trenchant statement of this view). To those who believe such things, Ricardo is held in great esteem, occupying a privileged position in an honourable intellectual tradition that had been broken by the 'neoclassicals' but gloriously revitalised by Sraffa. The subsistence treatment of wages, as in the traditional interpretation, was cause for congratulating him (and vicariously, oneself).

Depending on the writer's perspective, the traditional interpretation can be used to present Ricardo as a purveyor of 'good' economics or 'bad' economics. This has been one of its functions. But also, it is pedagogically attractive: the subsistence treatment of wages might be 'wrong', but it is certainly neat and amenable to pretty mathematical formulations (Pasinetti, 1960, is the classic example). Whether it is the correct interpretation has been questioned.

According to Alfred Marshall, Ricardo delighted in 'imagining strong cases' and confused the unwary reader by not repeating that 'he was omitting for the sake of simplicity the conditions and limitations that were needed to make his results applicable to real life' (Marshall, [1920] 1949, p. 422). His treatment of wages was therefore deliberately simplified and, apparently, should not be taken too seriously.

This did not amount to a wholescale revision of the traditional interpretation but it was enough to facilitate the claim that 'Economic science is, and must be, one of slow and continuous growth' (Marshall [1920] 1949, p. v). Interpreted 'generously', Ricardo's doctrine was conformable with those of the early 'neoclassicals' (*pace* Jevons) and, of course, with Marshall's own work, give or take the occasional ellipsis and difference in stress.

George Stigler was not so conciliatory, but his account also served to blur the edges of the received view by drawing attention to a passage in Ricardo's chapter 'On Wages' where there is a reference to market wages exceeding the natural rate for an 'indefinite period' in an 'improving society'. This, Stigler averred, should be recorded as a 'correct view' which 'Ricardo did not know how to incorporate into his theoretical system' (Stigler, 1952). It was 'correct' in the 'neoclassical' sense that it recognised wages to be competitively determined and essentially variable; but it was 'unintegrated knowledge' because Ricardo's theoretical system – particularly his theory of profit – required the assumption of wages at the subsistence level (something reaffirmed in Stigler, 1981).

For G. S. L. Tucker, the project was to integrate knowledge on Ricardo's behalf. The problem was that the explicit definition of the natural wage in the *Principles* required a stationary labouring population, yet in other passages Ricardo seemed to allow for market wages in excess of natural wages until the ultimate stationary state. To cope with this anomaly, Tucker redefined the natural wage as 'the wage that was necessary to ensure a given rate of growth of population', believing that Ricardo 'had this idea in mind, however imperfectly' (Tucker, 1960, p. 105).

Tucker's interpretation presaged the so-called 'new view' of Ricardo's analysis of wages. Two main variants may be distinguished, while a third can be viewed as a hybrid between this account and the traditional interpretation.

The first variant has been proposed by Casarosa. Having elevated the content of those passages singled out by Stigler and Tucker to the status of 'Ricardo's central propositions', Casarosa attempts, with some mathematical assistance, to put the ideas 'into a coherent whole' (Casarosa, 1985 p. 56, 1978). Without redefining the natural wage, a model is produced in which the market wage tends to converge on its 'dynamic equilibrium' value such that the rates of capital accumulation (hence the demand for labour) and population growth are equal. Before stationariness, the dynamic equilibrium market wage will initially rise and then fall; only in the stationary state, when growth rates are zero, will there be equality with the natural wage. Such a model, Casarosa claims, is 'closer to Ricardo's thought' than the traditional interpretation (Casarosa, 1978).

Hicks and Hollander share this judgement, although the variant advanced jointly by them, and developed at length by Hollander, is slightly different. In their model (Hicks and Hollander, 1977) it is differential growth rates between capital accumulation and population that account for the secular pattern of market wage movement described by Ricardo. In the 'improving society' the rate of capital accumulation increasingly outpaces the growth of population, so market wages rise higher and higher above the natural wage; thereafter, the rate of capital accumulation slackens (it is functionally related to profitability, which has eventually fallen because of higher wages) and market wages are reduced although, as with Casarosa, they remain above the natural wage until the economy has become static.

In developing this interpretation Hollander, 1979, does not deny that Ricardo sometimes assumed a given and constant wage, even at the subsistence level. But invoking the spirit of Marshall, such cases amount only to 'simplifying devices' rather than statements of fundamental doctrine (Hollander, 1979, pp. 1, 309, 646). They do not represent Ricardo's vision of the growth process occurring through historical time.

The historiographical implications of these variants of the 'new view' are spelt out by Hicks, 1979, who authoritively states that the

> 'fixwage' [traditional interpretation] is a travesty of Ricardo's meaning. The Ricardo theory is fully in the great tradition, which runs from Adam Smith through Ricardo and Mill to Marshall; modern 'linearists' [followers of Sraffa, for example] . . . have no business to claim Ricardo among their forerunners (compare Hollander, 1979, pp. 683–9).

Marshall is fully vindicated; by treating the wage as an essentially variable, competitively determined, price, Ricardo is proudly entitled to a place in the 'mainstream' tradition of economics.

With the interpretation of Caravale (building on earlier work – see Caravale and Tosato, 1980) we meet the hybrid: a bridge between the traditional interpretation – involving a *given* natural wage – and the insights of the 'new view'. The textual reason for doing so, according to Caravale, is Ricardo's claim that he wishes to consider the 'natural course' of distributive variables within the accumulation process, something that would be peculiar if the natural wage only prevails in the stationary state. The difficulty, as Tucker noticed, lies with Ricardo's definition of the natural wage. And so it is again redefined, this time as 'that constant level of the wage in correspondence with which rates of growth of population and of capital coincide', requiring that 'the rate of increase of population *instantaneously copies* the (declining) rate of accumulation' (Caravale, 1985 p. 143; his emphasis). This redefinition, far from being gratuitous, coincides 'with the dynamic definition of the natural wage given by Ricardo in the *Essay on . . . Profits . . .*' two years before the publication of the *Principles* (Caravale, 1985, p. 145). In this way it is commended as something we know Ricardo thought of himself. Crucially, it also facilitates his perception as a 'dynamic theorist' but one who falls outside the lineage of 'neoclassical' economics by taking the wage as a *datum* of analysis.

That completes my review of the main interpretations. I turn now to Ricardo himself.

II

The chapter 'On Wages' in the *Principles* is a good place to begin. It opens with the definition of the 'natural price of labour' as 'that price which is necessary to enable the labourers one with another, to subsist and to perpetuate their race, without either increase or diminution' (I, p. 93);[5] this depends on the prices of those commodities that have 'become essential . . . from habit' (I, p. 93; later in the chapter, from 'the habits and customs of the people', I, p. 97).

Ricardo subsequently introduces the 'market price of labour', this being 'the price which is really paid . . . from the natural operation of the proportion of the supply to the demand' (I, p. 94). 'However much the market price of labour may deviate from its natural price', he continues, 'it has, like commodities, a tendency to conform to it' (I, p. 94). He then elaborates:

> It is when the market price of labour exceeds its natural price, that the condition of the labourer is flourishing and happy, that he has it in his power to command a greater proportion of the necessaries and enjoyments of life, and therefore to rear a healthy and numerous family. When, however, by the encouragement which high wages give to the increase of population, the number of labourers is increased, wages again fall to their natural price, and indeed from a re-action sometimes fall below it.
>
> When the market price of labour is below its natural price, the condition of the labourers is most wretched: then poverty deprives them of those comforts which custom renders absolute necessaries. It is only after their privations have reduced their number, or the demand for labour has increased, that the market price of labour will rise to its natural price (I, p. 94).

Prima facie, this would seem to conflict with the 'new view': there is no restriction on the applicability of the natural wage to the stationary state, with the passage suggesting that it was regarded as a true 'centre of gravity' around which the market wage oscillates but with equality between the two rates periodically encountered.

Immediately following, however, we find one of the textual pillars for the 'new view':

> Notwithstanding the tendency of wages to conform to their natural rate, their market rate may, in an improving society, for an

indefinite period, be constantly above it; for no sooner may the impulse, which an increased capital gives to a new demand for labour be obeyed, than another increase of capital may produce the same effect (I, pp. 94–5).

This is clear enough: the tendency to conformity between market and natural rates may be suspended in an 'improving society'.[6] But it is back in operation when, in the following paragraphs, Ricardo distinguishes between the effect of an increase in both the quantity and (per unit) value of capital (capital consisting of 'food, clothing, tools, raw materials, machinery, &c' – I, p. 95) and the effect of an increase in quantity with the items of capital at an unchanged or even lower value:

> In the first case, the natural price of labour, which always depends on the price of food, clothing, and other necessaries, will rise; in the second, it will remain stationary, or fall; but in both cases the market rate of wages will rise, for in proportion to the increase of capital will be the increase in the demand for labour . . .
>   In both cases too the market price of labour will rise above its natural price; and in both cases it will have a tendency to conform to its natural price, but in the first case this agreement will be most speedily effected. The situation of the labourer will be improved, but not much improved; for the increased price of food and necessaries will absorb a large portion of his increased wages; consequently a small supply of labour, or a trifling increase in the population, will soon reduce the market price of labour (I, pp. 95–6).

In the other case, it 'will not be till after a great addition has been made to the population, that the market price of labour will again sink to its then low and reduced natural price' (I, p. 96). It might take some time, but the presumption was that the natural wage will prevail. Again, this appears to conflict with the 'new view'.

A few pages on in the chapter we meet this analysis:

> In the natural advance of society, the wages of labour will have a tendency to fall, as far as they are regulated by supply and demand; for the supply of labourers will continue to increase at the same rate, whilst the demand for them will increase at a slower rate. If, for instance, wages were regulated by a yearly increase of capital, at the rate of 2 per cent, they would fall when it accumulated only at the

rate of 1½ per cent. . . . and would continue to do so until the capital became stationary, when wages also would become stationary, and be only sufficient to keep up the numbers of the actual population (I, p. 101).

Given Ricardo's definition of the natural price of labour, this scenario is one in which market wages are above natural wages but falling until a stationary position is reached when market and natural rates coincide. But the scenario is not yet complete:

> I say that, under these circumstances, wages would fall, if they were regulated only by the supply and demand of labourers; but we must not forget, that wages are also regulated by the prices of the commodities on which they are expended (I, p. 101).

Having reminded himself of this he produces an integrated account:

> As population increases, these necessaries will be constantly rising in price, because more labour will be necessary to produce them. If, then, the money wages of labour should fall, whilst every commodity on which the wages of labour were expended rose, the labourer would be doubly affected, and would be soon totally deprived of subsistence. Instead, therefore, of the money wages of labour falling, they would rise; but they would not rise sufficiently to enable the labourer to purchase as many comforts and necessaries as he did before the rise in the price of those commodities (I, pp. 101–2).

Coupled with the 'improving society' passage, we now have the main textual support for the 'new view'.

However, the evidence is not yet exhausted. In his detailed exegesis, Professor Hollander (1979) can reasonably claim added confirmation from the chapter 'Taxes on Raw Produce' where Ricardo refers to 'Those who maintain that it is the price of necessaries which regulates the price of labour, always allowing for the particular state of progression in which the society may be' (I, p. 161). Furthermore, there is the opening to the chapter 'Taxes on Wages' where Ricardo quotes Adam Smith, approbatorily so it would seem, to essentially the same effect (I, p. 215). The 'new view' is not a total fiction.

Neither is it trouble-free. Passages have already been cited in which the natural wage is revealed as a meaningful centre of gravity: an 'attraction point' that is not explicitly constrained in operation to the stationary state. Underscoring this, consider the following from the chapter 'Taxes on Raw Produce':

> It generally happens indeed, that when a stimulus has been given to population, an effect is produced beyond what the case requires; the population may be, and generally is so much increased as, notwithstanding the increased demand for labour, to bear a greater proportion to the funds for maintaining labourers than before the increase of capital. In this case a re-action will take place, wages will be below their natural level, and will continue so, till the usual proportion between the supply and demand has been restored (I, p. 164).

Once again, it is the natural wage towards which market wages are gravitating, without the stationary state restriction.

This points in the direction of the traditional interpretation, although there is an important qualification. If conformity between market and natural wages rests on a mechanism involving marriage, procreation and resulting variations in the labour supply, it is obviously not something that can be instantaneously achieved. As described by Ricardo hereto, the population mechanism operates with a lag, and may well involve 'overshoot' or, as he puts it, 're-action'. This would seem to be the case unless the increase of capital providing the 'impulse' goes in tandem with a rise in value of the items of capital (see above, p. 111). Elsewhere, a different story is told.

In the chapter 'Taxes on Raw Produce' Ricardo writes: 'From the effect of the principle of population on the increase of mankind, wages of the lowest kind never continue much above that rate which nature and habit demand for the support of the labourers' (I, p. 159). It is not far-fetched to interpret this as saying that, for the 'lowest kind' of labour, wages persistently approximate to the natural level: the 'rate which nature and habit demand' is a phrase strikingly close to those used in the description of the natural rate (see above, p. 110). *Via* the population mechanism, then, the tendency to conformity between market and natural rates is in this case very powerful indeed.

There are other passages suggesting that the population mechanism operates with impressive celerity. From the chapter 'On Profits':

> Whilst the land yields abundantly, wages may temporarily rise, and the producers may consume more than their accustomed proportion; but the stimulus which will thus be given to population, will speedily reduce the labourers to their usual consumption (I, p. 125).

And in the chapter 'On Value':

> If the shoes and clothing of the labourer, could, by improvements in machinery, be produced by one fourth of the labour now necessary to their production, they would probably fall 75 per cent; but so far is it from being true, that the labourer would thereby be enabled permanently to consume four coats, or four pair of shoes, instead of one, that it is probable his wages would in no long time be adjusted by the effects of competition, and the stimulus to population, to the new value of the necessaries on which they were expended. If these improvements extended to all the objects of the labourer's consumption, we should find him probably at the end of a very few years, in possession of only a small, if any, addition to his enjoyments (I, p. 16).

In both these passages, population adjustment is speedily effected. We have the basis for the following stories:

Ia: The market wage is *always* tending towards the natural wage, but can be above or below it; the adjustment process takes considerable time and may produce oscillations of the market rate around the natural rate.

Ib: As with **Ia**, the natural wage is a true centre of gravity, although the gravitational pull is much stronger.

II: The natural wage is not a *centre* of gravity until the stationary state, before which the market rate exceeds the natural rate, to an increasing extent in an 'improving society', thereafter to a decreasing extent.

Can we say, along with proponents of the 'new view', that story **II** is the basis for the *true* 'Ricardian system'? Or, with defenders of the traditional interpretation, that **Ib** should be privileged? At this stage, if only superficially, the iconoclasts would seem to have the upper hand: they can argue that **II** represents the accumulation process in its full complexity, with **Ia** and **Ib** amounting to intentional simplifications. The traditionalists are in more of a quandary. Although they might be able to deal with **Ia** – after all, **Ia** and **Ib** share the property that the natural wage is a true centre of gravity, so **Ib** can be seen as an intentional simplification of **Ia** – that leaves unexplained the presence of story **II**.

At this juncture I will refrain from further comment. I turn instead to Ricardo's treatment of profitability: for some advocates of the traditional interpretation, their trump suit.

III

The chapter 'On Profits' in the *Principles* has the stated purpose of considering 'what is the cause of the permanent variations in the rate of profit, and the consequent permanent alterations in the rate of interest' (I, p. 110). After producing a detailed numerical analysis, illustrating that worsening agricultural conditions of production can depress general profitability through the effect on money wages, Ricardo expresses the related 'theory' (his word):

> profits depend on high or low wages, wages on the price of necessaries, and the price of necessaries chiefly on the price of food, because all other requisites may be increased almost without limit (I, p. 119).

And at the conclusion to the chapter:

> in all countries, and all times, profits depend on the quantity of labour requisite to provide necessaries for the labourers, on that land or with that capital which yields no rent (I, p. 126).

The central position occupied by agriculture is luminous, both in the numerical explication and these statements. Even so, it might be contended that there is no inconsistency with the 'new view': Ricardo was simplifying matters by leaving out of the picture the effect on profitability from those 'essentially variable' commodity wages. Read like this, he intended the dependency of profits on the price of necessaries, notably food, to be understood as a half-truth, since profits actually depend on both the prices of wage-goods and the current (real) market wage.

That would seem to be Professor Hollander's position. He quotes the following, also from 'On Profits':

> It may be said that I have taken it for granted, that money wages would rise with a rise in the price of raw produce, but that this is by no means a necessary consequence, as the labourer may be contented with fewer enjoyments. It is true that the wages of labour

may previously have been at a high level, and that they may bear some reduction. If so, the fall of profits will be checked; but it is impossible to conceive that the money price of wages should fall, or remain stationary with a gradually increasing price of necessaries; and therefore it may be taken for granted that, under ordinary circumstances, no permanent rise takes place in the price of necessaries, without occasioning, or having been preceded by a rise in wages (I, p. 118).

The thrust of this, for Hollander, is that 'money wages will rise even though real wages decline' (Hollander, 1979, p. 399). In this way, a reconciliation is effected between the analysis in 'On Profits' and, particularly, the passages in 'On Wages' that constitute the main basis for the 'new view'. Whether this reconciliation is fully justified may be doubted.

Ricardo's caveat applies to a situation in which 'the wages of labour may previously have been at a high level'. If so, that would check the fall in profits following a rise in the price of corn. But there are two ways in which this can be interpreted. One is Hollander's and the other takes 'high wages' to mean above-natural wages. Both can claim support from Ricardo's treatment of wages.

I suggest that the crux of the matter turns on whether permanent movements in profitability – Ricardo's object of analysis – were associated with variable commodity wages. They were not. In the chapter 'On Foreign Trade':

It has been my endeavour to shew throughout this work, that the rate of profits can never be increased but by a fall in wages, and that there can be no permanent fall of wages but in consequence of a fall of the necessaries on which wages are expended (I, p. 132).

By implication, a fall in wages resulting from altered supply and demand conditions in the labour market is a 'temporary' phenomenon and likewise the effect on general profitability.

This position is unequivocal in the chapter 'Effects of Accumulation on Profits and Interest'. Right at the beginning of the chapter, as a summary of his doctrine, Ricardo gives us this:

From the account which has been given of the profits of stock, it will appear, that no accumulation of capital will permanently lower profits, unless there be some permanent cause for the rise of wages.

. . . If the necessaries of the workman could be constantly increased with the same facility, there could be no permanent alteration in the rate of profit or wages, to whatever amount capital might be accumulated (I, p. 289).

The only 'permanent' variations in wages and profits are those that result from altered conditions of producing wage-goods; they are not associated with secular movements in the real wage.[7]

Just in case this had been overlooked by the reader the following was inserted in the second edition of the *Principles*:

however abundant capital may become, there is no other adequate reason for a fall of profit but a rise of wages, and further it may be added, that the only adequate and permanent cause for the rise of wages is the increasing difficulty of providing food and necessaries for the increasing number of workmen (I, p. 296).

The message is the same.

Now, the exclusive association of 'permanent' movements in profitability with altered conditions of producing 'necessaries', which implicitly relegates the effect of variations in the commodity wage basket to the status of a 'temporary' influence, is perfectly understandable so long as the natural wage is a true centre of gravity with only 'temporary' deviations between it and the market wage. It is less so if there are 'indefinite' excesses of market over natural rates. And if the excess persists until the stationary state, the permanent/temporary distinction becomes virtually pointless, with 'temporary' influences of co-ordinate importance with 'permanent' ones.

Advocates of the 'new view' must confront this. If their account represents 'what Ricardo believed', why should his central thesis on profitability not reflect that?

The response of Professor Hollander, who is alone in having seriously tackled this issue, is to downplay the 'agricultural' dimension in Ricardo's work:

Ricardo's primary objective, it would seem, was to provide an analytical framework whereby to investigate the various factors that play upon the profit rate, rather than one designed to yield a specific prediction (Hollander, 1979, p. 605).

This, I think embodies a serious confusion. For while it is true that Ricardo's 'framework' could be and was used to establish 'the general principle of the inverse profit-wage relationship' (Hollander, 1979, p. 12), I would say that his 'primary objective', from the inception of his writings on profitability, was rather to promulgate the theory of 'permanent' movements.[8] This was his central thesis in the field of distribution, which can hardly be described as a 'specific prediction' except by an imaginative use of language.

That is a stumbling block for the 'new view'. I will now consider some of Ricardo's writings prior to the *Principles*. My main purpose is to account for the presence of the various stories about wages that we have encountered. This will go some way towards an assessment of their relative significance to Ricardo. I will also comment on the hybrid between the traditional interpretation and the 'new view': an interpretative development which should now seem almost ineluctable.

IV

I have shown elsewhere that the 'early' Ricardo was preoccupied with 'permanent' variations in profitability resulting from changed conditions of production on the land; he often engaged in 'fixwage' analysis; and he did not explicitly associate 'permanent' movements in profitability with alterations in the wage basket (Peach, 1984). This doctrine was anathema to Malthus. In his letter of 23 November 1814 he wrote to Ricardo criticising his 'general position that the state of the land *regulates* profits' (VI, p. 152; Malthus's emphasis). One reason given for this dissent was a supposed 'constant tendency to a fall in the wages of labour' (VI, p. 152).

In his reply to Malthus, Ricardo first reaffirmed his position:

> I have been endeavoring to get you to admit that the profits on stock . . . are seldom permanently lowered or raised by any other cause than by the cheapness or dearness of necessities . . . Accumulation of capital has a tendency to lower profits. Why? because every accumulation is attended with increased difficulty in obtaining food, unless it is accompanied with improvements in agriculture . . . If there were no increased difficulty, profits would never fall, because there are no other limits to the profitable production of manufactures but the rise of wages (14 December 1814; VI, p. 162).

This is essentially the line on profitability that was subsequently espoused in the *Principles*, with context establishing that the 'rise of wages' is the result of the 'dearness of necessaries'. However, Ricardo later adds:

> A diminution of the proportion of produce,[9] in consequence of the accumulation of capital, does not fall wholly on the owner of stock, but is shared with him by the labourers. The whole amount of wages paid will be greater, but the portion paid to each man, will in all probability, be somewhat diminished (VI, pp. 162–3).

Does this betoken an acceptance of Malthus's position on wages or is the reduction an immediate or 'temporary' phenomenon? Since the letter to Malthus does not yield an answer to this question I suggest we pass on to the *Essay on . . . Profits . . .*, published two months later.[10]

In the detailed analysis that Ricardo launches into at the beginning of the *Essay*, one of the assumptions he makes is

> that capital and population advance in the proper proportion, so that the real wages of labour, continue uniformly the same; — that we may know what peculiar effects are to be ascribed to the growth of capital, the increase of population, and the extension of cultivation, to the more remote, and less fertile land (IV, p. 12).

By the 'proper proportion' he is evidently assuming that the rates of capital accumulation and population growth are equal and positive; his reason for doing so is unambiguous.

Further on, after allowing that general profits may rise with a 'fall of the real wages of labour', he comments that this 'is more or less permanent, according as the price from which wages fall, is more or less near that remuneration for labour, which is necessary to the actual subsistence of the labourer' (IV, p. 22). I take this to mean that 'permanent' movements in profitability were defined relative to the 'subsistence' real wage: formally the same notion which, I have argued, appears in the *Principles*.

An important point arises. Is the 'subsistence' wage the same as the 'uniform' wage that Ricardo had earlier assumed to prevail? In his hybrid interpretation Caravale seems to believe it is, hence his reference to 'the dynamic definition of the natural wage' in the *Essay* (Caravale, 1985, p. 143). One can understand the appeal of this reading for Caravale, in providing justification for his redefinition of the natural wage. But the justification is slender, at the most charitable. First, Ricardo makes no explicit linkage between the constant wage assumption and the idea of a 'subsistence' wage; and secondly, the specific category of the 'natural wage' only makes its appearance two years later in the *Principles*. I therefore suggest that we have no reasonable basis for imposing an identity between the 'uniform' and 'subsistence' wage in the *Essay*; and none at all for bracketing the two as a definition of the natural wage.

I return to the exchanges with Malthus, who was implacably opposed to the Ricardian analysis. Throughout 1815, 1816 and into 1817 he tirelessly bombarded Ricardo with the 'correct' view to take of wages: their variability coupled with the secular downward tendency. This elicited from Ricardo a general and much-quoted statement of their different theoretical approaches:

> you [Malthus] have always in your mind the immediate and temporary effects of particular changes – whereas I put these immediate and temporary effects quite aside, and fix my whole attention on the permanent state of things which will result from them. Perhaps you estimate these temporary effects too highly, whilst I am too much disposed to undervalue them. To manage the subject quite right they should be carefully distinguished and mentioned, and the due effects ascribed to each (24 January 1817; VII, p. 120).

This is presumably what Ricardo aspired to in the *Principles* with his discussion of labour supply lags, market wages oscillating around the natural level and, for that matter, the possibility of an 'indefinite excess' of market over natural rates in an 'improving society'.

Whether the inclusion of this material was a great success is doubtful.[11] It seems possible that Ricardo revised an early draft but did not do so comprehensively. Thus, at the close of the chapter 'On Natural and Market Price' (which may previously have incorporated a full discussion of wages) he clearly states that he is going to treat 'the laws which regulate natural prices, natural wages and natural profits' (I, p. 92). But this is lost sight of in the ensuing discussion, submerged by the attempt to 'manage the subject quite right'.

That may account for the presence of those 'qualifications' which leave unaffected the conception of the natural wage as a true centre of gravity, but what about the specific scenario of falling real wages with rising nominal wages?

For Malthus, the downward secular tendency for real wages

demolished Ricardo's inverse relationship between general profitability and worsening conditions of production on the land:

> When . . . the rise in the price of corn is occasioned solely and exclusively by the necessity of cultivating poorer land I am now convinced that the rise must be very small, and as the real price of labour must fall, I see no reason why the nominal price of labour must rise (22 December 1815; VI, p. 342).

Ricardo could not accept this argument. He rejoined:

> I cannot think it inconsistent to suppose that the money price of labour may rise when it is necessary to cultivate poorer land, whilst the real price may at the same time fall. Two opposite causes are influencing the price of labour[:] one the enhanced price of some of the things on which wages are expended, – the other the fewer enjoyments which the labourer will have the power to command, – you think these may balance each other, or rather that the latter will prevail, I on the contrary think the former the most powerful in its effects. I must write a book to convince you (10 January 1816; VII, p. 10).

From this, the scenario, so important to enthusiasts of the 'new view', may be seen as a direct attempt to challenge Malthus on his own ground.[12]

The possibility remains that Ricardo had internalised the view of secularly falling commodity wages and made it his own. If so, he had not done it in time to produce an integrated text; to stress, stories **Ia** and **Ib** told about wages cohere with the theory of permanent movements in profitability and story **II** does not (see above, p. 114).

To complete my exegesis I will consider the evidence from Ricardo's *Notes* on Malthus's *Principles of Political Economy*.[13] This will prove illuminating.

V

Malthus was scathing about Ricardo's definition of the natural price of labour:

This price I should really be disposed to call a most unnatural price; because in the natural state of things . . . such a price could not generally occur for hundreds of years. But if this price be really rare, and, in an ordinary state of things, at so great a distance in point of time, it must evidently lead to great errors to consider the market-prices of labour as only temporary deviations above and below that fixed price to which they will very soon return (II, pp. 227–8).

This criticism is highly pertinent. So too is Malthus's preferred definition:

that price which, in the actual circumstances of society, is necessary to occasion an average supply of labourers, sufficient to meet the average demand (II, p. 228).

This was a perfect opportunity for Ricardo to clarify his position. His first note began:

With every demand for an increased quantity [of labour] it [the market price] will rise above this [natural] price[;] therefore if capital and population regularly increase the market price may for years exceed its natural price (II, p. 228, n. 1).

This is a weak statement. The idea of the market wage exceeding its natural level 'for years' fails to conjure up the same time span as the 'indefinite excess' in an 'improving society', or the 'hundreds of years' predicted by Malthus before the stationary state arrives. But against this Ricardo continued:

I am . . . very little solicitous to retain my definition of the natural price of labour – Mr. Malthus's will do nearly as well for my purpose (II, p. 228, n. 1).

Here we must pause.

If we interpret Ricardo as accepting Malthus's criticism, the 'new view' or hybrid interpretation is strengthened. Advocates have not been slow to see this. Professor Hollander describes the note as 'conciliatory' (Hollander, 1979, p. 402) and quotes it *en route* to the conclusion 'that average commodity wages, in Ricardo's view, tend to decline in the course of secular expansion' (Hollander, 1979, pp. 402–

3). Similarly, Professor Caravale, who apparently failed to notice that Ricardo inserted 'nearly' in the note, claims that it reveals his '"flexibility" with respect to his own definition of the natural wage given in the chapter "On Wages" . . .' (1985, p. 137): more support for Caravale's redefinition.

The fact is that Malthus's definition did not do 'nearly as well'. The note was deleted and replaced with this one:

> By natural price I do not mean the usual price, but such a price as is necessary to supply constantly a given demand. The natural price of corn is the price at which it can be supplied affording the usual profits. With every demand for an increased quantity the market price of corn will rise above this price and probably is never at the natural price but either above or below it, – the same may be said of the natural price of labour (II, pp. 227–8).

Caravale's reaction to this is bizarre. Without quoting Ricardo's considered response to Malthus, he claims that the first note was only deleted 'to avoid repetitions' (and this is in a footnote Caravale 1985, p. 137, n. 10). That the sense of the two notes is entirely different seems to have passed him by.

What Ricardo has said is this. First, he wants to retain the definition of the natural wage given in the *Principles* (unless we ingeniously interpret 'a given demand' as 'a given rate of increase of demand'). And secondly, the natural price, so defined, is a true centre of gravity: like the relationship between the market and natural price of corn, the market wage will mostly be 'either above or below' the natural wage. From this, I conclude that he had not internalised the *Malthusian* vision of secularly declining market wages, with the applicability of the natural wage (as defined by Ricardo) at 'so great distance in point of time'.

What the *Notes* do confirm is Ricardo's firm conviction that he had 'managed the subject quite right'. For example:

> I refer to my chapter on wages with confidence to shew that I have admitted other causes besides the difficulty of producing food, for high wages and for periods too of considerable duration (II, p. 327)

But these 'other causes' were concessions to an adversary: insurance against Malthusian criticism. Thus:

Profits in all countries must mainly depend upon the quantity of labour given for corn . . . I say mainly depend, because I think wages mainly depend on the price of corn. After the observations of Mr. Malthus on the other causes which may affect labour, I must guard myself against being supposed to deny the effect of those other causes on wages (II, p. 291).

That was the reason for the discussion of 'temporary' wage-movements in the *Principles*.

VI

Sir John Hicks has been quoted as saying that the 'fixwage' (traditional) interpretation is a travesty of Ricardo's meaning (above, p. 109). My study suggests that the 'new view' advanced by Sir John and others is an even greater one. Leaving open the possibility that Ricardo might at one time have entertained the 'variable wage' scenario as an account of past and future wage behaviour, its elevation to the status of his 'true position' is surely a distortion: it detracts from, even obliterates, his theory of 'permanent' movements in profitability; and it erroneously represents the scenario as something which he had fully incorporated in his 'vision'.

The merit of the traditional interpretation is that it captures Ricardo's dominant treatment of the natural wage as a meaningful centre of gravity. The theory of profitability therefore retains its proper significance. But against this, the extreme form of the interpretation, which is common, downplays to vanishing point Ricardo's serious attempt to 'manage the subject quite right' – his discussion of 'temporary effects' – with the 'new view' scenario explained away by silence.

What has been happening? First, the preoccupation with model-building, referred to in my introduction. Since a good 'Ricardian model' must be logically consistent, offending portions of the text must either be 'constructively reinterpreted' to fit the system, or demoted in significance, which often means ignored. This goes some way to explaining how the 'new view' came to receive consideration. Quite rightly, its proponents recognised that the traditional account was not the whole story. That was a valuable advance. Unfortunately, the treacherous step was then taken of building an even more elaborate 'Ricardian model' which surpasses the earlier one in two ways, formal generality and misrepresentation. In turn, this accounts for any textually generated appeal that the hybrid interpretation may have – the lure of the 'middle way' – bogus as the textual foundation turns out to be.

Then there is the desire to 'place' Ricardo. So often, this plays the role of legitimising the 'school of thought' to which the commentator owes allegiance: if Ricardo 'belongs' it shows that there is a long and illustrious history for the 'correct' approach; if his place is elsewhere, his writings can serve as an object lesson in seriously deficient analysis. Examples of both these strategies have been given in my review of the secondary literature.

I doubt whether a proper textual appreciation is fostered in this way. Indeed, the attendant danger of distortion has long been recognised (see Ashley, 1891; Gonner, 1890). As recently emphasised by Hutchison, 1985, setting up a worthy progenitor, or a worthless ignoramus, tends to invite the construction of a monolithically consistent figure in order to 'prove' the point beyond doubt. The model-builders and teleologists serve each other well.

It seems to me that much of the continuing interest in Ricardo has been stimulated by distortion and counter-distortion, acquisitiveness and the desire to justify contemporary doctrine. Granted, the 'perfect reading' is an illusory conception, but there are some habits which commentators would do well to jettison, or justify, if textual understanding is to proceed less haphazardly.

NOTES

An earlier version of this paper was read to Section F of the British Association for the Advancement of Science in August, 1985. I would like to thank the participants at the conference for their comments; Paul Cammack, who read the first draft; and M. D. Kinzo for help and encouragement during the writing of this version. The responsibility for errors is mine.

1. Compare Hollander, 1983: 'Much depends on the precise assumption made regarding wages; the subsistence wage attribution, for example, has distorted the entire body of "Cambridge" historiographical doctrine relating to classical economics'. For future reference, the 'Cambridge' group should be taken to mean followers of Piero Sraffa. I discuss their position in the following section.

2. The 'short-circuit' metaphor is due to Samuelson, 1978 (compare Pasinetti, 1960:

    It is very impressive to notice how strongly Ricardo is convinced of the operation of this [population] mechanism. To be precise, he always speaks of a process which will operate 'ultimately' but the emphasis on it is so strong that his analysis is always carried on *as if* the response were almost immediate (Pasinetti's emphasis).

3. For those unfamiliar with Marx's writings, the reasoning is very roughly as follows. 'Labour-power' is the commodity that capitalists purchase from labourers for a specific period of time; it is the labourers capacity for work. 'Value' is the length of time computed to have been spent producing something, depending on both technical conditions of production and demand. The origin of profit is sought by Marx in the difference between the time required to produce a value equivalent to that of the given means of subsistence (that is the value of the given real wage-bundle) and the total time worked for the capitalist. This difference is 'surplus-value' or 'unpaid labour', while profit is its 'outward form' or 'appearance'. Labourers are 'dispossessed' in the sense that they do not own their own means of production and are therefore compelled to sell their labour-power to capitalists in order to live.

4. Schumpeter termed the same method of analysis the 'Ricardian vice': 'the habit of establishing simple relations between aggregates that then acquire a spurious halo of causal importance, whereas all the really important (and, unfortunately, complicated) things are being bundled away in or behind these aggregates' (1954, p. 668).

5. All references to Ricardo are from Sraffa (ed.) *The Works and Correspondence of David Ricardo*, (with the assistance of M. H. Dobb). I give the volume in Roman numerals, followed by the page reference.

6. Hicks and Hollander, 1977, interpret Ricardo's use of 'tendency' as 'a constant disposition to move or act in some direction or towards some point, end or purpose'. In other words, they ask us to believe that there is no conflict between the 'new view', with the natural wage only encountered in the stationary state, and Ricardo's pronouncements that market wages are tending to conform to the natural level. However, it is clear in the passage just quoted that the tendency is deemed inoperative ('Notwithstanding the tendency . . .'); moreover, in other passages (such as those I have cited on pages 110, 111, 113 and 114) the strength of the tendency would seem much greater than Hicks and Hollander suggest. I therefore conclude that this aspect of their interpretation is unsatisfactory.

7. The chapter from which the above quotation is taken is likened by Professor Hollander to Ricardo's *Essay on . . . . Profits* (1815) in which he 'consciously restricted the analysis in order to focus upon the effects of diminishing returns *alone*' (Hollander, 1979, p. 395, Hollander's emphasis); as part of this restricted focus, real wages were held constant; so too in the chapter on accumulation 'where the point he had in mind could more conveniently be conveyed if other complexities were (temporarily) set aside' (Hollander, 1979). The implication is that Ricardo's statements in the chapter should be taken with a pinch of salt. On my reading, in contrast, the passage quoted is a summary statement of fundamental doctrine (and similarly for the inserted passage which I quote in the following paragraph).

8. I have argued this in Peach, 1984.

9. The 'proportion of produce' is the ratio of profit to the wage bill (Peach, 1984).
10. *An Essay on the Influence of a low Price of Corn on the Profits of Stock*, published 14 February 1815.
11. See Sraffa's Introduction to *The Works and Correspondence of David Ricardo*, especially I, pp. xv–xix and p. xxvi.
12. Compare Rosselli, who suggests that the pre-*Principles* debate 'may have induced Ricardo to give a more rigorous form to his ideas, working out a theoretical argument designed to rule out possibilities suggested by Malthus' (1985 p. 244).
13. Malthus's *Principles* was published in April 1820 and Ricardo's notes were written three months later (see Sraffa, II, pp. vii–xviii).

REFERENCES

Ashley, W. J. 'The Rehabilitation of Ricardo', *Economic Journal*, vol. 1 (1891) pp. 474–89.

Caravale, G. A. (ed.) *The Legacy of Ricardo* (Oxford: Blackwell, 1985a).

Caravale, G. A. 'Diminishing Returns and Accumulation in Ricardo', in G. A. Caravale (ed.) *The Legacy of Ricardo* (Oxford: Blackwell, 1985).

Caravale, G. A. and D. A. Tosato *Ricardo and the Theory of Value, Distribution and Growth* (London: Routledge & Kegan Paul, 1980).

Casarosa, C. 'A New Formulation of the Ricardian System', *Oxford Economic Papers*, (N.S.) vol. 30 (1978) pp. 38–63.

Casarosa, C. 'The "New View" of the Ricardian Theory of Distribution and Growth', in G. A. Caravale (ed.), *The Legacy of Ricardo* (Oxford: Blackwell, 1985).

Garegnani, P. 'Value and Distribution in the Classical Economists and Marx', *Oxford Economic Papers*, (N.S.) vol. 36 (1984) pp. 291–325.

Gonner, E. C. K. 'Ricardo and His Critics', *Quarterly Journal of Economics*, vol. 4 (1890) pp. 276–90.

Hicks, J. 'The Ricardian System: A Comment', *Oxford Economic Papers*, (N.S.) vol. 31 (1979) pp. 133–4.

Hicks, J. and S. Hollander 'Mr. Ricardo and the Moderns', *Quarterly Journal of Economics*, vol. 91 (1977) pp. 351–69.

Hollander, S. *The Economics of David Ricardo* (Toronto: Heinemann, 1979).

Hollander, S. 'On the Interpretation of Ricardian Economics: The Assumption Regarding Wages', *American Economic Review*, vol. 73 (1983) pp. 314–18.

Hutchison, T. W. 'On the Interpretation and Misinterpretation of Economists and of the History of Economic Literature', in *Gli Economisti e la Politica Economica*, ed. P. Raggi. (Napoli: Edizioni Scientifiche Italiane, 1985).

Jevons, W. S. [1879] *The Theory of Political Economy* 4th edn, (London: Macmillan, 1970).

Marshall, A. [1920] *Principles of Economics* 8th edn (London: Macmillan, 1949).

Marx, K. [1862–3] *Theories of Surplus Value* (Part II) (London: Lawrence & Wishart, 1969),

Pasinetti, L. L. 'A Mathematical Formulation of the Ricardian System', *Review of Economic Studies*, vol. 27 (1960) pp. 78–98.

Peach, T. 'David Ricardo's Early Treatment of Profitability: A New Intepretation', *Economic Journal*, vol. 94 (1984) pp. 733–51.

Ricardo, D. in P. Sraffa (ed.) *The Works and Correspondence of David Ricardo* vols I–X, (Cambridge: Cambridge University Press, 1951–55) with the collaboration of M. H. Dobb.

Rosselli, A 'The Theory of the Natural Wage', in G. A. Caravale (ed.), *The Legacy of Ricardo* (Oxford: Blackwell, 1985).

Samuelson, P. A. 'The Canonical Classical Model of Political Economy', *Journal of Economic Literature*, vol. 16 (1978) pp. 1415–34.

Schumpeter, J. A. *History of Economic Analysis* (London: Allen & Unwin, 1954).

Sraffa, P. *Production of Commodities by Means of Commodities: Prelude To a Critique of Economic Theory* (Cambridge: Cambridge University Press, 1960).

Stigler, G. J. 'The Ricardian Theory of Value and Distribution', *Journal of Political Economy*, 60 (1952): 187–207.

Stigler, G. J. 'Review of Hollander (1979)', *Journal of Economic Literature*, 19 (1981): 100–2.

Tucker, G. S. L. *Progress and Profits in British Economic Thought* (Cambridge: Cambridge University Press).

6 The Relevance of John Stuart Mill: Some Implications for Modern Economics

SAMUEL HOLLANDER

1. INTRODUCTION

Sir John Hicks has recently lamented that John Stuart Mill 'as an economist, seems to have been de-throned' (Hicks, p. 60). It is my contention that his underevaluation has been at a great cost – intellectual and social. Professor Phelps-Brown, in his Presidential Address to the Royal Economic Society in 1971, charged that the profession had contributed little by its sophisticated theoretical and econometric techniques to the most pressing economic problems of our age, and explained this discrepancy by the argument that our models are 'built upon assumptions about human behaviour that are plucked from the air', rather than drawn from observation – 'that the behaviour posited is not known to be what obtains in the actual economy' (Phelps Brown, 1972, pp. 3–4). The President of the American Economic Association in 1971 made precisely the same point, that the 'consistently indifferent performance in practical applications is . . . a symptom of a fundamental imbalance in the present state of our discipline. The weak and all too slowly growing empirical foundation clearly cannot support the proliferating super-structure of pure, or . . . speculative economic theory'. What is needed, considering that by the nature of social systems the structural relationships (both their form and the parameters) are subject to continuous change, is 'a very difficult and seldom very neat assessment and verification of these assumptions in terms of observed facts'. In this context he characterised much econometric work 'as an attempt to compensate for the glaring weakness of the data base available to us by the widest possible use of more and more sophisticated statistical techniques' designed 'to stretch to the limit the meager supply of facts' – techniques which themselves are based on convenient assumptions of fact which can be seldom verified' (Leontief, 1971, pp. 1–3).

These laments portray the type of consequence against which J. S. Mill had sought to protect economics from 1830 onwards. His own council – and also his practice – justified a specialist economics but specifically on *empirical* grounds and thus provisionally; it implied a very modest estimate of the subject's forecasting or predictive potential; it demanded model improvement by way of verification against factual evidence; it disdained any notion of the *universal* validity of economic principles; it focused attention upon the mechanics of pricing in the real world of business rather than some ideal world; and it invited consideration of how economic mechanisms might operate under a variety of alternative institutional arrangements. His position took a stand against professional arrogance and narrow-mindedness. Most striking is Mill's remarkable prescience – he himself warned of the probable consequences of adopting the kind of hyper-specialist mathematical research program in the air, indeed already on the ground, during his last years.

We can trace the deflection of the subject to which I allude to the revolt against classicism in the early 1870s. Professor Black has argued that it is Jevons's emphasis upon 'the importance of the mathematical method' rather than the development of marginal utility theory as such, wherein lies 'the essence of his break with the classical tradition' (Black 1972a, p. 5). And this indeed seems to hit the nail on the head (compare Schabas, 1983a). Jevons's program was the mathematisation of economic theory: 'Economics, if it is to be a science at all, must be a mathematical science' (Jevons, 1924, p. 3) treating specifically *'the mechanics of utility and self-interest'* (Jevons, 1924, p. 21) – that is a science of economising behaviour (Black, 1972b, p. 372). Jevons's hope was for the transformation of economics from a 'mathematical' into an 'exact' science permitting application of statistical method; but economists were to proceed boldly 'in developing their mathematical theories in advance of their data' (Jevons, 1924, p. 6). For the 'mechanical' theory itself 'must be the true one'. Indeed, in a remarkable statement Jevons asserted that 'its method is as sure and demonstrative as that of kinematics or statics, nay, almost as self-evident as are the elements of Euclid, when the real meaning of the formulae is fully seized' (Jevons, 1924, p. 21); similarly, 'the first principles of political economy are so widely true and applicable that they may be considered universally true as regards human nature' (Jevons, 1905, p. 197).

Jevons by no means disdained the efforts of the historicists such as Cliffe Leslie. He observed in 1876:

I am far from thinking that the historical treatment of our science is false or useless. On the contrary, I consider it to be indispensable. The present state of society cannot possibly be explained by theory alone. We must take into account the long past out of which we are constantly emerging. Whether we call it sociology or not, we must have some scientific treatment of the principles of evolution as manifested in every branch of social existence' (Jevons, 1905, p. 195).

But theoretical work was to proceed unencumbered, for Jevons insisted firmly on division of labour: 'it will no longer be possible to treat political economy as if it were a single undivided and indivisible science' (Jevons, 1905, p. 197); '[it] is only by subdivision . . . that we can rescue our science from its confused state' (Jevons, 1924, pp. 20–1). And, in any event, historical economics (which apparently entailed different 'scientific' procedures from those appropriate in pure economics) would have a rather limited confirmatory function: 'so far from displacing the theory of economy, [historical economics] will only exhibit and verify the long-continued action of its laws in most widely different states of society' (Jevons, 1905, p. 197).[1]

In what precise ways did Mill differ from Jevons? There are obvious similarities. Mill too distinguished (as Ricardo had done) the 'science' from the 'art' of economics; and for him, too, scientific economics involved a form of maximisation theory. In fact, we must be quite clear that any revolutionary connotation attached to general pricing doctrine has to be avoided when treating the events of the 1870s. For the 'Ricardian' economics of Mill comprises in its essentials an exchange system consistent with the neoclassical elaborations (Hollander, 1979, 1985).

But even when we limit our perspective to pricing[2] there is a fundamental difference. The marginalists based their deductions on an *assumed* psychology acting within an *assumed* environment. From the limited number of hypothetical postulates relating to human psychology, and the social environment, was to be derived the entire body of economic doctrine; model improvement by the introduction of new material in the form of postulates, axioms, definitions and hypotheses derived by testing against real-world evidence played no part. This perspective threatened a reversion to the severe abstractions of James Mill, which had been undertaken on the basis of axioms adopted without serious empirical study – the state of affairs which induced J. S. Mill in 1829 and 1830 to compose in protest his celebrated essay on scope and method (Mill, 1836).[3] For, like Ricardo, he was concerned with the real world of business not some laboratory experiment. It is a failure of the profession to heed his warnings that delayed for decades the recognition of monopolistic competition, engendered ludicrous accounts of competitive price formation, and pushed such phenomena as conspicuous consumption into the footnotes. In these respects the 1870s encouraged intellectual regression.

I shall take for granted in what follows Mill's case (presented in his early essay on definition and method (Mill, 1836) and the *System of Logic* (Mill, 1843)) for a specialist economics – the empirical validity of the maximisation axiom, the role accorded 'verification' in model improvement, and the limitations imposed on the scope of economic science by empirical considerations – limitations which preclude 'prediction'. But one matter relating to formal method requires closer attention, Mill's famous assertion regarding the 'universality of the method of political economy', before we turn to the substance of our presentation. This concerns the empirical dimension of the *Principles of Political Economy* (Mill, 1848) with special reference to the analysis of price formation and the marginal utility issue. Mill's balanced and highly pertinent position regarding mathematical economics brings the paper to a close.

2.   THE UNIVERSALITY OF THE METHOD OF POLITICAL ECONOMY

In the course of a criticism in 1834 of English political economists who

attempt to construct a permanent fabric out of transitory materials . . . [and] presuppose in every one of their speculations, that the produce of industry is shared among three classes, altogether distinct from one another – namely, labourers, capitalists, and landlords; and that all these are free agents, permitted in law and fact to set upon their labour, their capital, and their land, whatever price they are able to get for it (Mill, 1834 – *CW*, IV 225),

Mill added a qualification which withdraws the barbs as far as concerns the method itself:

It must not, however, be supposed that the science is so incomplete and unsatisfactory as this might seem to prove. Though many of its conclusions are only locally true, its method of investigation is applicable universally; and as he who has solved a certain number of algebraic equations, can without difficulty solve all others, so he who knows the political economy of England, or even of Yorkshire, knows that of all nations actual or possible; provided he have sense enough not to expect the same conclusions to issue from varying premises. (This is cited in the *System of Logic* (*CW*, VIII, 904); and a similar position is taken in a reaction to Auguste Comte in 1865 (*CW*, X, 305–6).)

This claim regarding the universal applicability of the method of political economy has been said to conflict with the position laid down in the *Principles* that 'only through the principle of competition has political economy any pretension to the character of a science' (Winch, 1972, p. 340). Edgeworth (in Palgrave (ed.), 1910, II, p. 757), Winch observes, 'drew attention to this inconsistency when he pointed out that it was not really possible for Mill to retain belief in the *a priori* deductive method once "he began to doubt the universality of the principle of self-interest, which he once regarded as the foundation of economic reasoning"' (Winch, 1972, p. 340). Now the fact is that Mill had 'doubted' the universality of the principle of maximising behaviour from 1830 onwards. Are we then obliged to charge him with a self-contradiction throughout the essay?

The formulation relating to the applicability of the method of economics to 'all nations actual or possible' appears indeed to be too strongly stated on Mill's own terms. However, in his paper of 1834 Mill is quite explicit regarding his specific intentions. Mill insisted that:

The conclusions of the science, being all adapted to a society thus constituted, require to be revised whenever they are applied to any other. They are inapplicable where the only capitalists are the landlords, and the labourers are their property; as in the West Indies. They are inapplicable where the universal landlord is the

State, as in India. They are inapplicable where the agricultural labourer is generally the owner both of the land itself and of the capital, as in France; or of the capital only, as in Ireland. We might greatly prolongue this enumeration (*CW*, IV, 226).

In the *System of Logic* (Mill, 1843) he pointed out that:

the deductive science of society will not lay down a theorem, asserting in an universal manner the effect of any cause; but will rather teach us how to frame the proper theorem for the circumstances of any given case. It will not give the laws of society in general, but the means of determining the phenomena of any given society from the particular elements or data of that society (*CW* VIII, 899–900).

To this he adds that

whoever has mastered with the degree of precision which is attainable the laws which, under free competition, determine the rent, profits, and wages, received by landlords, capitalists, and labourers, in a state of society in which the three classes are completely separate, will have no difficulty in determining the very different laws which regulate the distribution of the produce among the classes interested in it, in any of the states of cultivation and landed property set forth in the foregoing extract. Mill was here alluding to the specific institutional arrangements listed in Harriet Martineau's *Political Economy* (1834).

The argument is referred to with enthusiasm by Torrens (1844, pp. xif) in his defence of Ricardian economics.

The strong statements regarding the applicability of the method of political economy 'to all nations and all times' do *not*, therefore, extend maximisation principles to all possible cases including (say) those involving custom or gift or force – alluded to in the *System of Logic* (*CW*, VIII, 900–1) as well as the *Principles* – which, Mill maintained, were not amenable to economic analysis and would have to be dealt with by 'some other' science. Mill was pointing rather to the working out of the maximisation hypothesis within a wide variety of specific institutional arrangements in addition to the capitalist-exchange system. This might be illustrated by reference to the treatment of peasant proprietorship, co-operation and the stationary-state issue, but the exercise would extend our present argument too far.

3. THE EMPIRICAL DIMENSION IN THE PRINCIPLES: SOME CASE STUDIES

The roles accorded 'induction' in the derivation of individual axioms and in model improvement are central to the early essay, and that essay Mill intended his readers to have at hand in 1848. It will be useful to take a brief overview of Mill's actual practice in the *Principles* from this perspective with particular reference to the self-interest axiom.

We must first set aside an unnecessary terminological complexity, turning on the technical usage of 'wealth' to exclude services. This usage has led some commentators to assert that Mill's maximising individuals concern themselves solely with material goods (for example, Bowley, 1937, pp. 46–7, 61, 63). In fact Mill had in mind nothing more than the rule that individuals seek to sell goods and services at the highest price attainable and to buy at the lowest price attainable, and possess the knowledge to do so (*CW*, III, 460 cited below). The consequence of such behaviour combined with other assumptions relating to large numbers and free entry is a single price for the same good (or service) in one market – the so-called 'Jevons rule' which characterises competition; and 'only through the principle of competition has political economy any pretension to the character of science' subject to 'principles of broad generality and scientific precision' (*CW*, II, 239).

That the maximising man in the *Principles* refers to the real man in the market-place rather than a psychological fiction comes to light with stark clarity in Mill's restriction of the economic analysis of pricing to the wholesale sector:

> The values and prices . . . to which our conclusions apply, are mercantile values and prices; such prices as are quoted in price-currents; prices in the wholesale markets, in which buying as well as selling is a matter of business; in which the buyers take pains to know, and generally do know, the lowest price at which an article of a given quality can be obtained . . . Our propositions will be true in a much more qualified sense, of retail prices; the prices paid in shops for articles of personal consumption (*CW*, III, 460).

This restriction turns on the observation that buyers at retail outlets do not typically make their purchases 'on business principles' – a reflection of their indolence, carelessness, satisfaction derived from paying high prices, ignorance, defective judgement and coercion, apart from high search costs (*CW*, III, 460). Equally conspicuous is the discussion of the motives governing employers of domestics (and of clerks) which explains why more is often paid than the 'competitive' wage in terms of 'ostentation' and a variety of 'more reasonable motives' all of which turn on the personal contact between employee and employer (*CW*, III, 398–9). This case-study provides a very clear indication that the assumption of wealth maximisation is pertinent to the anonymous market-place where personal contacts are reduced to a minimum precluding the range of considerations in question. Quite clearly Mill was fully at one with Smith regarding the supposed empirical accuracy of the maximising assumption in the capitalist-exchange environment, and more specifically the limitations imposed by that environment on a range of 'self-interested' forms of behaviour (but see Blaug, 1980, p. 61 for a quite different perspective).

Marshall maintained of Ricardo and his followers that they 'often spoke as though they regarded man as a constant quantity, and they never gave themselves enough trouble to study his variations' (Marshall, 1920, p. 762). While little harm was done in the contexts of money and trade they were 'led astray' particularly in that of distribution; they 'attributed to the forces of supply and demand a much more mechanical and regular action than is to be found in real life: and they laid down laws with regard to profits and wages that did not really hold even for England in their own time' (Marshall, 1920, pp. 762–3). Marshall did not include Mill of the *Principles* in this charge; it was rather Mill of the essay (Mill, 1836) who was supposedly guilty, Marshall presuming mistakenly that it was written under the influence of James Mill (Marshall, 1920, pp. 764–5n). As for the *Principles*, Marshall was right in that Mill did not there apply the principles of supply and demand 'mechanically', either in the context of commodity or of service pricing. Yet he took great pains to avoid disparaging competitive pricing, and in so doing *reinforced* the importance of classical theorising even from an empirical perspective.

His course of action involves the matter of 'disturbing causes' so central to the formal discussion of method. Consider the declaration that 'while there is no proposition which meets us in the field of political economy more often than this – that there cannot be two prices in the same market . . . yet every one knows that there are, almost always two prices, in the same market' (*CW*, II, 242). The solution adopted by Mill, in effect, is to treat non-maximising behaviour in the retail sector as involving 'disturbing causes' in pricing – in principle the responsibility of 'some other science'. But this, it must be emphatically stressed, has an empirical justification, in so far as the primary force at work – that governing the determination of the underlying wholesale price – remained pecuniary maximisation.

The latter procedure can be further illustrated by reference to the allowance in the essay that the 'perpetually antagonistic principles to the desire of wealth,' namely 'aversion to labour, and desire of the present enjoyment of costly indulgencies,' are in practice taken into account by economics 'to a certain extent' precisely because of their empirical pervasiveness (*CW*, IV, 322). This matter is much amplified in the *Principles*, where it is clarified that by desire of wealth is intended pecuniary maximisation, and by the two antagonistic forces in question a willingness to by-pass an opportunity to increase the return per hour or per unit of capital by movement between sectors, or to forego a bargain in commodity markets. Thus Mill observed regarding Continental Europe 'that prices and charges, of some or of all sorts, are much higher in some places than in others not far distant, without its being possible to assign any other cause than that it has always been so: the customers are used to it, and acquiesce in it' (*CW*, II, 244). Similarly, 'an enterprising competitor, with sufficient capital, might force down the charges, and make his fortune during the process; but there are no enterprising competitors; those who have capital prefer to leave it where it is, or to make less profit by it in a more quiet way'. The same could be said of labour. Now in the British case too, where 'the spirit of competition' is the strongest, custom was still a 'powerful influence'; but in other environments people were 'content with smaller gains, and estimate their pecuniary interest at a lower rate when balanced against their ease or their pleasure'. Clearly Mill intended more than a quantitative difference between Britain and the Continent. In the latter kind of environment the force of the wealth-maximisation motive was swamped by the antagonistic motives so that little could be said of the response to a newly-created wage or profit differential or a reduction in price; havoc was wrought as far as concerns 'predictions' regarding labour and capital flows, or rates of consumption with price change. In the British case there were strong empirical presumptions favouring the process of equalisation of returns to labour and to capital, and also the negative slope to the demand curve and thus a tendency to stable equilibrium in competitive markets – at least up to the wholesale stage.

Thus it is also that Mill appeals to the empirical accuracy of the behavioural axiom in his discussion of profit-rate equalisation (cost pricing):

> If the value of a commodity is such that it repays the cost of production not only with the customary, but with a higher rate of profit, capital rushes to share in this extra gain, and by increasing the supply of the article reduces its value. This is not a mere supposition or surmise, but a fact familiar to those conversant with commercial operations (*CW*, III, 472).

We recall too (see, pp. 140ff) the appeal to the real world of business and the complexity of entrepreneurial decision-making in the context of what we shall call 'internal adjustment' to cost variation.

The same perspective emerges in Mill's general analysis of the wage structure with special reference to his allowance for non-competing groups. A variety of features of the real world, conspicuously the impediments to mobility of a financial and social order, underlay his dissatisfaction with Smithian analysis, and it was his growing optimism regarding a breakdown of the impediments that ultimately led him to conclude that while 'there are few kinds of [skilled] labour of which the remuneration would not be lower than it is, if the employer took the full advantage of competition', yet competition 'must be regarded, in the present state of society as the principal regulator of wages, and custom or individual character only as a modifying circumstance, and that in a comparatively slight degree' (*CW*, II, 337).

Moreover, the existence of unusual cases is never denied. The most striking are the instances of excessive entry as in the literary professions (*CW*, II, 392) or the Canadian timber trade (*CW*, II, 383–4) generating negative returns even in equilibrium, – a consequence of that 'principal of human nature' whereby a few great prizes stimulates miscalculation. But this principle too was treated as a 'modifying circumstance' in going conditions.

That the primary behaviour axiom holds good as a first approximation is thus justified on purely empirical grounds as we are led to expect from the essay. But here we must note the fundamentally important caution regarding the allowances that have to be made in practice, a caution that appears following recognition of possible cases of permanent inequalities in the return on capital:

> These observations must be received as a general correction to be applied whenever relevant, whether expressly mentioned or not, to

the conclusions contained in the subsequent portions of this treatise. Our reasonings must, in general, proceed as if the known and natural effects of competition were actually produced by it, in all cases where it is not restrained by some positive obstacle. Where competition, though free to exist, does not exist, or where it exists, but has its natural consequences overruled by any other agency, the conclusions will fail more or less of being applicable. To escape error, we ought, in applying the conclusions of political economy to the actual affairs of life, to consider not only what will happen supposing the maximum of competition, but how far the result will be affected if competition falls short of the maximum (*CW*, III, 244).

Again this too reflects what is said in the essay, namely, that verification of the hypothesis is 'no part of the business of science, but of the application of science.' But it must be understood with qualification.[4]

As in the essay so in the *Principles*, we find that Mill allows the absorption into his economic models of market forms that do not fit the purely competitive case. What we have to say on this matter is pertinent to an evaluation of the view that, from Mill's perspective, 'we never test the *validity* of theories, because the conclusions are true as one aspect of human behaviour by virtue of being based on self-evident facts of human experience' (Blaug, 1980, p. 77). That the notion of 'self-evident' facts is suspect we know already; what emerges, however is the further circumstance that Mill does attempt model improvement based upon testing against the record; much more is involved than 'a search . . . for sufficient supplementary causes to close the gap between the facts and the causal antecedents laid down in the theory' (Blaug, 1980, p. 75).

Model improvement as defined in the essay is the hoped-for consequence of the process of testing against the evidence. In some instances a new disturbing cause would be discovered which in future use of theory has to be kept in mind – as instanced by the obstacles to wage-rate equalisation which Mill's empirical studies brought to light. But model improvement in consequence of verification might be more substantive, taking the form of 'inserting among its hypotheses a fresh and still more complex combination of circumstances, and so adding *pro hâc vice* a supplementary chapter or appendix, or at least a supplementary theorem to the abstract science'. Thus the exclusion of monopoly from the scientific domain and its treatment as disturbing cause turns out to be purely a formal matter; in practice Mill admitted that it had 'always been allowed for by political economists' and himself applied the tools of analysis to this case (Hollander, 1985, pp. 300–1). Even more striking, he allows in practice for the absorption of custom – again formally a 'disturbing cause' – where custom establishes prices yet competition acts to reduce profits to the economy-wide rate by reducing market size – the 'monopolistic competition' model (*CW*, II, 243, 409–10). Here then we have two splendid illustrations of the observation in the essay that 'a disturbing cause . . . which operates through the same law of human nature out of which the general principles of the science arise . . . might always be brought within the pale of the abstract science, if it were thought worthwhile'.[5]

Equally striking is Mill's recognition of (short-run) excess demand for money to hold. This too illustrates model improvement, in this case a consequence of the 'anomaly' of contemporaneous excess labour and capital which forced itself on his attention after his escape from his father's influence. And the idea of an endogenous trade cycle is better developed by Mill than any contemporary and clearly related to real-world events.[6]

4. ON PRICE FORMATION

Much of the apparent ambiguity surrounding Mill's formulations of cost price in its relation to demand-and-supply dissipates on a close inspection of the texts. For it becomes apparent that it arises from an impressive attempt to get a grip on the notoriously complex issue of long-run price and output adjustments in unconventional terms from the perspective of the modern reader precisely because Mill is attempting to deal with the complexity of real-world business.

We take as the standard case the adjustment to a new equilibrium following a technological change that reduces natural price. Mill's approach allows a price-setting role to individual (competitive) entrepreneurs who, aware of the likelihood of entry into the industry by firms in response to super-normal profit, act to forestall them. It is, therefore, not increase in supply that works to reduce price to the lower cost level, but price that is lowered directly, at a rate depending upon the estimate of the immediate danger of entry made by existing entrepreneurs who calculate the risks of entry as viewed by prospective entrants, a calculation which turns partly upon demand elasticity (*CW*, III, 473–4).

It is expectation of increased supply that brings about the price reduction to cost, for which reason precisely 'if the supply *could* not be increased no diminution in the cost of production would lower the value'. Next to be noted is the actual output expansion, in the usual case of non-zero elasticity of demand, by existing firms who will be faced by larger markets which they can serve at the going (economy-wide) profit rate. In the limiting case of zero-demand elasticity (characterising basic foodstuffs) there will, of course, be no such opportunities at all; this possibility Mill emphasised in order to counter the view that there necessarily occurs an output expansion to assure that price falls to cost.

There arise a number of complications. Before these expansions have been accomplished there will be excess demand at cost price and one must suppose that consumers or perhaps retailers, for their part, will put upward pressure on the price. This kind of complexity is actually raised by Mill in his treatment of a tax:

Again, reverse the case, and suppose the cost of production increased . . . The value would rise; and that probably immediately. Would the supply be diminished? Only if the increase of value diminished the demand. Whether this effect followed, would soon appear, and if it did, the value would recede somewhat, from excess of supply, until the production was reduced, and would then rise again (*CW*, III, 474).

In this case, as before, price changes 'immediately' (although the counterpart to the logic of fear of entry is not clarified). At the higher price, in the first instance, supply exceeds demand in the event that demand contracts, generating some downward pressure on the price, although it seems that the market does not fully clear until the adjustment is completed; only after output is actually reduced can the higher price level be permanently maintained. The implication is that, in our case of technological change, prices will rise somewhat from the initial (lower-cost) level although firms would be reluctant to accept improved offers for fears of attracting new entrants and would be engaged in attempting to expand capacity to meet the expected demand at the cost price, even if current price should be held somewhat above it. But again, the market does not actually clear until the adjustment process is completed. (That a degree of trial and error is involved is also clarified by the remark that 'the permanent tendency of supply is to conform itself to the demand which is found by experience to exist for the commodity when selling at its natural value'.)

There are, of course, complexities. Mill's firms are supposed to engage in a passive form of collusion to satisfy what amounts to an implicit market division arrangement. A characteristic of the analysis is its failure to indicate the long-run optimum size of the firms, each of which is apparently presumed to have the technical ability to expand at constant cost without limit; what constraint exists, is self-imposed.[7] Secondly, it would be going too far to attribute to Mill sole reliance on internal adjustment. That mechanism applies where the disturbance is amenable to treatment in partial-equilibrium terms, where the economy-wide profit rate can be taken by firms in a particular industry as given. It would not apply to a disturbance such as a general wage change. And it is difficult to see how it would operate effectively alone in variable-cost industries where there is no unambiguous level of costs to which firms can attempt to adjust price. Even in the standard case of adjustment to technological change in a constant-cost industry, the smaller the success of existing firms in maintaining price near the new cost level, the greater will be the attraction for newcomers. And the mechanism will be irrelevant in the case of newly-established industries. Yet despite all this we have here a remarkable attempt, of which we have simply lost sight in the literature, to get to grips with an exceedingly complex issue. This case illustrates my contention that even in their own domain of price theory, the marginalists failed to build on their predecessors – a failure accountable by their model-building in isolation from the real business world.

5. MILL AND MARGINAL UTILITY

We proceed to the marginal utility issue – the fact that the classical approach to the law of demand (the negative slope to the demand curve) eschewed reference to the principle of satiability of wants. How to explain what, from a neoclassical perspective, is often represented as a 'failing' (compare de Marchi, 1972, p. 350). Is the marginal utility episode not a case of unambiguous progress?

It is possible that the marginal utility concept itself was long familiar to Mill (de Marchi, 1972, p. 347; Bowley, 1972; Hollander, 1977); in fact, Mill utilised a version of diminishing utility in his case for income redistribution (Hollander, 1985, p. 880). That Mill 'inherited from Ricardo a bias against giving consumption a place equal to that held by production and distribution in the schema of economic science' (de Marchi, p. 350 – compare pp. 354, 363) is also true, provided that this is not understood as downplaying the law of demand itself which was so central to Ricardian economics, or as a blanket denial that the ultimate motive governing production and employment is final purchase. By his statements in the essay regarding consumption Mill merely intended to convey that the 'laws of consumption' – which are identified with the 'laws of human enjoyment' – fall outside the domain of the economist (*CW*, IV, 318n). The existence of such laws, however, seems to be conceded. Indeed, Mill removes some potential roadblocks along the path. There is his insistence in *Utilitarianism* (Mill, 1861) that 'rules of arithmetic are applicable to the valuation of happiness, as of all other measurable quantities' (*CW*, X, 258). In *A System of Logic* he took strong issue with Comte and others who

> prefer dogmatically to assume that the mental differences which they perceive, or think they perceive, among human beings, are ultimate facts, incapable of being either explained or altered, rather than take the trouble of fitting themselves, by the requisite process of thought, for referring those mental differences to the outward causes by which they are for the most part produced, and on the removal of which they would cease to exist (*CW*, III, 859).

He maintained that 'the commonest observation shows that different minds are susceptible in very different degrees to the action of the same psychological causes. The idea, for example, of a given desirable object, will excite in different minds very different degrees of intensity of desire' (*CW*, VIII, 865, compare 857); but he was ready enough to allow the usefulness of 'approximate generalizations' albeit that they constituted the lowest kind of empirical law: 'that which is only probable when asserted of individual human beings indiscriminately selected, being certain when affirmed of the character and collective conduct of masses' (*CW*, VIII, 847).

There is then no categorical rejection of an investigation of the 'laws of human enjoyment'. And the question would have arisen for Mill whether it might be fruitful to seek a basis in psychology for the law of demand.

As a matter of principle Mill maintained (in a famous letter to Cairnes) that 'the wants of the time' required 'that scientific deductions should be made as simple and as easily intelligible as they can be made without ceasing to be scientific' (letter of 5 December 1871; *CW*,

XVII, 1863). Now the law of demand had already been rationalised in terms of the income effect by Ricardo, and more than that may not have been found necessary. We can be rather more specific. Our researches have shown that when pressed to consider the details of consumer reaction to relative price variation, purchasing power held constant, Mill applied brilliantly and effortlessly a 'revealed preference' analysis, thereby confirming a liking for as simple a rationale as possible – eschewing psychologism in favour of the pure logic of choice (Hollander, 1985, pp. 270–71). This illustrates nicely his complaint to Cairnes in the letter just referred to regarding Jevons's 'mania for encumbering questions with useless complications' (letter of 5 December 1871; *CW*, XVII, 1862). Jevons, for his part, simply asserted that 'it is surely obvious that Economics does rest upon the laws of human enjoyment; and that, if those laws are developed by no other science, they must be developed by economists' (Jevons, 1924, p. 39). Mill probably did not see the *Theory* (Schabas, 1983a, p. 39); but he was closer to the truth than Jevons by his realisation that recognition of the need for a theory of demand does not necessarily imply need for a psychological theory of consumption.[8]

But the appeal for simplicity alone might not have led to a refusal to follow through along a route which otherwise promised a more profound comprehension of behaviour. There is a further consideration – Mill's appreciation that consumer goods are usually characterised by some degree of durability imposing a 'capital' dimension upon decisions to purchase. For the production process comes to a halt when things are 'in place where they are required for use' (*CW*, II, 48); to focus on psychology to explain the stage of acquisition would have appeared inappropriate without the further complication of a discount factor, since the 'laws of human enjoyment' come into play only with the *use* of (durable) consumer goods.

There is also the belief that much consumer activity at the retail level is governed by non-maximising motivation. (From this point of view, it is doubtful whether Mill would have accorded diminishing marginal utility the status even of 'empirical law'.)[9] To the extent that consumer behaviour is not undertaken on terms of 'business principles' economics had nothing much to say. It is not that Mill was 'prevented' from defining optimum consumption patterns because he lacked the principle of marginal utility (de Marchi, 1972, pp. 356–7); rather, maximising behaviour was, empirically speaking, an inappropriate axiom in the first place. But to the extent that the consumer was envisaged as a maximiser – or at least as behaving consistently – an 'objective' approach was preferable. Important matters of principle govern Mill's neglect of diminishing marginal utility; to refer to it as a 'failure' and imply that the contributions of the 1870s were an unambiguous advance is inappropriate.

6.   MILL AND MATHEMATICAL ECONOMICS

Schwartz maintains that 'Mill was no mathematician, either by training or, which is more important, by inclination', and accordingly 'resisted the trend towards the formalisation of new knowledge' (Schwartz, 1972, p. 238). As an indication of this perspective he cites the letter to Cairnes regarding Jevons's *Theory of Political Economy* (1871) already referred to:

> I have not seen Mr. Jevons' book, but as far as I can judge from such notices of it as have reached me, I do not expect that I shall think favourably of it. He is a man of some ability, but he seems to me to have a mania for encumbering questions with useless complications, and with a notation implying the existence of greater precision in the data than the questions admit of. His speculations on logic, like those of Boole and De Morgan, and some of those of Hamilton, are infected in an extraordinary degree with this vice.

The notion that Mill's mathematics were inadequate can be dismissed (de Marchi, 1972, p. 347; Schabas, 1983a, p. 283). A key to Mill's reaction to Jevons will rather be found in an observation by Cairnes regarding *The Theory of Political Economy* (Jevons, 1871) in the letter which elicited the foregoing citation – 'I own', Cairnes wrote, that 'I have no faith in the development of economic doctrines by mathematics. What you have said on the subject of nomenclature in the second vol. of your Logic seems to me decisive upon this point' (23 October 1871, cited by Schwartz, 1972, p. 295). Cairnes is here referring to Mill's generalisation in *A System of Logic* that

> whenever the nature of the subject permits our reasoning processes to be, without danger, carried on mechanically, the language should be constructed on as mechanical principles as possible; while in the contrary case, it should be constructed that there shall be the greatest possible obstacles to a merely mechanical use of it' (*CW* VIII, 707).

This is followed by a statement of presumption against the widespread applicability of mathematical language suitable only for the 'mechanical' approach:

> [The] admirable properties of the symbolic language of mathematics have made so strong an impression on the minds of many thinkers, as to have led them to consider the symbolic language generally; to think that names in general, or (as they are fond of calling them) signs, are fitted for the purposes of thought in proportion as they can be made to approximate to the compactness, the entire unmeaningness, and the capability of being used as counters without a thought of what they represent, which are characteristic of the *a* and *b*, the *x* and *y* of algebra. This notion has led to sanguine views of the acceleration of the progress of science by means which, I conceive, cannot possibly conduce to that end, and forms part of that exaggerated estimate of the influence of signs, which has contributed in no small degree to prevent the real laws of our intellectual operations from being understood (*CW*, VIII, 708).

It is likely that this perspective governed at least in part the allusion to Jevons's 'use of a notation implying the existence of greater precision in the data than the questions admit of'. The observation extends far beyond the application of mathematics to consumption theory. Quite generally, Mill's fear was that the inappropriate use of mathematical language would act as a positive hindrance to scientific progress; Jevons's mathematical program for economics must have seemed to Mill an invitation to set out on a false trail.

Of crucial import here is the reaction to the argument that the adoption of a mathematical approach to the deductive sciences 'would reduce all reasonings to the application of a technical form, and enable their conclusiveness to be rationally assented to after a merely mechanical process, as is undoubtedly the case in algebra' (*CW*, VIII, 709). This case could only be applied 'where the practical validity' of the reasoning derives from the reasoning itself as in geometry and the 'science of number'. But where there arises the problem of 'composition of causes' involving propositions valid only in the absence of countervailing causes and thus having only 'hypothetical certainty' – the key problem in economics – what is called for is an attitude of mind alert to the specifics of the case and the empirical 'meaning' of the axioms:

A conclusion . . . however correctly deduced, in point of form, from admitted laws of nature, will have no other than an hypothetical certainty. At every step we must assure ourselves that no other law of nature has superseded, or intermingled its operation with, those which are the premises of the reasoning; and how can this be done by merely looking at the words? We must not only be constantly thinking of the phenomena themselves, but we must be constantly studying them; making ourselves acquainted with the peculiarities of every case to which we attempt to apply our general principles (*CW*, VIII, 710).

Mill's fear that a mathematical program would encourage a perspective deflecting attention from 'the meaning of our signs' is very nicely illustrated from the theory of consumption. I refer again to his approach towards the retail sector – consumers, in many cases, were not he believed, maximisers. The science of economics based upon maximising behaviour had much to offer regarding the determination of outputs and prices up to the wholesale level, but not beyond; the assumption of marginal calculation by final consumers might be totally inappropriate from an empirical perspective.

From this viewpoint the transformation of economics into a mathematical subject would entail an episode in scientific regression. And, in point of fact, the marginal treatment of consumption did throw overboard Mill's sophisticated empirical approach to demand – the recognition of 'disturbing causes' which generate failures of the 'law of demand' – in favour of Jevons's excessive simplification in the interest of mathematisation such as the assumptions of independent goods and independent consumers. More generally, Mill's potentially fruitful approach to competitive price formation involving the relation between firm and industry and expectation regarding entry fell on unreceptive soil, Jevons and Walras resorting to totally artificial expedients in order to proceed. This loss of 'realism' is particularly conspicuous in the case of Walras who, as Jaffé has strenuously argued, was concerned with the workings of an 'ideal' system not a 'real' capitalist economy, and whose *tâtonnement* process was unrelated to price adjustments in actual markets (Jaffé, 1980; but see the counter-argument by Walker, 1984).

Mill's warnings were remarkably prescient considering the fact that he was unfamiliar with the writings of the early 1870s. And equally striking, some of the dangers of over-simplified models had been long before formulated in a letter of 1829 to d'Eichthal. There he had emphasised that French procedure, by neglecting 'disturbing causes', distorted the operation even of those causes allowed for:

> They deduce politics like mathematics from a set of axioms & definitions, forgetting that in mathematics there is no danger of partial views: a proposition is either true or it is not, & if it is true, we may safely apply it to every case which the proposition comprehends in its terms: but in politics & the social science this is so far from being the case, that error seldom arises from our assuming premises which are not true, but generally from our overlooking other truths which limit, & modify the effect of the former (*CW*, XII, 35–6; compare *A System of Logic*, *CW*, VIII, 894).

There is an interesting parallel here with Keynes's celebrated warnings of 1939 regarding econometrics in his paper on 'Professor Tinbergen's Method'.[10]

This is not the end of the matter. There are various pronouncements in *A System of Logic* which together amount in effect to a case against mathematical 'forecasting' in economics – an exercise that requires precise numerical data – and which also may have played a part in Mill's actual (or potential) response to Jevons. First, consider the positive overview in the case of the physical sciences:

> The immense part which those laws ['which are the peculiar subject of the sciences of number and extension'] take in giving a deductive character to the other departments of physical science, is well known; and is not surprising, when we consider that all causes operate according to mathematical laws. The effect is always dependent on, or is a function of, the quantity of the agent; and generally of its position also. We cannot, therefore, reason respecting causation, without introducing considerations of quantity and extension at every step; and if the nature of the phenomena admits of our obtaining numerical data of sufficient accuracy, the laws of quantity become the grand instrument for calculating forward to an effect, or backward to a cause (*CW*, VII, 620).[11]

Here the reader is referred to volumes I and II of Auguste Comte's *Cours de Philosophie Positive* for further elaboration, and to volume III for the 'limits to the applicability of mathematical principles' – limits which cover economics:

Such principles are manifestly inapplicable where the causes on which any class of phenomena depend are so imperfectly accessible to our observation, that we cannot ascertain, by a proper induction their numerical laws; or where the causes are so numerous, and intermixed in so complex a manner with one another, that even supposing their laws known, the computation of the aggregate effect transcends the powers of the calculus as it is, or is likely to be; or lastly, where the causes themselves are in a state of perpetual fluctuation; as in physiology, and still more, if possible, in the social science. The solutions of physical questions become progressively more difficult and imperfect in proportion as the questions divest themselves of their abstract and hypothetical character, and approach nearer to the degree of complication actually existing in nature; insomuch that beyond the limits of astronomical phenomena, and of those most nearly analogous to them, mathematical accuracy is generally obtained 'at the expense of the reality of the inquiry' (*CW*, VII, 620–1; compare 459).

Mill concludes that the application of mathematical principles would be 'chimerical' in chemistry and physiology and in 'the still more complex inquiries, the subjects of which are phenomena of society and government'.

There are thus two conceptually distinct but complementary cases pointing away from the fruitful applicability of mathematics to economics – one based on the danger of attributing a bogus precision to symbols thereby opening the door for excessively simple 'geometric' procedures; the other turning upon the paucity of numerical data and the complexity of causal relations which rule out precise computation of the combined effect of causes.

In her account of the reaction to Jevons by Cairnes and Mill, Dr Schabas has remarked upon Mill's own recognition that, in so far as scientific knowledge involves the pursuit of causal laws, it is 'ultimately quantitative and thus mathematical in principle', so that, she concludes, 'Mill would have to concede, given this claim, that political economy, as the study of the causes which regulate wealth, was in the very same sense as it was for Jevons, inextricably mathematical. Mill, however, did not reach these conclusions'. (Schabas, 1983b, p. 291). Yet as Dr Schabas proceeds to show, Mill went a long way along the Jevonian path. I take issue only with her representations of Mill's position as 'inconsistent' (Schabas, 1983b, p. 293). A word of explanation.

Concern with the excessive simplifications characterising French geometrical procedure, and doubts regarding mathematical forecasting, do not necessarily rule out the use of mathematics in aid of clear logical thought. Mill himself, after all, had engaged in elementary algebraic formulations (*CW*, III, 611). A formal statement of his recognition of a legitimate role for mathematics appears in the *System of Logic* itself where reference is made to 'the value of mathematical instruction as a preparation for those more difficult investigations' (chemistry, physiology, social science and government, and aspects of astronomy) 'in the applicability not of its doctrines, but of its method', by providing training in the deductive procedure of employing 'the laws of simpler phenomena for explaining and predicting those of the more complex' (*CW*, VII, 621). In *An Examination of Sir William Hamilton's Philosophy* (Mill, 1865), in the chapter containing Mill's reply to a hypocritic of the study of mathematics, the contrast appears very strikingly. Here (following Comte) Mill defends mathematical instruction as an 'indispensible first stage of all scientific education worthy of the name' on the grounds that it sets high standards of 'proof', encourages precise logical thought based upon given axioms, postulates and definitions, and teaches 'the importance of quantities' (*CW*, IX, 472f).[12] Thus even though

in the achievements which still remain to be effected in the way of scientific generalization it is not probable that the direct employment of mathematics will be to any great extent available [Mill here includes the moral and social sciences] the nature of the phenomena [precluding] such an employment for a long time to come – perhaps for ever, [yet (applied) mathematics] affords the only sufficiently perfect type (*CW*, IX, 480–1).

For

the process itself – the deductive investigation of Nature; the application of elementary laws, generalized from the more simple cases, to disentangle the phaenomena of complex cases – explaining as much of them as can be so explained, and putting in evidence the nature and limits of the irreducible residuum, so as to suggest fresh observations preparatory to recommencing the same process with additional data: *this* is common to all science, moral and metaphysical included; and the greater the difficulty, the more needful is it that the enquirer should come prepared with an exact understanding of the requisites of this mode of investigation, and a mental type of its perfect realization (481; compare also *CW*, XXI, 235–7).

But there was a danger. Once again the perspective of 1829 is reiterated:

And here we come upon the one really grave charge which rests on the mathematical spirit, in respect of the influence it exercises on pursuits other than mathematical. It leads men to place their ideal of Science in deriving all knowledge from a small number of axiomatic premises, accepted as self-evident, and taken for immediate intuitions of reason . . . Nearly everything that is objectionable, along with much of what is admirable, in the character of French thought, whether on metaphysics, ethics, or politics, is directly traceable to the fact that French speculation descends from Descartes instead of from Bacon. All reflecting persons in England, and many in France, perceive that the chief infirmities of French thinking arise from its geometrical spirit; its determination to evolve its conclusions, even on the most practical subjects, by mere deduction from some single accepted generalization: the generalization, too, being frequently not even a theorem; but a practical rule, supposed to be obtained directly from the fountains of reason: a mode of thinking which erects one-sidedness into a principle, under the misapplied name of logic, and makes the popular political reasoning in France resemble that of a theologian arguing from a text, or a lawyer from a maxim of law (*CW*, IX, 485).

Thus unlike Cliffe Leslie – indeed unlike Cairnes (Checkland, 1951, p. 166) – Mill warned only against the abusive use of mathematics not mathematics *per se*. This is further confirmed by his defence of political economy against Comte's low opinion, in the course of which he insisted on the applicability to the social sciences of the methods designed for the natural sciences – the 'scientific artifice familiar to students of science, especially for the application of mathematics to the study of nature':

When an effect depends on several variable conditions, some of which change less, or more slowly, than others, we are often able to determine either by reasoning or experiment, what would be the law of variation of the effect if its changes depended only on one of the conditions, the remainder being supposed constant. The law so found will be sufficiently near the truth for all times and places in which the latter set of conditions do not vary greatly, and will be a basis to set out from when it becomes necessary to allow for the variations in those conditions also. Most of the conclusions of social science applicable to practical use are of this description (*CW*, X, 309).

Comte's system, Mill complained, 'makes no room for them. We have seen how he deals with the part of them which are the most scientific in character, the generalizations of political economy'.

By his various allowances Mill is certainly not 'inconsistent'; his balanced perspective defining the role of mathematics in economics bears consideration in our own day. For it is one thing to doubt the usefulness of 'calculating forward' to a precise numerical forecast, or to condemn the application of maximisation principles without discrimination, however empirically inappropriate the exercise may be. It is quite another to employ mathematics as a check to sound reasoning. Mill's position was in effect taken up by Marshall who certainly allowed for mathematics as an aid to 'clear thought' while at the same time he objected to contrived 'appearance[s] of lucidity' (Marshall, 1920, pp. 357n, 368; compare also pp. 781f).

Our discussion helps lighten a further grey area in the literature – the notion that the adoption of algebra requires for Mill that the science in question afford precise numerical data (compare J. N. Keynes, 1891, p. 249; Schabas, 1983a, p. 288; 1983b, p. 27). This view was strongly opposed by Jevons in his Preface:

> Many persons entertain a prejudice against mathematical language, arising out of a confusion between the ideas of a mathematical science and an exact science. They think that we must not pretend to calculate unless we have the precise data which will enable us to obtain a precise answer to our calculations (Jevons, 1924, p. 5).

But Mill recognised the quantitative dimension to economic phenomena notwithstanding the absence of precise data – their basis in 'the psychological law . . . that a greater gain is preferred to a smaller' (*CW*, VIII, 901) – and more specifically, he was prepared to countenance the (limited) use of algebra in economics, notwithstanding the absence of precise data; indeed, he himself supplemented his verbal account of price formation in the trade context by an attempt to generalise in algebraic terms. The pronouncement that mathematical 'solutions of physical questions became progressively more difficult and imperfect in proportion as the questions divest themselves of their abstract and hypothetical character, and approach nearer to the degree of complication actually existing in nature' (see above, p. 149) creates no difficulty for us. He intended thereby the ambitious task of mathematical forecasting and the derivation of axioms à la Newton cf n11; much easier is the more mundane task of formulating causal relations of the order 'more or less'.

7. CONCLUDING REMARKS

Mill himself was suspicious of Jevons's approach. But to be fair we must allow for Jevons's own realisation of the limits of mathematics in the 'dynamical' branches of economics (Black, 1972a, pp. 7–8), and recall his own brilliant inductive contributions. The true danger of a specialist program for mathematical economics divorced on principle from applied economics has proved to be a long-term liability from the perspective of professional trends – an 'objective' result (to use a Marxian term) of the kind of recommendation characterising the 'innovators' of the early 1870s.

Mill's awareness of the danger has been our topic. But we must at all costs avoid any notion of Mill as averse to deductive theory as such. Professor Winch has argued that Walter Bagehot carried further Mill's 'conciliatory stance' towards the historicists – which 'provided an opportunity to undermine claims to universality' – 'by restricting the science to "a single kind of society – a society of grown-up competitive commerce, such as in England"' (Winch, 1972, p. 340). Mill certainly warned of unjustified applications of theory, and this even *within* the advanced British system – these instances illustrate his insistence on the non-universality of the standard axioms of economics. But it is also true that he demonstrated the empirical relevance of the science to a far broader range of institutions – both existing and prospective – than those allowed by Bagehot. There is no 'conciliation' here. We must not, for example, presume (as Winch presumes) that Mill's observations on co-operation or the stationary state imply the 'replacement' of competition. The same holds for the study of peasant proprietorship. Competition, and thus economic theory, is accorded a very extensive (though not universal) scope.[13]

Some like to call Mill self-contradictory. But this is gratuitous. His strength lay precisely in his demonstration that the range of applicability of economic science – in terms of the empirical accuracy of the maximisation axioms – was narrower than 'extremist' deductivists imagined, but broader than 'extremist' opponents of theory imagined. This balanced attitude cannot but encourage a habit of mind which, while ready to seek out and experiment with alternative institutional arrangements, yet retains, in their consideration, a healthy awareness of possible limits – flowing from behavioural as well as physical constraints – to what can be accomplished. Unfortunately this lesson has always, so it seems, to be learned the hard way.

NOTES

A version of this paper was delivered at the Third History of Economic Thought Society of Australia Conference held at La Trobe University, Melbourne, 17–20 May 1985. I am grateful to the participants, particularly to Philip Williams and Michael White, for their criticisms.

1. Similar recommendations were made by Walras. He too championed a sharp demarcation between pure, applied and social economics, confining the first – represented as 'a science which resembles the physico-mathematical science in every respect' – to the 'theory of the determination of prices under a hypothetical regime of perfectly free competition' (Walras, 1954, pp. 71, 40); and representing 'any value in exchange' as 'partak[ing] of the character of a natural phenomenon, natural in its origins, natural in its manifestations and natural in its essence,' a reference to the scarcity property (Walras, 1954, p. 69).

   Menger in Austria was unenthusiastic about mathematics, but went even further than his confrères in insisting firmly on the independent status of pure theory. For he denied, on methodological grounds, any meaning to the verification of the principles of rational action (compare Winch, 1972, pp. 330, 343).

2. The notion that a classicism without the population-growth mechanism cannot be conceived (Winch, 1972, p. 336) is questionable. The inverse wage-profit relation, turning on principles of allocation theory, applies even with population treated as a constant. And although population plays so large a part in Mill's work, 'the strictness of purely scientific arrangement [is] thereby somewhat departed from for the sake of practical utility' (*CW*, IV, 323) since a variety of motives apart from wealth maximisation are at play. There are other similar enlargements relating to knowledge creation and health.
   Note: *CW* throughout this chapter stands for *Collected Works of John Stuart Mill* and the references to this are written in the form *CW*, IV (vol.), 225 (page).

3. Mill was quite at one with those members of the Historical School who did not object to deduction as such – on the contrary – but insisted that 'deductions should be made from categorical premises obtained from

historical material' (Viner, 1962, p. 109); Roscher's work on 'historicism' reads like Mill's (Roscher, 1878, I, p. 110).

In an account of the marginalist developments Professor Winch refers to Mill's 'concessions' to the 'prevailing intellectual tide' of the second half of the century – the evolutionist and inter-disciplinary critics of economic theory (1972, p. 341); similarly, 'Mill went further than any of his immediate neoclassical successors were willing to go in meeting the historical and sociological critics of political economy' (p. 340). These formulations by alluding to Mill's 'concessions' fail to recognise that the later British historicists, such as Cliffe Leslie, were themselves nourished by Mill's *Principles* (Hollander, 1985, p. 926); and that Mill's own positive objections on 'historical' lines to Jevons's type of approach to theory extend back to the early 1830s.

My reaction is similar to the formulation by Hutchison which assumes a belated response by Mill to the historical critics (Hutchison, 1978, p. 55n).

4. The stage of *verification* in the deductive process, although it may indeed contribute towards establishment of the axioms or correction of the logical process of deduction, is not itself a device for the derivation of complex causal relations; that remains the function of '*ratiocination*'. Verification contributes only indirectly by indicating the need for improvement in the axiomatic foundation (or in the logical process itself). It would, therefore, not be misleading to say that the present axiomatic framework, perhaps incorporating refinements shown to have been required by an *earlier* verification, constitutes the first stage for any *subsequent* ratiocination; and to describe the scientific work at hand as involving ratiocination on the basis of the axiomatic framework – again without reference to the possibility that the framework owes something to a preceding verification, or that further modifications might be proven necessary by a new verification as additional evidence accumulates.

We will not enter into the details of Mill's position on the proof of hypotheses except to say that he took a stricter line than did William Whewell, objecting to the latter's 'Friedmanesque' position whereby the verification of predictions flowing from a hypothetically-based theory constituted a proof of the 'truth' of that theory; in Mill's view this was insufficient since the 'condition of accounting for all the known phenomena is often fulfilled equally well by two conflicting hypotheses' (*CW*, VII, 501).

5. It is scarcely surprising that Mill excluded 'small numbers' market structures from the domain of political economy. Edgeworth later observed regarding indeterminacy that 'among those who would suffer by the new regime . . . would be . . . the abstract economists, who would be deprived of their occupation, the investigation of the conditions which determine value. There would survive only the empirical school, flourishing in a chaos congenial to their mentality' (Edgeworth, 1925, I, pp. 138–9).

6. Allowance for varying quality is a further interesting illustration; compare Mill's explanation of the failure of prices to rise as expected in consequence of gold inflows which runs in terms of a deterioration of the quality of commodities (letter of 15 September 1863, *CW*, XV, 882).

7. In some contexts Mill implies a U-shaped or possible a ⊔⁄-shaped cost curve. Compare his proposal for a test of scale economies (*CW*, II, 133, 140, 141; on this matter see Williams, 1978, pp. 54–5; 1982); and his treatment of monopolistic competition (*CW*, II, 243, 409–10; Williams, 1978, pp. 56–7).

8. It is most regrettable that the profession cannot be shaken from the opinion that Ricardo and Mill were unable to resolve the paradox of value; and that the utility contributions of the 1870s were required to break the deadlock. For the latest example of this error see Cooter and Rappoport (1984, p. 510).

   If there is any doubt of the sophistication of classical analysis consider the fact that as early as 1825 Mill, in a study of the corn tariff, effortlessly applied the 'compensation' principle of welfare economics published by Nicholas Kaldor in 1939 in formal utility terms (Stigler, 1968, p. 97).

9. de Marchi (1972, pp. 352–3) characterises the law of diminishing marginal utility as an empirical law; and argues that Mill's associationist psychology would not have provided an adequate underpinning for that law. He concludes that an adherence to associationist psychology made it unlikely that Mill would enunciate even this 'empirical law' for himself (de Marchi, 1972, p. 354).

10. Am I right in thinking that the method of multiple correlation analysis essentially depends on the economist having furnished, not merely a list of the significant causes, which is correct as far as it goes, but a *complete* list? For example, suppose three factors are taken into account, it is not enough that these should be in fact *verae causae*; there must be no other significant factor. If there is a further factor, not taken account of, then the method is not able to discover the relative quantitative importance of the first three (Keynes, 1973, XIV, p. 308).

11. Compare also 'Inaugural address to the University of St. Andrews' (Mill, 1867) regarding the potential of applied mathematics in the appropriate physical sciences:

    We are able, by reasoning from a few fundamental truths, to explain and predict the phenomena of material objects: and what is still more remarkable, the fundamental truths were themselves found out by reasoning, for they are not such as are obvious to the senses, but had to be inferred by a mathematical process from a mass of minute details, which alone came within the direct reach of human observation. When Newton, in this manner, discovered the laws of the solar system, he created, for all posterity, the true idea of science (*CW*, XXI, 236).

12. Ricardo's famous complaint against Malthus's opinion that Political Economy 'is not a strict science like mathematics' (Ricardo, 1951, VIII, p. 331) has been read as evidence of 'dogmatic, *a priori* deductivism' (Hutchison, 1978, p. 56n). But this is doubtful. Ricardo's statement proceeds to specify that Malthus, in consequence of his viewpoint, 'thinks he may use words in a vague way, sometimes attaching one meaning to

them, sometimes another and quite different'. Mill pleaded against dogmatic, *a priori*, deductivism throughout his career yet saw a place for mathematics in deductive theory, basing himself partly on precision of thought; his position, as usual, was fully in line with Ricardo's.

13. See also the misleading reference by Professor George Stigler to the 'astonishing and absurd deficiences which [Mill] assigned to private enterprise' (Stigler, 1982, pp. 14–15).

REFERENCES

Black, R. D. C. 'Jevons, Marginalism and Manchester' *The Manchester School*, XL (1972a) March 1972, 2–8.

Black, R. D. C. 'W. S. Jevons and the Foundation of Modern Economics' *History of Political Economy* IV (1972b) 364–78.

Blaug, M. *The Methodology of Economics* (Cambridge: University Press, 1980).

Bowley, M. *Nassau Senior and Classical Economics* (London: 1937).

Bowley, M. 'The Predecessors of Jevons. The Revolution that wasn't'. *The Manchester School*. XL (1972a) 9–29.

Checkland, S. G. 'Economic Opinion in England as Jevons Found It'. *The Manchester School*, XIX (1951) 143–69.

Comte, A. *Cours de Philosophie Positive*, (6 vols) (Paris: Bachelier, 1830–42).

Cooter, R. and P. Rappaport 'Were the Ordinalists Wrong About Welfare Economics?' *Journal of Economic Literature*, XXII (1984) 507–30.

Edgeworth, F. Y. 'John Stuart Mill', in R. H. I. Palgrave (ed.) *Dictionary of Political Economy*, II (1910) 756–63.

Edgeworth, F. Y. *Papers Relating to Political Economy* (London: Macmillan, 1925).

Hicks, J. *Collected Essays on Economic Theory*, Vol. III, *Classics and Moderns* (Oxford: Basil Blackwell, 1983).

Hollander, S. 'The Reception of Ricardian Economics'. *Oxford Economic Papers*, XXIX (1977) 221–57.

Hollander, S. *The Economics of David Ricardo* (London: Heinemann, 1979).

Hollander, S. *The Economics of J. S. Mill* (Oxford: Basil Blackwell, 1985).

Hutchison, T. W. *On Revolutions and Progress in Economic Knowledge*. (Cambridge: Cambridge University Press, 1978).

Jaffé, W. 'Walras's Economics as others see it', *Journal of Economic Literature*, XVIII (1980) 528–49.

Jevons, W. S. *The Principles of Economics*, rev. edn (London: Macmillan, 1905).

Jevons, W. S. [1871] *The Theory of Political Economy*, 4th edn (London: Macmillan, 1924).

Keynes, J. M. *The General Theory and After*, Part II, in D. Moggridge (ed.) *Collected Writings*, vol. 14 (London: Macmillan, 1973).

Keynes, J. N. (1891) *Scope and Method of Political Economy* (New York: Kelley, 1955).

Leontief, W. 'Theoretical Assumptions and nonobserved Facts', *American Economic Review*, LXI (1971) 1–7.

de Marchi, N. 'Mill and Cairnes and the Emergence of Marginalism in England'. *History of Political Economy*, IV (1972) 344–63.

Marshall, A. *Principles of Economics*, 8th edn (London: Macmillan, 1920).

Martineau, H. *Illustrations of Political Economy*, (London: Fox, 1832–1834).

Mill, John Stuart (1834) 'Miss Martineau's Summary of Political Economy', *Monthly Repository*, in *Collected Works of John Stuart Mill*, IV, 1967, 223–8.

Mill, John Stuart (1836) 'On the Definition of Political Economy and on the Method of Investigation Proper to it', in *Collected Works*, IV, 1967, 309–39.

Mill, John Stuart (1843) *A System of Logic Ratiocinative and Inductive*, in *Collected Works*, VII–VIII, 1973.

Mill, John Stuart (1848) *Principles of Political Economy*, in *Collected Works*, II–III, 1965.

Mill, John Stuart (1861) *Utilitarianism*, in *Collected Works*, X, 1969, 203–59.

Mill, John Stuart (1865) *An Examination of Sir William Hamilton's Philosophy*, in *Collected Works*, IX, 1979.

Mill, John Stuart (1867) *Inaugural Address Delivered at the University of St. Andrews*, in *Collected Works*, XXI, 1984, 215–57.

Mill, John Stuart *The Earlier Letters 1812–48*, in *Collected Works*, XII–XIII, 1963.

Mill, John Stuart *The Later Letters 1849–73*, in *Collected Works*, XIV–XVII, 1972.

Phelps Brown, E. H. (1972). 'The Underdevelopment of Economics', *Economic Journal*, 82 (1972) 1–10.

Ricardo, D. *The Works and Correspondence of David Ricardo*, vol. VIII (Cambridge: Cambridge University Press, 1951).

Roscher, W. *Principles of Political Economy*, 2 vols, J. J. Lalor (ed.) (New York: Holt, 1878).

Schabas, M. L. *W. S. Jevons and the Emergence of Mathematical Economics in Britain* PhD thesis (Toronto: University of Toronto, 1983a).

Schabas, M. L. 'J. S. Mill to W. S. Jevons: An Unpublished Letter', *The Mill Newsletter*, XVIII (1983b) 24–8.

Schwartz, P. *The New Political Economy of John Stuart Mill* (London: ???, 1972).

Stigler, G. J. 'Mill on Economics and Society'. *University of Toronto Quarterly*, XXXVIII, (1908) 96–101.

Stigler, G. J. *The Economist as Preacher and Other Essays* (Chicago: ???, 1982).

Torrens, R. *The Budget* (London: Smith, Elder, 1844).

Viner, J. [1917] 'Some Problems of Logical Method in Political Economy', in E. J. Hamilton *et al.* (eds) *Landmarks in Political Economy* (Chicago: University of Chicago Press, 1962) pp. 101–24.

Walker, D. A. 'Is Walras's theory of general equilibrium a normative scheme?' *History of Political Economy*, XVI (1984) 445–69.

Walras, L. in *Elements of Pure Economics*, W. Jaffé (ed.) (London: George Allen & Unwin, 1954).

Williams, P. L. *The Emergence of the Theory of the Firm. From Adam Smith to Alfred Marshall* (London: Macmillan, 1978).

Williams, P. L. 'Welfare and Collusion: A Comment', *American Economic Review*, vol. 72 (1982) 272–5.

Winch, D. 'Marginalism and the Boundaries of Economic Science'. *History of Political Economy*, IV (1972) 325–43.

7 Marx's *Capital* Today

ANTHONY BREWER

Most of the creations of the intellect or fancy pass away for good after a time that varies between an after-dinner hour and a generation. Some, however, do not. They suffer eclipses but they come back again, and they come back not as unrecognisable elements of a cultural heritage, but in their individual garb and with their personal scars which people may see and touch. These we may call the great ones . . . Taken in this sense, this is undoubtedly the word to apply to the message of Marx (Schumpeter, 1954, p. 31).

Marx's *Capital*[1] has a status quite different from that of any other work of economics. It is the masterpiece of one of the handful of thinkers who have shaped the modern world. It is bought, sometimes even read, by many who are not professional economists or students facing an examination in economics. Even if its economics were shown to make no sense at all, its status as a classic of modern thought would remain secure. But *Capital* is not a compendium of Marx's views, or a political tract. It is a treatise on economics, dealing with all the main subjects normally covered in a nineteenth-century 'principles of economics'. It covers other topics as well, but as digressions; the main structure of the work is a systematic exposition of Marx's analysis of capitalism as an economic system.

The question I want to pose is: what (if anything) can economists still learn from Marx? I intend to pay him the compliment of judging his work by the highest modern standards of rigour, in the light of modern theory and of the issues that concern us today. There are many different questions that one can legitimately ask about a classic text, and correspondingly there are many different ways of writing about the history of economics. I am not arguing that judging a text by modern standards is always the right approach, only that it is one legitimate approach among many. The fact that Marx's economics still has many adherents who argue its continuing relevance is a particular reason for examining it in this way.

If one were to judge by the recent literature on Marx's economics, one might think that Marx was the author of a rather peculiar form of the labour theory of value, and little else. Debates over value theory have dominated the literature, with neo-Ricardians, Sraffians, and others attacking Marx's theory, and more traditional Marxists defending it.[2] The debate is about played out now, and the inescapable conclusion is that Marx's value theory has been discredited. If Marx's economics had nothing more to offer, it could safely be ignored.

However, Marx's work continues to attract interest, not because of his value theory, but because readers are interested in bigger questions. Will capitalism survive? Should capitalism be overthrown and replaced by some other system? Value theory is not important in itself, but as a technical device which provided a consistent theoretical framework in which Marx could present his insights into the dynamics of capitalism. It is now time to ask what remains of Marx's economics after the debates on value.

I will divide Marx's economics into two parts: statics, the study of an economy at a single instant, and dynamics, the study of how an economy changes (or does not change) over time. I will argue that Marx's statics has little or nothing to teach us now, but that his dynamics contains important insights which can be and should be disentangled from his value theory.

MARX'S STATICS: VALUE AND SURPLUS VALUE

One of Marx's aims in setting out his theory of value and surplus value was to explain observed levels and trends in wages, profits and prices. This was not his only aim, but it takes up a great deal of space in *Capital*, and was clearly an important part of Marx's project. If his theory were to fail in this, it would lose contact with real life experience, and it is hard to see how it could be taken seriously at all.

The value of a commodity is defined as the labour required, directly or indirectly, to produce it (*Cap*. I, chapter 1). There are some qualifications to this definition (only 'socially necessary' labour is to count, for example), but they do not affect the argument. Marx did not make the elementary mistake of thinking that market prices are in fact proportional to values. In the first two volumes of *Capital* he asked what would happen if prices were proportional to values, and in the third volume he tried to show how prices of production (in modern terms, long-run equilibrium prices) could be derived from the value analysis of volumes one and two (*Cap*. III, chapter 9). His theory has been the subject of intense debate; I will not go over the debate in detail, but will summarise what I see as the main results.

Marx's procedure for 'transforming' values into prices of production is known to be faulty.[3] There two equivalent ways of correcting Marx's method. Following Bortkiewicz (1907) and others, prices, wages and the profit rate can be derived by solving an appropriate set of simultaneous equations. However, this is equivalent to solving directly for prices of production without using values at all. As Samuelson (1971, p. 400) put it, values are 'transformed' into prices by simply erasing the former and writing down the latter. Alternatively, following Shaikh (1977), Marx's procedure can be seen as the first stage in an iterative process which converges on the Bortkiewicz solution. Marx himself hinted at this approach. However, there is no need to start from values; almost any first approximation to prices will do equally well as a starting point. Values again seem to be an unnecessary 'fifth wheel'. Values, it is said, are a pointless detour, and should be eliminated on the basis of Occam's razor.[4] This is a damaging criticism, but not by itself conclusive; the use of value analysis might be justified on other grounds, since Marx did not intend it to be merely a method for calculating prices.

A much more serious criticism, put forward particularly by Steedman (1977, chapters 10 to 12), is that Marx's theory cannot encompass joint production. Joint production is the case where one production process produces two or more saleable outputs; the rearing of sheep, for example, produces both wool and meat. The problem is that there is no obvious way to identify the labour embodied in each output individually, in order to assign values to them. Joint production is important in its own right, but it gains decisive importance from the fact that production using fixed capital (which means almost all production) is for analytical purposes equivalent to joint production. A process using fixed capital can be thought of as producing used capital equipment jointly with its primary output. The problem is to assign a value to the used capital equipment (Steedman, 1977, chapter 10). Marx did consider production with fixed capital, of course, but his method applies only to certain special cases.

The definition of value must clearly be extended to deal with joint production. Several alternative definitions have been proposed. I will not go into detail, but will simply report that none of them preserves the basic framework of Marx's analysis. If values are defined as Steedman suggests, then they may turn out negative, with absurd results; this is precisely Steedman's point. Steedman's definition, however, can only be used in the special case where the number of production processes in use happens to equal the number of products. If on the other hand, Morishima's (1974) approach is adopted, and the value of a good, or a collection of goods, is defined as the minimum labour required to produce it, equally severe difficulties arise. The value of a collection of goods taken together need not equal the sum of their values taken individually, since the labour required may be reduced by producing two or more goods jointly, while the labour expended in a production process need not be equal to the value created, because techniques which minimise costs do not necessarily minimise the labour required. The whole framework of volume one of *Capital*, and thus the whole framework of Marx's economics as it is presented in *Capital*, must be abandoned if this definition is adopted. There is no question of finding some alternative definition which evades these problems, since Steedman's definition amounts to writing down the consistency conditions needed for Marx's analysis to work. Marx's value analysis simply fails to perform the task that Marx set it.[5]

I turn now to the substance of Marx's theory of surplus value, considered as a theory of income distribution. Put very crudely, workers get a socially-determined subsistence wage, and capitalists get the rest of output. In this Marx followed Ricardo, though he gave a different account of how wages are held down to subsistence level. Marx asserted that 'in a given country, at a given period, the average quantity of the means of subsistence necessary for the labourer is practically known' (*Cap.* I, p. 171), and he defined the value of labour power as the value of this quantity of the means of subsistence. How actual market wages are linked to the value of labour power is unclear. Marx argued that wages are held down by competition for jobs from the reserve army of the unemployed. What he did not do was to explain how, or even whether, these market pressures would hold wages down to the particular socially-determined subsistence level corresponding to the value of labour power. How, for example, could the simple fact that wages in Britain have increased massively since Marx's time be explained in terms of Marx's theory? (see Meek, 1967, p. 119). If Marx is read as predicting fixed real wages, then his theory is falsified by the facts. If not, then the theory becomes either empty (wages are what they are) or incomplete (wages are governed by unspecified social factors).

It might be argued that Marx was not primarily concerned to predict, or even to explain, quantitative trends in income distribution, but to show that profit is the result of exploitation. He defined exploitation as the extraction of surplus labour, where surplus labour is defined as the excess of the labour actually performed by the workers over the labour necessary to produce the goods which the workers actually get.[6] It is easy to show that profits (or any other non-wage incomes) correspond to exploitation in this sense, provided that the labour required in production is a monotonically increasing function of the output vector. Given this assumption, it takes more labour to produce wage goods plus something than it would to produce wage goods alone, so if any non-worker gets any part of output, it is as a result of (or is associated with) exploitation in Marx's sense. The elaborate mechanics of the labour theory of value are not needed for this result, which is neither very surprising nor very interesting.

To summarise; Marx's value theory cannot cope with joint production, or with any but the simplest cases of fixed capital. If these difficult cases are excluded, his theory is at best an awkward and roundabout way of explaining wages, prices and profits. His positive theory of income distribution is either vacuous or empirically falsified, and his theory of exploitation is mainly a matter of definition. It is hard to find anything in Marx's statics that an economist could learn from today.

If value theory is rejected, can any of Marx's economics be salvaged? *Capital* seems to hang together, starting from simple, abstract premises and deducing complex consequences in a Hegelian style. It might seem that the whole argument stands or falls with the labour theory of value. I will argue that there are valuable insights in Marx's account of the dynamics of capitalism which do not depend on values, and which should not be thrown away.

MARX'S MICRODYNAMICS: TECHNICAL CHANGE AND THE LABOUR PROCESS

The heart of Marx's analysis of the dynamics of capitalism is his theory of technical progress (*Cap.* I, chapter 12). Capitalists aim to maximise profits. Any individual capitalist who can reduce costs by introducing new methods of production will make additional profits for as long as the cost advantage over other producers lasts. As others catch up, which they will, the extra profits of the innovator will be competed away, and those who fail to keep up will not survive. The general level of efficiency throughout the industry will be raised. There is therefore a very strong pressure to try to stay ahead of the average level of efficiency, and it is necessary for survival at least to keep up. Continuous cost reducing innovation is built into the system, driven by the pressure of competition. Note that the labour theory of value is not in any way essential to the argument, though Marx, of course, originally presented it in value terms, as the theory of 'relative surplus value'.

Although writers before Marx had discussed technical change, none had seen it as a continuous process inherent in the workings of the capitalist system. Subsequent writers, too, have rarely stressed it as Marx did. The obvious exception is Schumpeter, who took Marx's analysis and transplanted it into a Walrasian general equilibrium framework; he is often wrongly thought of as its inventor. Even Schumpeter presented innovation as an intermittent phenomenon, produced by the efforts of a few gifted individuals ('entrepreneurs'), rather than as a continuous and inevitable concomitant of capitalist economic organisation.

According to Marx, the competitive pressure to innovate leads to a constant state of turmoil at the level of individual industries and firms. New processes and new products undermine established firms, throwing them out of business, and throwing the workers out of jobs. Whole industries are wiped out, when their products become obsolete. The resulting state of insecurity is perhaps more important than the over-all level of unemployment in weakening the bargaining position of workers. Existing skills are constantly devalued, and working-class organisations find the ground cut from under their feet.

A capitalist does not aim to raise productivity for its own sake, still less to lighten the workers' burdens, but to cut costs. In a capitalist framework, costs depend not only on output per unit of effort, but also on the intensity of work (and on wage rates). Workers have no reason to work any harder than they have to, since the product does not accrue to them but to their employer. Once they have sold their labour power, their capacity to work, it is up to the employer to extract the work from them. The function of the capitalist is not simply to co-ordinate the technical process of production, but also to exercise authority over a reluctant workforce. Technical change can, and often does, reduce the effort required to achieve a given result. It also can be, and often is, a means of intensifying work, and maintaining the employer's control over the production process.

Marx traces the effects of technical change on the actual process of work in one of the most important (and most readable) sections of

Capital (part four of volume one). I will sketch out some of the main points in his argument, but there is no substitute for reading the original. Marx's treatment blends theory with economic history and with empirical material from his own time. The particular examples he quotes may not be directly relevant a century later (though fairly direct modern parallels often spring to mind), but the method cries out to be applied to modern issues. This part of Marx's work was rediscovered by Braverman (1974), and has inspired a rapidly growing literature, under the name of 'the labour process'.[7] Some of the points Marx stresses seem very obvious, but non-Marxist economists have a distressing tendency to treat technology and technical change as if they involved only a technical relation between outputs and inputs, quite overlooking their effects on bargaining power and on the character of work.

Marx distinguishes three ways in which a capitalist labour process can be organised; simple co-operation, manufacture, and modern industry. They form a broad historical sequence, though earlier forms persist both within and alongside later forms. Manufacture is a developed form of co-operation in which specialised workers each carry out a particular operation, while in modern industry the actual activity of production is carried out by machines. Marx's discussion of mechanisation is remarkably forward looking; indeed it is the best starting point I know of for thinking about the likely effects of the revolution in technology caused by the use of microprocessors. Braverman's analysis of the computerisation of clerical work (1974, pp. 326–48), for example, springs very directly from the analysis in *Capital*.

A number of themes emerge. Unskilled workers can be paid less than skilled workers, they require less training, and can more easily be replaced. Technical change has, in general, tended to eliminate skills, cutting costs both directly and by strengthening the bargaining position of the employers. New skills are created, such as those required to build and maintain machines, but they are outweighed by those that are destroyed. Control of the work process and understanding of the technology are centralised into the hands of the capitalist, or of specialised managerial and technical staff. Mental and manual labour, conception and execution (Braverman's terms), are progressively separated. In a handicraft system of production, the main body of technical knowledge is embodied in the craft skills of the workforce, and passed from one generation to the next by apprenticeships. In the manufacturing division of labour, over-all control is taken over by management, though capital still has to 'wrestle with the insubordination of the workmen' (*Cap*. I, p. 367). In modern industry, technology is embodied in the design of the machine, and workers simply carry out the tasks assigned to them by the designer. Control of the pace of work is also centralised. As long as production by hand predominates, workers can, to a degree, resist pressures to speed up, but in a mechanised system the machine sets the pace.

The progressive subordination of the worker by the machine is one of the most important elements of Marx's indictment of capitalism. From the beginning, the capitalist, as buyer and therefore owner of labour power has formal command over the labour process, but the character of technical progress in a capitalist system is such that work comes under ever closer control, destroying the freedom and autonomy of the worker. It should be noted that nothing in this analysis depends on the labour theory of value. If Marx's argument has a weakness, it is that it underrates the bargaining power of workers, and their capacity to resist (Friedman, 1977, chapter 4), but it is at least a starting point.

To be competitive, a firm has to achieve a certain level of employment, output and capital invested. Marx asserts that this minimum grows over time, as a result of technical change. Workers are brought together in larger numbers, laying the basis for working-class organisation and for the eventual overthrow of capitalism. The number of firms falls, and it becomes increasingly difficult for a new firm to establish itself. Large firms are more efficient, and hence more profitable, than small ones, so they grow faster, increasing the gap. Marx calls this the concentration of capital; it is reinforced by the centralisation of capital, in which large firms take over failed small firms. Together, concentration and centralisation lead to an increasing predominance of a few large firms, a tendency to monopoly (*Cap*. I, chapter 25, section 2). Marx's argument has a gap in it, since the innovation process destroys old industries, dominated by large, established firms, and creates new industries, perhaps relatively more competitive in structure. In addition, the assertion that economies of scale become more important over time is an empirical judgement that might turn out wrong. None the less, Marx's prediction has proved pretty accurate so far.

Marx implicitly assumed that each firm was owned by an individual capitalist (or a family, or a small group of partners), so he expected the concentration of capital into a few large units to correspond to a concentration of personal wealth into a few hands. 'Along with the

constantly diminishing number of the magnates of capital, . . . grows
the mass of misery, oppression, slavery, degradation, exploitation; but
with this too grows the revolt of the working class . . .' (*Cap.* I, p. 763).
It has not worked out quite like that, because the corporate form of
organisation allows a single firm to have many 'owners'. Marx's
analysis of concentration and centralisation, like that of the labour
process, does not rely in any important way on labour values.

MARX'S MACRODYNAMICS: ACCUMULATION AND TECHNICAL CHANGE

The framework for Marx's analysis of growth and technical change at
the level of the whole economy is provided by his schemes of
reproduction (*Cap.* II, part 3). The basic idea is simple; if an economy
is to continue functioning smoothly from one period to the next, it is
essential that the right mix of goods be produced. Marx used a three-
sector model, distinguishing means of production, means of subsistence, and luxuries, though it is easy to disaggregate further. Time is
divided into a succession of periods, with output available at the end of
each period for use in the next. The amount of each good produced in
each period must match the demand for it in the next, and so on. Given
this insight it is possible to analyse both the relations between sectors at
a given moment and the process of change over time. Marx found the
case of simple reproduction (a stationary system) fairly straight-
forward, but he had great difficulty with the case of expanded
reproduction (a growing system). The analysis is conducted in terms of
values, but it is fairly easy to reconstruct it in terms of prices.

For its time, Marx's unfinished analysis of reproduction was a
brilliant achievement. If economists with adequate technical equipment had taken up where Marx left off, the history of economics could
have been dramatically different. But Marx was too far ahead of his
time, and this potential went unfulfilled for more than 50 years after
the publication of the second volume of *Capital*, until the work of
Keynes, Kalecki, von Neumann, Leontief, and others (some of whom
were quite unaware of Marx's pioneering work). The few Marxists
who did work on the subject, such as Rosa Luxemberg, lacked the
technical skills to make any progress.

What the models of reproduction show, or would show if fully
developed, is that it is possible in principle, given an appropriate rate
and pattern of investment, for a capitalist economy to grow smoothly,

with output matching demand. Marx did not think it likely that any capitalist economy would actually do so. His discussions of the business cycle are scattered and incomplete; they do not amount to a worked-out theory. Like the reproduction models they were well ahead of their time, but have been superseded by subsequent work.

The main lines of Marx's macrodynamics pose a rather difficult problem for my argument, since they are constructed in terms of trends in various key magnitudes and ratios expressed in value terms, and are harder to disentangle from the theory of value. In this part of Marx's argument, the main function of values is to deal with index number problems. There may even be a case for using values as a rough and ready solution, since no index is wholly satisfactory in dealing with cases in which the commodity composition of output and of the stock of means of production is changing over time. I will argue that the main problem is not Marx's use of values, but his habit of making rather speculative assertions about the relative importance of counteracting trends in different variables.

The crucial variable in Marx's macroeconomics is the ratio of employment, or of living labour, to the total value of capital, or dead labour. Marx takes the flow of expenditure on labour power, in value terms, as an index of employment, implicitly assuming that the value of labour power remains constant. He also assumes, to begin with, that all capital is circulating capital, used up in a single cycle of production. Given these two assumptions, employment per unit value of capital is determined by the ratio of expenditure on means of production to expenditure on labour power, in value terms. Marx expected this ratio, the value composition of capital, to increase over time as a result of technical change. What it boils down to is this; employment per unit value of capital is inversely related to (1) the physical mass of means of production handled by each worker, (2) the value of each physical unit of means of production, (3) the average turnover time of capital (the ratio of the stock of capital to the flow of expenditure), and (4) the value of labour power. The first of these will probably, but not certainly, rise over time, the second will fall, and the third and fourth might go either way. Marx confidently expected the first of these factors to predominate, so that employment per unit value of capital would fall over time. It is, I think, generally agreed now that Marx did not provide a firm basis for this (empirical) judgement, and that one cannot make any definite predictions.

Marx's 'law' of the tendency of the rate of profit to fall (*Cap*. III, part 3) follows fairly directly from his discussion of the value composition of capital. According to Marx, the profit rate is equal to total surplus value divided by the total value of capital. Since living labour is the only source of surplus value, a falling ratio of living labour to capital would entail a falling profit rate, if surplus value per unit of living labour were constant. The criticisms of this argument are well known. I have already argued that employment per unit value of capital need not fall, while the rate of surplus value might increase (as Marx recognised). The whole argument depends on the discredited labour theory of value, and it can in any case be shown that capitalists have no incentive to adopt any innovations that reduce the profit rate. This part of Marx's theory is best forgotten (see Hodgson, 1974; Roemer, 1979).

The existence of a 'reserve army' of unemployed workers is important to Marx's argument both from a positive and from a normative viewpoint. Competition for jobs, which keeps wages down, plays an essential role in his positive theory of income distribution. At the same time, the miseries of unemployment and insecurity are a major count in his normative indictment of capitalism.

Marx's analysis of the trend in employment and unemployment is to be found in the penultimate part of volume one of *Capital*. Accumulation without technical change (that is, with a constant ratio of employment to capital) obviously increases the demand for labour power. But, as we have seen, Marx expected technical change to reduce employment per unit of capital, offsetting the effect of accumulation. The trend of unemployment depends on the relative rates of growth of the demand for, and the supply of, labour power. The supply grows over time for demographic reasons, and also because of migration from country to town. (Marx was, implicitly, only considering urban employment.) Marx asserted: 'The greater is social wealth . . . the greater is the industrial reserve army' (*Cap.* I, p. 644). It is, however, clear that the net effect depends on the relative strength of a large number of offsetting factors, and no general conclusion can be drawn.

Another, stronger, argument is sketched out in some of Marx's comments on the business cycle. Suppose that accumulation proceeds fast enough for labour to become scarce, forcing up wages. Profits will be threatened (if the wage increase outruns productivity increases), accumulation will slow or halt, reducing the rate of growth of demand for labour power, while high wages will encourage labour saving innovations. Unemployment will rise, and wages will be forced back down. This mechanism ensures that the reserve army will always be large enough to serve its function in maintaining a balance of power in the labour market favourable to the capitalists (*Cap.* I, pp. 619–21). It does not justify a prediction that unemployment will grow over time, or that real wages will fall.

Marx's macrodynamics, then, is marred both by his use of the labour theory of value, and by incautious and ill-founded empirical judgements. He did, however, raise important questions and pick out the important factors at work, and his writings can still be an important source of insight and inspiration. The long run dynamics of capitalism is still pretty well uncharted territory.

MARX AS A PREACHER

Marx did not write *Capital* simply as a contribution to economic theory; he wrote to advocate and predict the overthrow of capitalism and its replacement by a better system. His main arguments have already been described, but I will gather them together and attempt a preliminary evaluation by way of conclusion.

Marx's indictment of capitalism rests on several grounds. First, he argues that capitalism is inherently exploitative; it could not exist without profit, and profit is the result of exploitation. I have argued that this conclusion follows very directly from a particular definition of exploitation. If it is more than a matter of words, an arbitrary definition, it must be based on a moral premise that ownership of capital should not confer any right to profit (or some equivalent). Marx does not present any explicit argument of this sort. He does present a number of subsidiary arguments. Capitalism originated in the forcible expulsion of peasants from the land, and came into the world 'dripping from head to foot, from every pore, with blood and dirt' (*Cap.* I, p. 760). This is hardly relevant to the ethical status of capitalism as a system, once it exists. Marx concedes that an individual capitalist may have started out by saving from wages and working hard, but argues that the capitalist can only stay in business as a result of subsequent profits (*Cap.* I, chapter 24). True, but this begs the question by assuming that profits are unmerited in order to prove that they are. There is a strong ethical case to be made against profit, but Marx does not make it explicitly.

Secondly, Marx argues that although the exchange between capitalist and worker is, on the face of it, a free exchange between equals, the worker has in fact no option but to sell labour power or starve. Once sold, labour power becomes the property of the capitalist, who controls its disposal, so the worker surrenders freedom and autonomy during the period of the working day. This argument parallels the discussion of 'alienation' in Marx's early writings (see Marx, 1844), but it is made far more concrete in *Capital*, in Marx's detailed analysis of the effects of technical change on the labour process. It is, perhaps, the strongest part of his indictment of capitalism, though it could be argued in reply that large-scale production (which Marx seems to have expected to continue in a socialist system) requires centralised co-ordination (as Marx recognised; *Cap*. I, pp. 330–1), so some loss of individual autonomy is inevitable.

Thirdly, Marx argued that capitalism necessarily produces growing misery, through unemployment and underemployment, insecurity, low wages, ill health caused by poor conditions of work, and so on. 'The greater the social wealth . . . the greater is the industrial reserve army . . . Accumulation of wealth at one pole is . . . at the same time accumulation of misery, agony of toil, slavery, ignorance, brutality, mental degradation, at the opposite pole' (*Cap*. I, pp. 644, 645). I have argued that Marx's prediction of increasing unemployment is based on unsupported empirical judgements. In the event, the miseries Marx described have decreased rather than increased over time, though they have certainly not been eliminated.

Logic would require Marx to complement his assault on capitalism with a demonstration that a better system is possible. He never did so, maintaining that it would be 'Utopian' to provide a blueprint of a future society, and his moral criticism of capitalism remained implicit in the tone of his description and in his choice of words, without any explicit ethical underpinnings. On the surface, *Capital* is an entirely objective, scientific analysis. Marx claimed that he viewed 'the evolution of the economic formation of society . . . as a process of natural history' (*Cap*. I, p. 10). Ostensibly, then, Marx predicted the downfall of capitalism, rather than advocating it.

The grounds for Marx's prediction that capitalism is doomed are not at all clear. Many commentators have read into his work a prediction that capitalism will eventually fail to function effectively in some way, perhaps through increasingly severe economic crises, or through prolonged stagnation and depression. I cannot find any definite and explicit prediction to this effect in his mature work, though there are ambiguous statements that can be read in this way by those who want to do so. It may be that Marx thought that his 'law' of the tendency of the rate of profit to fall would produce the desired result; certainly many of his followers have thought so. His comments on the implications of the law (*Cap*. III, chapter 15) are, however, rather vague. The tendency of the rate of profit to fall cannot be taken seriously anyway.

An alternative argument is stated rather more explicitly, though still not argued in detail. On this argument, capitalism will not collapse for purely economic reasons, but will be overthrown by conscious action by workers. As capitalism develops, an increasing fraction of the population is proletarianised, workers are gathered into increasingly large production units, and the potential for united action is increased. At the same time, polarisation of wealth increases the incentives to dispossess the capitalists.

> Along with the constantly diminishing number of the magnates of capital . . . grows the mass of misery, oppression, slavery, degradation, exploitation; but with this too grows the revolt of the working class, a class always increasing in numbers, and disciplined, united, organised by the very mechanism of the process of capitalist production itself . . . The knell of capitalist private property sounds. The expropriators are expropriated (*Cap*. I, p. 763).

This is, of course, prophecy, not detailed argument, involving implicit assumptions about the sociology of revolution as well as forecasts about the evolution of economic variables. It cannot be regarded as conclusive. So far capitalism remains intact in the main economic centres, and successful revolutions have been confined to relatively backward countries. The future of capitalism remains an open question.

NOTES

1. The three volumes of *Capital* (Marx, 1867; 1885; 1894) will be referred to as *Cap*. I, II and III.
2. See Steedman *et al.* (1981) for a variety of views. The debate will be discussed further below.
3. See, for example, Howard and King (1985), pp. 134ff.
4. The literature is immense. For a survey of the issues and an excellent bibliography see Howard and King (1985). The best known, and most comprehensive, assault on the labour theory of value is Steedman (1977).
5. On the issues raised in this paragraph, see the debate between Steedman and Morishima (Steedman, 1975; Morishima, 1976; Wolfsetter, 1976; Steedman, 1976a; Steedman, 1976b; Steedman, 1977).

6. In Marx's framework, of course, profit derives from surplus value, and surplus value from surplus labour. For various theorems linking profit, surplus labour, and surplus value (appropriately defined), see Morishima (1973, chapter 5; 1974) and Roemer (1981, chapter 2); see also the references cited in note 5.
7. See, for example, Braverman (1974), Friedman (1977) and Thompson (1983).

REFERENCES

Bortkiewicz, L. von (1907) 'On the correction of Marx's fundamental theoretical construction in the third volume of "Capital"', in P. M. Sweezy (ed.) *Karl Marx and the Close of his System* (New York: Kelley, 1969).

Braverman, H. *Labor and Monopoly Capital* (New York: Monthly Review Press, 1974).

Friedman, A. L. *Industry and Labour* (London: Macmillan, 1977).

Hodgson, G. 'The falling rate of profit', *New Left Review*, 84 (1974).

Howard, M. C. and J. E. King *The Political Economy of Marx*, 2nd edn (London: Longman, 1985).

Marx, K. (1844) *Economic and Philosophic Manuscripts of 1844* (London: Lawrence & Wishart, 1970).

Marx, K. (1867), *Capital*, vol. I (Moscow: Foreign Languages Publishing House, 1961).

Marx, K. (1885), *Capital*, vol. II, F. Engels (ed.) (Moscow: Foreign Languages Publishing House, 1957).

Marx, K. (1894), *Capital*, vol. III, F. Engels (ed.) (Moscow: Foreign Languages Publishing House, 1962).

Meek, R. *Economics and Ideology and other Essays* (London: Chapman & Hall, 1967).

Morishima, M. *Marx's Economics* (Cambridge: Cambridge University Press, 1973).

Morishima, M. 'Marx in the light of modern economic theory', *Econometrica*, 42 (1974): 611–32.

Morishima, M. 'Positive Profits with negative surplus value: a comment', *Economic Journal*, 86 (1976): 599–603.

Roemer, J. 'Continuing controversy on the falling rate of profit: fixed capital and other issues', *Cambridge Journal of Economics*, 3 (1979): 379–98.

Roemer, J. *Analytic foundations of Marxian economic theory* (Cambridge: Cambridge University Press, 1981).

Samuelson, P. A. 'Understanding the Marxian notion of exploitation: a summary of the so-called transformation problem between Marxian values and competitive prices', *Journal of Economic Literature*, 9 (1971): 399–431.

Schumpeter, J. A. *Capitalism, Socialism and Democracy*, 4th edn (London: Allen & Unwin, 1954).

Shaikh, A. 'Marx's theory of value and the "transformation problem"', in J. Schwartz (ed.), *The Subtle Anatomy of Capitalism* (Santa Monica: Goodyear, 1977).

Steedman, I. 'Positive profits with negative surplus value', *Economic Journal*, 85 (1975): 114–23.

Steedman, I. 'Positive profits with negative surplus value: a reply', *Economic Journal*, 86 (1976a): 604–8.

Steedman, I. 'Positive profits with negative surplus value: a reply to Wolfstetter', *Economic Journal*, 86 (1976b): 873–6.

Steedman, I. *Marx after Sraffa* (London: NLB, 1977).

Steedman, I. *et al. The Value Controversy* (London: Verso Editions and NLB, 1981).

Thompson, P. *The Nature of Work* (London: Macmillan, 1983).

Wolfstetter, E. 'Positive profits with negative surplus value: a comment', *Economic Journal*, 86 (1976): 864–72.

8 The Continuing Relevance of Alfred Marshall

JOHN WHITAKER

It is hardly controversial to suggest that Alfred Marshall, the Cambridge economist who lived from 1842 to 1924, was a leading figure in the development of economics as a discipline.[1] His influence came both from his economic ideas and from his roles as professional leader and mentor. His most famous protégés were John Maynard Keynes and Arthur Cecil Pigou, while his masterwork, *The Principles of Economics*, dominated the subject for decades after the appearance of the first edition (Marshall, 1890). Historians of economics have been intensively engaged in elucidating and assessing, or reassessing, all aspects of Marshall's thought and professional impact, and this interest will doubtless continue apace; a definitive interpretation, that will stand unchallenged by posterity, is hardly possible in the case of so complex and central a figure as Marshall. In fact, interest in the study of Marshall as a historical figure currently seems to be in the ascendant. But the fact that Marshall's contribution to the development of economics is a major concern of historians of economics does not imply that it is, or should be, of much interest to economists who profess to have no interest in their subject's past. I will, indeed, suggest later that economists *ought* to be interested in the rich body of past economic thought, and probably would be if they took a more realistic view of the nature of their subject.[2] But for the present I want to consider what relevance Marshall might have for the non-historically minded economist of today. To what extent is Marshall's thought still relevant to the concerns, interests and activities of such a person? My impression is that non-historians, who happen to read some Marshall, do often come away impressed and stimulated, and this is perhaps a prima-facie indication that vitality remains. But in what does it consist?

There is (as I have perhaps already demonstrated) a danger of lapsing into excessive generality and vagueness in the kind of broad-gauged discussion I am attempting here. As a corrective, I propose to start with some relatively concrete matters. First I will consider what one might call the 'fossil remnants' of Marshall's theoretical contribution – those theoretical tools and concepts still embodied in the main corpus of modern economics and remaining part of the common intellectual baggage of most economists even today. I will handle this topic rather briefly. It deserves notice in any consideration of Marshall's continuing relevance, but it hardly needs detailed exegesis. After this, I turn to a sample of Marshall's overlooked analytical contributions. Here the focus is on Marshall as a continuing storehouse of novel theoretical insights and results within the dominant neoclassical tradition. The third topic addressed will be the general character of Marshall's method and his vision of economic reality. The spotlight now turns from Marshall, the technical economic theorist, to Marshall, the sage: a potential source of insights into the aims and purpose of economic analysis and the issues it needs to tackle, a supplier of awkward questions rather than answers. Now the emphasis is on Marshall's differences from modern 'mainstream' economics, rather than his affinities to it. After sections devoted in turn to each of these three topics, the concluding section offers some more general speculations.

1. THE FOSSIL REMNANTS

Any competent graduate student should be able to draw up a list of certain familiar concepts and arguments which derive directly from Marshall. If the student is particularly learnèd, he (or she) will be aware that sometimes Marshall was not the initial propounder, but rather the rediscoverer or populariser, but even in such cases Marshall's espousal was largely responsible for embedding the concept firmly in economists' consciousness.

What are the main items on this list? I would suggest (with brief reference to Marshall's main statement)[3]

1. The partial equilibrium analysis of price determination in a competitive market by the intersection of curves indicating

demand price and supply price as functions of the total quantity
sold on, or supplied to, the market (Marshall, 1879; 1920,
pp. 323–80).

2. The analysis of the stability of such an equilibrium on the
   assumption that quantity supplied increases or decreases as
   demand price exceeds or falls short of supply price at the quantity
   currently supplied (Marshall, 1879; 1920, pp. 345–7). This is
   often referred to as the 'Marshallian adjustment process'.

3. The distinction between short-period and long-period supply and
   the associated concept of quasi-rent as a price-determined short-
   period return to an input whose supply is less elastic in the short
   period than in the long (Marshall, 1920, pp. 363–80, 394–424).

4. The concept of the (price) elasticity of market demand as the
   percentage change in total quantity demanded in consequence of
   a one per cent change in market price (Marshall, 1920, pp. 102–
   3, 838–40).

5. Consumers' surplus as the excess of the demand price over the
   market price on any unit sold in a given market over a specified
   period (a monetary measure of the net benefit to the buyer of that
   unit) summed over every unit sold (Marshall, 1879; 1920,
   pp. 124–32, 841–3).

6. The market derived demand curve for an input, assuming
   maintained equilibrium in the market for the final good the input
   produces and in the markets for co-operating inputs (Marshall,
   1920, pp. 381–93, 846–56).

7. The offer curve in international trade, and the associated analysis
   of trading equilibrium and its stability by means of intersecting
   offer curves (Marshall, 1879; 1923, pp. 330–60).

One could doubtless add further items to the list, but these are the
most familiar, and all remain abundantly represented in modern
textbooks, testimony to the fecundity of Marshall's constructive
genius.

All the listed concepts share certain family characteristics. Although
based on specific assumptions about individual behaviour, they are all
focused on market-level phenomena. And they all have a certain
robustness and lack of refinement. They are effective tools, but only
rough and ready ones, deficient in logical rigour and completeness. I
will argue in Section 3 below that they were meant to have these
characteristics in consequence of Marshall's views on the uses of
economic analysis. Because modern economists tend to place a high

value on logical rigour and completeness, Marshall's rough tools have been largely expelled from the frontiers of academic research, but they still retain their hold on elementary pedagogy and, one suspects, play a larger role in applied work and the sifting and focusing of preliminary ideas than is apparent from the finished products published in academic journals. They are unlikely to be entirely discarded for many years to come.

2. NEGLECTED ANALYTICAL CONTRIBUTIONS

In this section I want to suggest that Marshall's work may be an unexhausted store of new theoretical insights. The most compelling procedure would be to show that significant theoretical developments of the next 20 years are implicit, or at least signposted, in his writings. The obvious difficulty with such a plan is that I lack the prescience to know what these developments will be: otherwise I would not be spending time writing this. Consequently, I attempt the more modest task of arguing that some significant, and mainly recent, twentieth-century developments are clearly foreshadowed in his work. I will give three instances, dealing with the latter two rather cursorily.

The first, and I think most interesting, example is Marshall's treatment of optimal public-utility pricing when taxation is burdensome. In discussing the theory of monopoly, Marshall (1920, pp. 487–93) raises the question of the rule for optimal behaviour of a monopolist, public or private, who 'regards a gain to the consumers as of equal importance with an equal gain to himself' (p. 487). The proposed criterion is the maximisation of 'total benefit', which is the 'sum of the monopoly [net] revenue and the consumers' surplus' (p. 487n). This leads, as I will show shortly, to the standard marginal-cost pricing rule. However, for a public enterprise, net surplus contributes to general government revenue, while any loss must be met from this revenue. A reduction in monopoly revenue will therefore force the government to turn to some alternative revenue source. Marshall (1920) is very clear that this will impose an excess burden elsewhere in the economy:

Even a government which considers its own interests coincident with those of the people has to take account of the fact that, if it abandons one source of revenue, it must in general fall back on others which have their own disadvantages. For they will necessarily involve friction and expense in collection, together with some injury to the public, of the kind which we have described as a loss of consumers' surplus (p. 488).

He therefore proposes as the appropriate criterion the maximisation of 'compromise benefit' which modifies 'total benefit' by giving consumers' surplus only a fractional weight, n, in the sum.[4] This is equivalent to maximising consumer surplus plus $(1/n)$ times monopoly net revenue. The magnitude $1/n$, which exceeds unity, can be interpreted as the opportunity cost of raising an extra unit of government revenue from the next best alternative source.

Marshall analyses the implications of the maximisation of compromise benefit very thoroughly. He argues geometrically, using average curves in his monopoly diagram with its superimposed grid of rectangular hyperbolae. And he gives a full calculus treatment in the Mathematical Appendix (1920, pp. 856–8). The concepts of marginal revenue and marginal cost are implicit in his treatment, but not explicitly recognised, so that he fails to invoke what now seems the most lucid interpretation of his results. As shown in the Appendix below, the maximisation of compromise benefit, for any value of n between zero and unity, requires

n (price) $+ (1 - n)$ (marginal revenue) $=$ marginal cost.

Thus, when $n = 1$, and total benefit maximisation applies, we get the rule 'price equals marginal cost'; while when $n = 0$, and consumer surplus does not count at all, we get the familiar rule 'marginal revenue equals marginal cost' for maximised monopoly net revenue. As Marshall showed (see Appendix below), the larger is the value of n, then the greater is the level of monopoly output at which compromise benefit is maximised.

What is important is that we have here a very explicit treatment, the first to my knowledge, of a second-best problem in public finance which recognises that all sources of government revenue impose deadweight losses. The subject was raised again in Hotelling's classic paper (1938), while Ramsey's tax-theory classic (1927) later proved to have close formal relevance. But it was only after 1950 that a proper understanding of these issues began to take hold (see Baumol and Bradford, 1970). The modern treatments which have emerged are more general in that they deal with multiproduct cases and use a general-equilibrium framework rather than a partial-equilibrium one. Thus, the shadow price of the government funds needed to replace a cut in the net revenue of a public enterprise is determined endogenously, and interrelations between the demand or cost conditions of different products are recognised. But Marshall's treatment is correct as far as it goes, and has an appealing robustness and simplicity.

The other two examples of Marshall's theoretical prescience will be described more perfunctorily. On the first there is really nothing more to say than that Marshall gave a very clear description of the von Neumann and Sraffa device for handling fixed capital in a circulating-capital framework with joint production. His statement is so clear that it must be quoted:

> Sometimes it is convenient to speak as though all the capital applied were circulating capital applied at the beginning of the year or during it: and in that case everything that is on the farm at the end of the year is part of the produce . . . The farm implements may even be treated in the same way, their value at the beginning of the year being taken as so much circulating capital applied to the farm, and at the end of the year as so much produce . . . It is often the best plan for general reasonings of an abstract character, particularly if they are expressed in a mathematical form (Marshall, 1920, p. 172).

The puzzle is that there is no indication that Marshall himself ever exploited this insight into what nowadays seems the most satisfactory and comprehensive framework for the analysis of fixed capital. Again, it was not until the 1960s that this approach became widespread among economic theorists.

The final instance I will point to is Marshall's clear understanding of the differing principles governing the returns to renewable and non-renewable resources (1920, pp. 166–7, 438–9).

> The supply of agricultural produce and of fish is a perennial stream; mines are as it were nature's reservoir . . . The rent of a mine is calculated on a different principle from that of a farm. The farmer contracts to give back the land as rich as he found it: a mining company cannot do this; and while the farmer's rent is reckoned by the year, mining rent consists chiefly of 'royalties' which are levied in proportion to the stores that are taken out of nature's storehouse (p. 167). The royalty itself on a ton of coal, when accurately adjusted, represents that diminution in the value of the mine, regarded as a source of wealth in the future, which is caused by taking the ton out of nature's storehouse (p. 439).

So acute a theorist as F. Y. Edgeworth had difficulty in grasping Marshall's distinction, which is now a fundamental basis for the theoretical treatment of non-renewable resources.[5] The classic modern source on this is yet another seminal paper by Hotelling (1931), but the full-scale development of the theory occurred only in the 1970s (see Dasgupta and Heal, 1980; Fisher, 1981, for useful surveys).

I do not want to claim that 'it is all in Marshall': only that he had acute insights which might have helped expedite theoretical progress had they been widely recognised at a sufficiently early date. Whether the same will hold true for future developments is another matter. I would not be surprised if this proved so, but there could well be an upper bound to the extent by which even the most creative thinker can be ahead of his time.

3.   MARSHALL'S VISION AND METHOD

I come now to a range of issues where I must paint with the broadest of brushes, without any serious attempt at detailed documentation.[6] I start with Marshall's vision of economic reality and then turn to his method of analysing it.

Marshall's vision of economic reality was of a complex evolutionary process of economic growth in which individual abilities, characters, preferences and knowledge develop jointly, along with social institutions, markets, and technologies of production and communication. Economic motivation – that part of human behaviour which can be calibrated against the measuring rod of money on the opportunity-cost principle – was seen as ubiquitous in this evolutionary process, an ever-acting source of change and adaptation. But the pursuit of broadly-conceived self-interest was far from operating frictionlessly or on the basis of theoretically-complete information or fixed preferences. The inertia and limited knowledge and foresight of many economic actors was emphasized. Even the 'principle of substitution' – often thought of as the archetypal concept of neoclassical economics – was seen by Marshall as a 'special and limited application of the law of survival of the fittest' (1920, p. 597). He envisaged savings in cost obtained by one producer, through experiment or serendipity, as only gradually forced on others by the pressures of competition. Marshall's producers are far from having access to a set of blueprints fully characterising current production technology. However, considerable stress was placed on the secular growth of 'deliberateness' of action, regarded as both historical tendency and normative goal. Stress was placed also on the radical improvements in communication which had transformed the world economy during Marshall's lifetime. Customs and social institutions (for example, land tenure practices) were viewed as molding themselves over time into conformity with the dominant forces of self-interest, but meanwhile as themselves exerting an independent constraining influence on the path of social evolution. Self-interest itself did not necessarily lead to atomistic competition and perfect markets, but often to exclusive combinations and joint action in the interests of a narrow group, although combined action was in turn frequently undermined by the eroding forces of individual opportunism and economic change.[7]

Unfortunately, Marshall was unable to provide much beyond a descriptive evocation of this underlying vision of the manifold nature of economic reality and vague discussions of the complex processes at work. 'The Mecca of the economist lies in economic biology rather than in economic dynamics' (Marshall, 1920, p. xiv), but the only analytical tools to hand were the comparative-static ones based on individual optimisation and market equilibrium. These were employed by Marshall with great effectiveness, but within a limited sphere of application and with a continual awareness of the provisional, tentative, and incomplete nature of the results.

> The main concern of economics is thus with human beings who are impelled, for good and evil, to change and progress. Fragmentary statical hypotheses are used as temporary auxiliaries to dynamical – or rather biological – conceptions: but the central idea of economics, even when its Foundations alone are under discussion, must be that of living force and movement (Marshall, 1920, p. xv).

It might be said that in extending his statical tools to embrace increasing returns and a loose notion of 'free competition' as a process, Marshall pushed them beyond their proper limits. It cannot be charged that he did so without due warning,[8] but his efforts on these lines were certainly a source of confusion and controversy. Later generations of economists were more inclined to pursue equilibrium theory to its logical conclusions and not attuned to Marshall's attempts to maintain a delicate balance between the statical tools and the complexly-evolving subject matter to which they were to be applied: 'economic problems are imperfectly represented when they are treated as problems of statical equilibrium, and not of organic growth' (Marshall, 1920, p. 461).

Facing this complexly-evolving reality, and equipped only with grossly inadequate tools for understanding it, the economist must avoid two extremes. On the one hand there is the danger of over-elaborate and artificial extensions of the statical theory, based on misleading or overstretched analogies to physical science, which fail to recognise the limited and provisional nature of the theory's effective applicability. For example, Marshall would have nothing to do with elaborate theorising about the stationary state, even though he recognised it as the culmination of the inner logic of the statical approach. Nor would he reason elaborately about complex indirect market interdependencies, a path which leads ultimately to the merely formal elegance of Walrasian general equilibrium.

The pragmatic imperative is perhaps clearest in Marshall's time or period analysis which uses statical tools as a rough and ready means of coming to grips with developments occurring through time. The alternative, an explicit analysis of time paths by methods of dynamical mechanics, seemed to Marshall too rigid and falsely-precise to be worth pursuing far.[9]

The other extreme to be avoided was excessive empiricism and reliance on direct induction from history. Marshall's distaste for overly-elaborate economic theorising was exceeded only by his scorn for those who denied the need for a machinery of economic analysis and believed that they could decipher the economic past, or understand the future, unaided by an 'organon' of systematic thought. Economic analysis or theory was to Marshall an invaluable and indispensable instrument for coming to terms with complex economic reality. But it was a tool which could only supplement and not replace common sense. Its effective use had to be grounded on good judgement and thorough acquaintance with the facts of the situation: its historical background, quantitative dimensions, institutional setting, and non-economic elements. Economics was not a set body of doctrines, but an art of approaching the complex world with some simple, robust machinery of thought. The machinery was an indispensable aid to understanding, but did not itself constitute empirical knowledge. It was not an end, but a means, and it was not to be used without continuous questioning of the appropriateness of the assumptions used and continuous awareness of changing non-economic circumstances.

Marshall had no great profundity as a philosopher of science and had little patience with metaphysics. His discussions of methodology largely reflect the philosophical presuppositions of his day. His method, which was in the general deductive tradition of Ricardo, John Stuart Mill and Cairnes, was described by John Neville Keynes as 'deductive political economy guided by observation' (Keynes, 1891, p. 217n). Keynes's chapter 'On the Deductive Method in Political Economy' (J. N. Keynes, 1891, pp. 204–35) is as good a rationalisation of Marshall's method as one can find, but the most striking characterisation was provided by John Neville Keynes's famous son, whose views on the role of economic analysis seem to have been very close to Marshall's. In a letter of 1938 to Roy Harrod, John Maynard Keynes argued that

> Economics is a science of thinking in terms of models joined to the art of choosing models which are relevant to the contemporary world, . . . The object of a model is to segregate the semipermanent or relatively constant factors from those which are transitory or fluctuating so as to develop a logical way of thinking about the latter, and of understanding the time sequences to which they give rise in particular cases . . . the gift for using 'vigilant observation' to choose good models . . . appears to be a very rare one (J. M. Keynes, 1973, pp. 296–7; see also pp. 299–300).

This kind of essentially nineteenth-century view of economic method is no longer in good odour with methodologists, and it conflicts with the naïve positivistic beliefs one would probably find on scratching the typical modern economist, impatient of methodological matters.[10] I do not advocate turning back the methodological clock in an attempt to rehabilitate Marshall's approach as a distinct and superior mode of economic explanation, although there is perhaps more to it than modern methodologists are prone to admit. But I do believe that economists might learn (if only humility) from Marshall's cautious and eclectic views on the role of economic theory, his keen awareness of the intrinsic difficulty and changeability of the subject matter of economics, and his concern to build alliances with cognate areas of social and philosophical enquiry, rather than to extend the economists' empire roughshod.

4. CONCLUDING REMARKS

The understandable ambition to establish economics as a science like the physical sciences has not so far been fulfilled. The goal of systematically explaining and predicting a widening range of persistent empirical phenomena remains largely (although not entirely) unmet. Perhaps the goal should be modified. Perhaps we should even be content to view economics as a specialised realm of discourse whose adherents are better equipped to argue coherently and effectively about some parts of social organisation and policy than are those unfamiliar with its language.[11] If reappraisal proves called for – and persistent rumblings of discontent and the recent rise of heterodoxy suggest it might be – we may go back to the earlier economists with a kinder and more alert eye. If economics is not clearly established to be an empirically progressive science like physics, so that its future path remains mist enshrouded, there is a strengthened case for continuing to expose economists to the classic works of the past. Their authors knew things we have forgotten or missed, and this knowledge is often tacit and uncommunicable except by osmosis from submergence in the original text.[12] There is, too, the salutary benefit of experiencing directly the play of mind of a major thinker. For these reasons, if no other, Marshall should continue to be read, along with other important past economists.

There is, however, a risk of going too far in giving credit to the vaguely formed and half-expressed insights of past writers. They can be a source of inspiration to us, without being viewed as bricks in some alternative conceptual structure. Much of what Marshall has to offer to us today may fall into this category. What is most distinctive is his general vision of reality, not his formal theoretical structure, although, as I have tried to demonstrate, the latter is not without its interest and merits. This vision, and the consequent attitude to economics, distance Marshall somewhat from the modern mainstream or neoclassical approach to economics, which he did so much to foster, and align him to some degree with various heterodox approaches.[13] But it would have been anathema to Marshall to be regarded as a fount of doctrine or ideology. He remains unique.

APPENDIX: THE MAXIMISATION OF COMPROMISE BENEFIT

Let $R(x)$ and $C(x)$ be, respectively, the total revenue and cost of a public enterprise when its output is x. Consumers' surplus is given as a function of x by

$$\int_0^x [R(u)/u]\,du - R(x),$$

while monopoly revenue is $R(x) - C(x)$.
Hence compromise benefit is

$$n\int_0^x [R(u)/u]\,du + (1-n)R(x) - C(x). \tag{A}$$

Maximising (A) by choice of x gives the first-order condition (a prime denoting differentiation)

$$nR(x)/x + (1-n)R'(x) - C'(x) = 0. \tag{B}$$

Since $R(x)/x$, $R'(x)$ and $C'(x)$ are, respectively, average revenue (or price), marginal revenue, and marginal cost, this gives the result stated in the text.

Totally differentiating the implicit function (B) with respect to n gives

$$R(x)/x - R'(x) + M(dx/dn) = 0$$

where M is the second derivative of (A) with respect to x, evaluated at the x satisfying (B). If the second-order condition for compromise-benefit maximisation holds in sufficient form, then $M < 0$. Hence, $dx/dn > 0$, given that the demand or average revenue curve is negatively sloped, so that $R(x)/x > R'(x)$.

This argument holds at any n between zero and unity, so that x is an increasing function of n over this interval, providing (as Marshall explicitly notes, 1920, p. 857) that (A) has a unique maximum at each such n. (At any singular n where $M = 0$ this function will not be differentiable, but the argument is not otherwise affected.)

Condition (B) may be written in the alternative form

$$\frac{P - MC}{P} = \frac{(1-n)}{e} \tag{B*}$$

where P, MC, and e are, respectively, price, marginal cost and Marshallian demand elasticity, all evaluated at the x satisfying (B). The discrepancy between price and marginal cost is thus greater the lower is n and the smaller is e. Formula (B^*) brings out very clearly the similarity to the modern literature on Ramsey prices (see Baumol and Bradford, 1970).

NOTES

1. For further details on Marshall's life see the classic essay (Keynes, 1924). For a useful compact survey of Marshall's work see O'Brien (1981).
2. See Section 4 below.
3. I will refer throughout to the final (eighth) edition of Marshall's *Principles* (1920), although all the arguments are to be found in the first edition of 1890.
4. Marshall also hints that this concept might apply to a public-spirited private monopolist who is willing to sacrifice his own interest somewhat for the sake of consumers, but such an extension does not seem very convincing.
5. I draw this conclusion from unpublished letters to be included in an edition of Marshall's correspondence I am currently editing.
6. The interested reader may obtain a general impression of Marshall's views by consulting Marshall (1920, pp. v-xvii, 1–48, 723–84) and Pigou (1925, pp. 295–318, 323–46). Some aspects I will have to ignore here are dealt with in Whitaker (1977) (see also Loasby, 1978).
7. This last range of issues is particularly prominent in Marshall (1919).

8. The Statical Theory of equilibrium is only an introduction to economic studies; and it is barely even an introduction to the study of the progress and development of industries which show a tendency to increasing return. Its limitations are so constantly overlooked, especially by those who approach it from an abstract point of view, that there is a danger in throwing it into definite form at all (Marshall, 1920, p. 461).

9. I would like to interject two warnings here: (1) Marshall's heavy emphasis on long-period analysis must be seen as partly directed to doctrinal issues of value theory and can hardly be justified by its pragmatic interest. This (as Marshall conceded) is small because of the implausibility of holding background circumstances, such as technology, constant for very long periods (see Whitaker, 1982); (2) Since Marshall (1920) is only the first part of a never-completed larger project, it can give a misleading impression of the over-all balance in his thinking (for example, short-period analysis was to assume a much more prominent role in the unfinished parts).
10. Paradoxically, though, I discern certain parallels between the views of Marshall and the currently-influential ones of Milton Friedman (see especially Friedman, 1953). Both take a pragmatic view of economic theory and both distrust the tendency to pluck complex formal systems out of the air. But, of course, where they differ fundamentally is in the significance attached to verisimilitude of assumptions.

11. See Solow (1985) and McCloskey (1983) for interesting discussion of these and related issues.
12. See Whitaker (1985) for a fuller discussion along such lines.
13. The affinities are perhaps closest to 'Post-Keynesians', in part because Maynard Keynes and Marshall had much in common. Affinities to Institutionalists and neo-Austrians are present, but less marked.

REFERENCES

Baumol, W. J. and Bradford, D. F. 'Optimal Departures from Marginal Cost Pricing', *American Economic Review*, vol. 60 (1970) pp. 265–83.
Dasgupta, P. S. and Heal, G. M. *Economic Theory and Exhaustible Resources* (Cambridge: Cambridge University Press, 1980).
Fisher, A. C. *Resource and Environmental Economics* (Cambridge: Cambridge University Press, 1981).
Friedman, M. 'The Methodology of Positive Economics' in his *Essays in Positive Economics* (Chicago: University of Chicago Press, 1953).
Hotelling, H. 'The Economics of Exhaustible Resources', *Journal of Political Economy*, vol. 39 (1931) pp. 137–75.
Hotelling, H. 'The General Welfare in Relation to Problems of Taxation and of Railway and Utility Rates', *Econometrica*, vol. 6 (1938) pp. 242–69.
Keynes, J. M. 'Alfred Marshall, 1842–1924', *Economic Journal*, vol. 34 (1924) pp. 311–72, reprinted in Pigou (1925) and in J. M. Keynes, *Essays in Biography* in *Collected Writings* vol. 10 (London: Macmillan, 1972).
Keynes, J. M. *The General Theory and After: Part II Defense and Development* in D. Moggridge (ed.) *Collected Writings* vol. 14 (London: Macmillan, 1973).
Keynes, J. N. *The Scope and Method of Political Economy* (London: Macmillan, 1891).
Loasby, B. J. 'Whatever Happened to Marshall's Theory of Value?', *Scottish Journal of Political Economy*, vol. 25 (1978) pp. 1–12.
McCloskey, D. N. 'The Rhetoric of Economics', *Journal of Economic Literature*, vol. 21 (1983) pp. 481–517.
Marshall, A. *The Pure Theory of Foreign Trade: The Pure Theory of Domestic Values* (Privately printed, 1879; reprinted, London: London School of Economics, 1930). An amplified version is reproduced in J. K. Whitaker (ed.) *The Early Economic Writings of Alfred Marshall, 1867–1890* (London: Macmillan, 1975).
Marshall, A. *Principles of Economics*, vol. I (London: Macmillan, 1890).
Marshall, A. *Industry and Trade* (London: Macmillan, 1919).
Marshall, A. *Principles of Economics*, 8th edn (London: Macmillan, 1920). This is reproduced as the first volume of the ninth (variorum) edition edited by C. W. Guillebaud (London: Macmillan, 1961).
Marshall, A. *Money Credit and Commerce* (London: Macmillan, 1923).
O'Brien, D. P. 'A. Marshall, 1842–1924', in D. P. O'Brien and J. R. Presley (eds) *Pioneers of Modern Economics in Britain* (London: Macmillan, 1981).

Pigou, A. C. (ed.) *Memorials of Alfred Marshall* (London: Macmillan, 1925).
Ramsey, F. P. 'A Contribution to the Theory of Taxation', *Economic Journal*, vol. 37 (1927) pp. 47–61.
Solow, R. M. 'Economic History and Economics', *American Economic Review*, vol. 75 (1985) pp. 328–31.
Whitaker, J. K. 'Some Neglected Aspects of Alfred Marshall's Economic and Social Thought', *History of Political Economy*, vol. 9 (1977) pp. 161–97.
Whitaker, J. K. 'The Emergence of Marshall's Period Analysis', *Eastern Economic Journal*, vol. 8 (1982) pp. 15–29.
Whitaker, J. K. 'Must Historians of Economics Apologize?', *History of Economics Society Bulletin*, vol. 6 (2) (1985) pp. 9–15.

9 Modern Monetarist Ideas: A British Connection? *

JOHN R. PRESLEY

Media debate on economic issues is naturally and justifiably inclined to over-simplification. The terms 'monetarism' and 'Keynesian' are often used freely without any clear specification of what these terms mean. The difference between them is summarised as that of 'money matters' or 'money does not matter'. Unfortunately this disguises a host of complex differences and omits many similarities. In truth no economist, not even Keynesian, has argued that money does not matter; neither would a monetarist argue that money is the only thing that matters; it is more a question of emphasis than of extremes.

This paper has has two major objectives. The first is to enquire as to the meaning of 'monetarism'. The second is to investigate the existence of monetarist ideas in the earlier writings of British economists. In this second objective it concentrates upon the writings of Alfred Marshall, Arthur Pigou, Ralph Hawtrey, the pre-*General Theory* Keynes, Frank Lavington and Dennis Robertson. If a title must be put to such a group, might I suggest the 'Cambridge School' although it cannot be pretended that all their views on economic theory and policy shared such common ground as to merit a collective title; but then this is no less true of the monetarist or the Keynesian school. What will be demonstrated, in particular, are two themes developed in the presidential address, the relationship between theory and policy, as strong in the Cambridge School as in monetarism, and

* I am grateful to Professor Milton Friedman, Professor D. Collard, Professor E. Davis, Professor B. Tew and Professor D. O'Brien; I also wish to thank the Wincott Foundation and the British Academy for financial support on related research topics.

the repetition and rediscovery in economic thought in the context of monetarism. In other words there is an affirmative answer to the question posed in the title to this paper. Many of the essential features of 'monetarism' did appear in the writings of the Cambridge School, particularly in the period 1870–1930.

DEFINING 'MONETARISM'

On looking below the surface at monetarism it is not too difficult to comprehend why economic commentators generally avoid defining it. There is no clear definition available in the literature; entire books (Mayer 1978; Macesich 1983) have been written to clarify the term; yet no fully acceptable definition emerges. The term was first employed by Brunner (1968) but it was quickly popularised by the media; Milton Friedman, the father figure of 'monetarism' in the same manner that Alfred Marshall could be regarded as the father figure of the Cambridge School, dislikes the term 'monetarism' and prefers the 'quantity theory of money' as a description of his views; he has nevertheless been forced by the conventions of others into accepting it (Friedman, 1982, p. 1). Friedman argues that a monetarist stresses the 'relationship between the nominal quantity of money on the one hand and such aggregate variables as the price level, real output, nominal income on the other' (letter to the author dated 8.5.85). Brunner's original definition (1968) in fact agrees with Friedman's view here. If this is acceptable as a definition then there is little doubt that all of the Cambridge School could also be labelled 'monetarist'. Indeed, Friedman regards J. M. Keynes's *Tract on Monetary Reform* (Keynes, 1923) as the most explicitly monetarist work amongst the writings of the Cambridge School (letter to the author 8.5.85).

Contemporary literature, however, is inclined to require much more detail in the features of monetarism, and it is these essential features which must be isolated and identified in the Cambridge School if it is to be accepted to any degree as its ancestor. It cannot be pretended that the list of features selected here will meet unanimous approval. Certainly there are a number of controversial boundaries to be drawn. To ascertain where one school or research programme ends and another begins is open to debate. Cross identifies orthodox monetarism and shows supply-side economics and new classical economics as separate research programmes leading on from 'monetarism' (Cross,

1982, chapters 8 to 10). Others regard 'monetarism' as an ongoing, expanding and pragmatic programme which may well embrace the 'new' research programmes recognised by Cross (Mayer, 1978). There has to be a clear divide between schools, some major differential in approach to merit separate treatment. For many economists the application of rational expectations in the macroeconomic process is sufficient to warrant the use of 'new classical' to describe those who seek to apply it. For others rational expectations is simply one further development within the monetarist research programme.

Mayer provides perhaps the standard reference (Mayer, 1978, p. 2), listing 12 sets of propositions which are a feature of monetarism and which distinguish it from Keynesianism. This list (see Appendix to this chapter) offers a pot-pourri of theoretical, empirical and policy characteristics which have met with an equally mixed reception from monetarists and Keynesians alike (Mayer, 1978, pp. 47ff). This kind of approach begs the question, of course, that monetarism should be defined according to its distinguishing features compared to Keynesian economics; clearly for some it may be more advantageous to define it according to differences from Marxism or some other 'ism', or without reference to any other school at all. Nevertheless let me persist with the old habit, if only on the basis that monetarism has for most people been regarded as a counter revolution against the so-called Keynesian revolution.

Of course, Mayer's comprehensive list of all possible ingredients in monetarism leads to the reaction that some would prefer greater portions of particular ingredients. Laidler is correct to assert that 'monetarism', like beauty, lies in the eye of the beholder (Laidler, 1981, p. 1). Hence Stein, for example, sees monetarism as a 'set of propositions in direct opposition to Keynesian fiscal policy', and chooses to emphasise policy aspects (Stein, 1976, p. 183). Consequently, the key ingredient is the monetarist belief that fiscal policy can have little effect upon total spending in an economy and therefore upon output, employment or the price level, and that monetary policy alone can be used to regulate spending and the price level over a long period. This emphasis is enforced by those who see no crucial difference in theoretical issues between monetarists and Keynesians. This view is most lucidly put forward by Modigliani in his Presidential Address to the American Economics Association (Modigliani, 1977, p. 1) and by Laidler (Laidler, 1981, p. 18). B. Friedman chooses to isolate the 'empirical' propositions of monetarism (Mayer, 1978, pp. 94–112): 'What distinguishes most of these "monetarist" propositions is their explicit statement about the magnitude of one or more of the parameters of the common underlying theoretical framework accepted by monetarists and Keynesians' (Mayer, p. 95).

Laidler (1981, pp. 1ff, also Mayer, 1978, p. 133) offers different ingredients from both sides of the Atlantic. The British monetarist is viewed as paying more attention to unemployment than his American counterpart and also to international aspects of inflation and trade; the former refers to inflation as an international occurrence, to the transmission of inflation between countries, and to the question of the monetarist solution to international monetary problems. The American monetarist in contrast is single-minded in his pursuit of the control of inflation. There is some natural rate of unemployment to which the level of unemployment always returns irrespective of economic policy, rendering discretionary employment policy ineffective. In Britain, the monetarist would at least attempt to *lower* the natural rate of unemployment by, for example, striving to increase the occupational and geographical mobility of labour.

From this plethora of monetarist preferences a selection needs to be made. I make advanced apologies if my selection fails to conform to everyone's taste, but in the time and space available I choose to stress the following as the main ingredients of monetarism:

1. An approach to macroeconomic analysis through the Demand for Money

Friedman's pioneering article (Friedman, 1956) consisted primarily in a reformulation of the Quantity Theory of Money, emanating from Fisher's equation of exchange (Fisher, 1911), as a theory of the demand for money. Macroeconomic analysis consequently proceeded through the demand for money function; this was in sharp contrast to the Keynesian approach which, although having a demand for money function, sees the income-expenditure approach as central to macroeconomic analysis. The focus of analysis therefore in monetarism is upon exploring the reasons why people wish to hold money. This translates into a belief that monetary factors are of the utmost importance in the determination of nominal income in an economy. The income expenditure approach, in contrast, concentrates upon the determinants of particular types of expenditure.

2. A 'broad' view of the demand for money

This is less of a meaningful distinction when compared to modern Keynesian economics, but certainly early interpretations of Keynes's *General Theory* (1936) show an emphasis upon the rate of interest as the relevant cost of holding money (Gordon, 1977, p. 11). Friedman's view of the individual's demand for money is much broader, although there are still a limited number of variables affecting it:

$$\frac{M}{P} = f\left\{y,\ w,\ r_m^e,\ r_b^e,\ r_e^e, \frac{1}{P}\frac{dP}{dt} ; u\right\}$$

Where M is the stock of money; P is the price level; y is the nominal income at constant prices; w is the fraction of wealth in non-human form (proportion of income derived from property); r_m^e is the expected nominal rate of return on money; r_b^e is the expected nominal rate of return on fixed value securities (incorporating the expected price changes); r_e^e is the expected rate of return on equities; $\frac{1}{P}\frac{dP}{dt}$ is the expected rate of return on real assets (the expected rate of change of the price of goods); u is an all embracing term for all other variables affecting the utility attached to holding money.

Fundamentally, the monetarist position is that of seeing a wide range of assets as possible substitutes for holding money balances. The individual, in deciding his money holding, looks at the benefits derived from holding money in relation to rates of return on a range of financial and real assets available to him. The 'early' Keynesians saw only a limited range of financial assets as being potential substitutes for money balances; real assets were not regarded as substitutable for money; hence this placed an over-emphasis upon the importance of the rate of interest on the demand for money. Let me stress, however, that contemporary Keynesians would not share this 'narrow' view of the demand for money.

3. A particular model of the monetary transmission process

Given the demand for money function in 2, the mechanism which links increased money balances to increased spending is one of portfolio adjustment. Given our individual's holding of money balances alongside a wide range of real and financial assets, any increase in money balances will essentially reduce the marginal rate of return on these balances making the alternative, real and financial assets more attractive. The individual, in other words, changes his portfolio, taking account of his perceptions of all the rates of return listed in 2. In this manner an increase in the money supply would work its way through on to aggregate spending in the economy.

Again if reference is made to the Keynesian stance, one can see very little difference between modern Keynesianism and monetarism on this issue (Tobin, 1969). However, there was a disposition amongst Keynesians in the 1950s, compounded by macro-economics textbook interpretations at that time, to emphasise the impact of changes in the money supply upon the rate of interest; these, in turn, influenced aggregate spending, more especially investment and not consumption. This was undoubtedly the popular translation of Keynes's *General Theory*.

4. The stability of the demand for money

This is the linchpin between economic theory and policy in monetarism. Friedman's assertion is that the demand for money is a stable function of its determinants, not necessarily a stable absolute quantity. His empirical investigation with Schwartz (Friedman and Schwartz, 1963) of the US economy indicated a reasonably stable demand for money along an upward trend, during a period of rising income (1867–1960). One would instinctively assume that a demand for money which had several determinants, that is, the monetarist case, would show greater stability than one where only one determinant existed – as in the case of the extreme Keynesian position with the rate of interest as the only key variable. Variations in one determinant may offset the effects on another. It is not on this basis, however, that monetarists argue that demand is stable; it is more on the basis that the major determinants of money demand historically have changed very slowly. In contrast the *General Theory* implied instability in liquidity preference as changes in the rate of interest brought with them variations in the velocity of circulation of money.

5. The superiority of monetary policy

The theoretical foundations in 1–4 are the justification for the advocacy of monetary policy to control movements in nominal income. If the demand for money is stable, then it follows that changes in the value of money must necessarily be caused by changes in its supply. If money supply growth is controlled, so must be movements in the value of money. The private sector is regarded as inherently stable and therefore government intervention is not a requirement. In one of the more recent additions to monetary analysis, the 'expectations-augmented Phillips Curve' has been used to portray, as mentioned earlier, some long-run natural rate of unemployment towards which the level of unemployment will always gravitate; this is irrespective of whatever short-term policy may be adopted by a government. This is a partial argument in favour of greater attention being paid by monetarists to prices than to unemployment.

There is no role to be played by either fiscal or incomes policies in the monetarists' scheme. Indeed, not all monetary policies are acceptable. The preference is for a long-run monetary policy which expresses itself in some monetary growth rule. Short-term monetary policy in the form of periodic changes in the money supply can be damaging. This conclusion results from the time lags indicated by the empirical evidence on the correlation between money supply changes and their eventual effects on prices and nominal income.

These key ingredients could, of course, be extended. I have intentionally omitted any reference to the international aspects of monetarism which some would see as perhaps the latest development. This relates to the monetary approach to the balance of payments and to exchange rate analysis. There is no sinister motive in this omission, simply one of time and space; if anything I suspect that the argument here would be strengthened by its inclusion (see Humphrey, 1980).

RECOGNISED ANCESTRY

Friedman has never disguised the fact that his own brand of monetarism owes much to earlier works. His restatement of the quantity theory (1956) acknowledges the importance of Fisher's work in his analysis; he is indebted to the Chicago oral tradition which through Simons, Mints, Knight and Viner continuously retained the study of macroeconomic problems via the quantity theory, rather than through the Keynesian income-expenditure analysis (Patinkin, 1981). But Friedman's earlier writings do much to establish the American ancestry of 'monetarism', perhaps to the neglect of its British counterpart. In fairness to Friedman he has made no claim to a revolution in monetary theory or policy; his theory has evolved, as he sees it, from the earlier quantity theory.

On the 'Cambridge School' he writes:

'My training as an economist included exposure to the works of Robertson, Pigou, Keynes, Marshall etc. Their work undoubtedly influenced my own work in the monetary approach. But it is hard at this distance to make that statement any more definite or to compare their influence with the influence, for example, of Irving Fisher to whom I regard myself as much closer in detail' (letter to the author 8.5.85).

This exposure must have come to some extent during his research in Cambridge in the mid 1950s, and one would suspect, whilst he was editor of the Cambridge Economic Handbooks in 1957. By the time he wrote 'A Theoretical Framework of Monetary Analysis' (Friedman, 1970) he displayed a not insignificant knowledge of the monetary analysis of the Cambridge School. In answer to the question, 'Was Friedman unaware of the Cambridge School?', the answer is definitely, 'No'; but whether he was totally cognisant of the links between his own early writings and their work, must remain in doubt. There still remains the question whether or not any of the ingredients of monetarism isolated above were present in the writings of the Cambridge School.

ON MATTERS OF THEORY

The contention in this section is that, on questions of economic theory, monetarism is much closer to the Cambridge School than to the acknowledged American ancestry seen in the work of Fisher.

The kind of oral tradition that existed in Chicago was also a feature of Cambridge in the period 1890–1930. It is impossible to overestimate the importance of Marshall in all of this. Hutchison has commented: 'for some time theoretical economics in England con- sisted very largely of discussion and interpretation, often textual, of Marshall's *Principles*' (Hutchison, 1953, p. 62). There is much truth in this and, although in the context of monetary theory, Marshall did not provide a totally new approach, he did nevertheless develop significantly the work of earlier writers, particularly Thornton, Senior and Cantillon (Eshag, 1963, p. 13). His approach was very much that of later monetarists. He focused attention on the reasons why people should demand money balances, rather than upon the rate at which money changes hands (the velocity of circulation of money). In this respect he was much closer to Friedman than was Fisher. The development of Marshall's approach, labelled the 'Cambridge Cash Balance Approach', was taken up by his pupils and colleagues, particularly Pigou, Robertson, Keynes and Lavington. In the more sophisticated versions of it (Pigou, 1917; Robertson, 1922), Friedman later appreciates its advantages over the quantity theory, and in so doing implies that his own approach is a more direct descendent of the Cambridge School. He writes: 'The cash balances approach . . . leads to stress being placed on the variables affecting the usefulness of money as an asset: the costs and returns from holding money instead of other assets, the uncertainty of the future and so on' (Gordon, 1977, p. 10). This was, of course, precisely the emphasis in his *restatement* of the quantity theory.

Most members of the Cambridge School were convinced of the advantages of the cash balance approach over the quantity theory. Robertson believed it to be more useful in analysing the psychological forces determining the demand for money (Robertson, 1915, p. 39). Pigou (1917) elaborates the Marshallian cash balance approach and offers what he calls a more completely fool-proof tool of analysis than Fisher's quantity theory. Indeed Friedman regards Pigou's main contribution here as making clear: 'the relationship between Fisher's transaction approach to money and the Cambridge cash-balance approach' (letter to the author 8.5.85). In general the cash balance approach was favoured by the Cambridge School because it enabled an enquiry as to the determinants of the velocity of circulation to take place, that is, as to why people hold on to money balances and what impact changing economic conditions have upon liquidity preference. (Eshag, 1963, chapter 1).

Of course, the cash balance approach was attractive because it conformed to the general approach of the neoclassical school; it was a part of the theory of value, with the value of the money being determined by both demand and supply. It enabled the 'neoclassical' equimarginal principle to be applied. Money, like any other commodity, possesses utility; for Marshall, holding money balances 'allows business transactions to be "easy and smooth" and puts the holder at a bargaining advantage' (Marshall, 1923, p. 45); it also allows the holder to speculate, to postpone expenditure until prices fall (Marshall, 1923, pp. 227–8). The individual therefore, in assessing the level of his money holdings, balances:

> the benefits, which he would get by enlarging his stock of currency in the hand, against those which he would get by investing some of it in either a commodity – say a coat or a piano – from which he would derive a direct benefit; or in some business plant or stock exchange security which would yield some money income (Marshall, 1923, pp. 38–9).

The individual decides upon his money holdings by balancing 'at the margin'; by a consideration of the marginal benefits derivable from a wide range of assets, including not only financial but real assets (the coat or piano in the quotation). Pigou, Lavington, Keynes and Robertson followed on from Marshall in analysing the individual's demand for money as a balancing act 'at the margin', balancing the benefits of holding money derived from satisfying the desire for liquidity and its function as a store of value against the benefits available from both real and financial assets. Robertson, for example, wrote: 'We must picture the individual distributing his real income between the uses of immediate consumption, of adding to his income bearing property, and of adding to his store of ready value in such ways as to make equal the marginal utility derived from each one' (Robertson, 1963, p. 22).

Keynes (1923) adopted a similar view, arguing that the amount of cash that people wish to hold: 'depends partly on the wealth of the community and partly on its habits. Its habits are fixed by its estimation of the extra convenience of having more cash in hand compared with the advantages to be got from spending the cash or investing it . . .' (Keynes, 1923, pp. 78–9). Lavington's analysis is a little more developed; he explains the rate of return on different types of assets in terms of their marketability; the more readily they are transferable into cash the lower will be the rate of return upon them and the more they will yield in terms of 'convenience' and 'security' to their holder (Lavington, 1921, pp. 30–1).

There is an interesting digression here. Friedman lays great virtue in the Chicago tradition in persisting with the quantity theory despite the Keynesian Revolution. The implication is, of course, that the quantity theory was neglected elsewhere. Perhaps, most surprisingly, this was not totally true of Cambridge. Despite the Keynesian Revolution taking place there and the enthusiasm of Keynes's Cambridge disciples in spreading the message (I am thinking particularly of Joan Robinson and Richard Kahn), the 'ancient ceremony' of the quantity theory remained the central analysis of at least one course given in Cambridge in the post-war period. I refer to Robertson's 'Lectures on Economic Principles', published as a book in 1963 under that title. He had succeeded to the chair of economics on Pigou's retirement in 1947 and held the chair to his own retirement in 1957; he continued to recommend Marshall's *Principles* (1890), Pigou's *Economics of Welfare* (1920) alongside Keynes's *General Theory*; his lectures on money were given entirely by using the framework offered by the cash balance approach, to the relative neglect of the Keynesian income-expenditure analysis. There was a partial attempt therefore to keep the Cambridge oral tradition going on issues of money even into the post-war period! (Although most of what concerns us here was seen before 1930.)

It is a fairly modest step, given that the Cambridge School saw the possession of both financial and real assets competing with the holding of money balances, to the list of variables influencing the demand for money in Friedman's analysis. The balancing act outlined above has to be undertaken by first assessing the rate of return on *all* the available assets which compete with money balances in the individual's portfolio. Keynes was keen, not only to establish the role of wealth and habits of individuals as determining the amount of purchasing power which they thought necessary, but the rate of interest (Keynes, 1923, pp. 62–8). This was not new to the literature. Thornton had put forward a demand for money function incorporating the state of business confidence, the rate of interest, and the cost of converting assets to cash, as early as 1802 (Thornton pp. 90–7), Most members of the Cambridge School included the rate of interest as *one* determinant of money demand.

Marshall discussed the role of price expectations in the demand for money in 1887 (Pigou, 1925, p. 201). He argued that if the value of a metal has been increasing for some time, this will lead to the expectation of a further increase and will heighten its demand. Keynes and Robertson too concluded in 1926 that expectations of price increases influenced the demand for money: 'If prices are expected to go on rising, people tend to hurry on with the purchase of goods (such as clothes and motor cars) of which the exact moment of purchase can be varied within pretty wide limits' (Robertson, 1926, p. 75). Pigou, in 1917 (p. 48), concluded that if the purchasing power of money is expected to increase this will bring about a greater demand for money balances; as with other Cambridge writers, he stressed the role of business confidence in affecting the demand for money balances (Pigou, 1917, p. 60). Hawtrey too developed Marshall's money demand function by considering the determinants of not only the transactionary and precautionary reasons for holding money, but also the investment motive. His analysis centred upon the 'unspent margin'; this he saw as a function of the individual's income and wealth; wealth incorporated both accumulated and expected wealth, with expected wealth in this case being largely determined by future prices (Hawtrey, 1919, pp. 34–43).

Robertson was later to develop his analysis (1963, pp. 336–7) and to comment upon the Cambridge approach in the light of the *General Theory*. In this he again stressed that business habits, the structure of industry, the 'general conditions of social and business life' and the state of the capital goods market (given that, for example, land and houses are partial substitutes for money) were all factors determining the proportion of real income which people wished to keep as money balances. But of more importance, he was anxious to emphasise the rate of return on alternatives to holding money as key determinants. In this he remarked 'it is . . . once more necessary to remind you that the purchase of gilt-edged securities is by no means the only, or normally the most economically important, alternative use of resources to holding money' (Robertson, 1963, p. 337). In summary, the only significant departure by Friedman from this analysis was his identification and inclusion of human wealth in money demand analysis, alongside non-human wealth (human wealth consisting of discounted expected future earnings.)

There are two fundamental issues relating to the question of the monetary transmission mechanism. First, it must be ascertained whether or not the Cambridge School favoured 'a portfolio adjustment' approach in analysing changes in the money supply, or the early Keynesian disposition to emphasise the changes in spending brought about by the interest rate movement associated with money supply changes. Secondly, without disputing that nominal income will increase with the money supply, it is essential to discover how the nominal income change is distributed between price and output changes; in this the monetarist view would recognise only price changes resulting from monetary growth; the 'early' Keynesian views would stress the stability of prices at least in situations of less than full employment.

From what has been said already, it must be apparent that the Cambridge School, in general, emphasised the portfolio adjustment route of money supply changes to spending; but at the same time they *did not underestimate* the 'indirect' route that money supply changes may take via the rate of interest. If anything Marshall perhaps favoured the 'indirect' route as a more important explanation of money supply changes (Marshall, 1926, pp. 38–45). Keynes, in contrast, wrote: 'When people find themselves with more cash than they require . . . they get rid of the surplus by buying goods or investments, or by leaving it for a bank to employ or, possibly by increasing their hoarded reserves' (Keynes, 1923, p. 75). The logical mechanism, given the cash balance approach, is that an increase in money supply will leave people with more money balances than they desire to hold; the natural outcome must be a switch to the alternatives to holding money; this may be to consumer or capital goods, or to financial assets. Nevertheless most members of the Cambridge School (particularly Robertson, Keynes and Hawtrey) also gave the interest rate effect of money supply changes some weight in their analysis (Robertson, 1915, pp. 213–5; Hawtrey, 1919, pp. 247–8).

Our discussion of the second issue, the distribution of the change in nominal income between price and output changes, can be linked to the final question of the *stability* of the demand for money in the writings of the Cambridge School. At the outset it is essential to distinguish between short- and long-run analysis in the Cambridge School. Both types of analysis were present in Marshall's work and were carried on by Robertson, Keynes, Pigou and Hawtrey. As with monetarism, there is a tendency to believe that, in the long run, any change in the money supply will be neutral; its effects are felt entirely upon prices and not upon output and employment. In the short run, however, a money supply change may have repercussions on prices, output and employment. Certainly Marshall expected prices to adjust quickly to a change in money supply, but this, in turn, affected profit margins and would lead to some readjustment of output and employment (Marshall, 1926, pp. 7–10, 286–7). Keynes presented a similar argument in the short run analysis of the *Tract* (Keynes, 1923) and Robertson also, in the complex jargon of *Banking Policy and the Price Level* (Robertson, 1926), saw the money supply affecting business activity as well as prices. Nevertheless, despite the difference between the short and long view in the Cambridge School, there is clearly much more attention paid to price changes than is present in early Keynesian theory.

This kind of distinction between short and long run extended to the discussion of the behaviour of the velocity of circulation of money V, or its reciprocal, k, the proportion of income which people wish to hold as cash balances. The monetarist policy position ultimately depends upon the *stability* or, at least, the *predictability* of V and k. Instability in the demand for money, reflected in changes in V and k would render a policy which focused entirely upon money supply changes as potentially ineffective if not dangerous. Mayer has remarked: 'It is the proposition that there is a stable demand for money that differentiates monetarism from the classical quantity theory of money tradition and "monetarism" from its Keynesian rival' (Mayer, 1978, p. 127). Friedman takes refuge in a vast volume of empirical evidence which has supported his claim for stability in the demand for money.

The Cambridge School, despite Robertson's trust in empirical investigation (Robertson, 1915), did not enquire empirically as to the stability of the demand for money, but relied, instead upon theoretical judgement. Robertson is fairly typical of their approach in the 1920s. He writes:

> the volume of bank loans has permanently increased by, let us say, 10% and so has the volume of money in the hands of the public. But since prices have risen by 10%, the aggregate real value of the public's money supply is no greater than it was before' (Robertson, 1922, 1928 edn, p. 92).

In other words, in the long run individuals act so as to restore the real value of their money balances disturbed by an increase in the money supply. Even in *Banking Policy and the Price Level* (Robertson, 1926, chapter 5, appendix 2), which was much more detailed in its analysis than *Money* (Robertson, 1922), Robertson upholds the proportionality of the money supply and the price level in the long run. As for the short run there may again be proportionality if 'normal' conditions prevail; that is, if there exists either moderate inflation or deflation. However, it was much more common to examine the short run as a period of instability. The interchange between Keynes and Robertson is very illuminating here (Presley, 1978, part II). As early as the *Tract* (1923) Keynes saw the demand for money varying over the course of the cycle; k is inclined to diminish during the boom and increase during the depression (Keynes, 1923, pp. 81–3). In particular, if, as the money supply increases, people expect further price increases, so a more than proportionate increase in the price level may result (pp. 75–81). Persuaded by Keynes, Robertson was to utilise this 'expectational' effect and, in addition, to appreciate the instability in the aggregate demand for money brought about by the redistribution of income and wealth taking place between fixed income groups and others during a period of changing money supply (Robertson, 1926, chapter 5). Robertson, particularly writing in 1928, had the experience of the higher inflation in Germany to draw upon, and this undoubtedly had some bearing upon his view of the stability of money demand.

Contrary to monetarist belief, Robertson, unlike others in the Cambridge School, saw the private sector as *inherently* unstable; the very nature of investment – the indivisibility of capital goods, the long gestation period associated with their purchase and manufacture and their durability – all worked to make the trade cycle an inevitable feature of industrial progress (Robertson, 1926, chapter 1). Following on from Marshall, Pigou, Keynes and Hawtrey all assembled theories of the trade cycle, generally stressing either monetary or psychological factors as causes of the cycle (Presley, 1978, part I); but none believed the economy to be *inherently* unstable, or that fluctuation itself may be desirable in the interest of progress, as did Robertson.

Friedman has placed much relevance upon empirical work to elucidate the time lags present in the monetary transmission process. Although the Cambridge School were aware that time lags did exist, there was no attempt to quantify these and consequently policy recommendations were formulated without a precise account being taken of the 'empirically perceived' dynamic nature of monetary transmission.

TOWARDS MONETARY POLICY

On monetary theory there is sufficient common ground between our authors to merit the description 'Cambridge School'. On matters of policy, however, there are some major dissimilarities in approach. For each author, whether it is the extreme of Robertson or Hawtrey, there is consistency between their own theoretical scheme and their policy outlook; but economic policy is *not* decided by reference to monetary theory alone. For Robertson money was only of secondary importance to the real forces at work in the economy (Robertson, 1922, Preface); Hawtrey, at the other extreme, believed that 'the trade cycle is a *purely* monetary phenomenon' (Hawtrey, 1913, p. 141). Despite this, *all* the major members of the Cambridge School were advocates of monetary policy to control prices and employment; albeit not necessarily advocates of 'long term' monetary policy, or for that matter, exclusively monetary policy to the neglect of other policies (except in the case of Hawtrey).

Despite some support for the long run proportionality between money supply and the price level, the Cambridge School never advocated a monetary growth rule, some long term mechanistic monetary policy to regulate prices. In policy matters most of their analysis and discussion focused upon the short or medium term; Keynes most quoted statement is perhaps: 'in the long run we are all dead'. Discretionary government policy, *short-term* government intervention was a feature of the Cambridge School; for the monetarists, the time lags in monetary effects indicated by empirical evidence led to the conclusion that long-term monetary policy will out perform any short-term discretionary monetary policy. (Mayer, 1978, pp. 90–1).

Robertson at times was the nearest, and at other times the farthest, from monetarism in policy issues. In the economic conditions of the 1930s he was the foremost proponent of fiscal policy, of public works expenditure to raise the level of employment (Robertson, 1930), and he doubted the ability of monetary policy, in the form of lower rates of interest, to create more investment. Yet, in the inflationary conditions of the 1950s, he was perhaps the strongest advocate in Britain of monetary policy. Inflation, he believed was caused by *monetary flabbiness* and should be counteracted by strict control of the growth of the money supply (Presley, 1978, part III). At the time his views were not popular; history tells us that the Radcliffe Report resulted in the fall from favour of monetary policy in the late 1950s in Britain. Clearly matters would have been much different had the Cohen Council on Prices, Productivity and Incomes been more adhered to in 1958. This Council of 'three wise men' which included Robertson, strongly recommended control of the money supply to remedy inflation. It concluded that the plentiful supply of money in the 1950s had created a situation of excessive monetary demand which was responsible for inflation. But even so, it believed that control of the money supply had its limitations, arguing that changes in the demand for money could either offset or reinforce such a monetary policy: 'Even if the quantity of money is not increased, the stream of monetary demand can be fed' (Cohen Council, 1958, appendix III, p. 71).

Unfortunately, with the exception of Hawtrey, the other members of the Cambridge School did not live into the late 1950s and 1960s, otherwise their policy views may well have been modified in the light of the economic conditions of the time.

Returning to the 1920s, the policy pronouncements of the Cambridge School were not only dictated by their theoretical stance, but by the economic conditions prevailing. Much of the debate focused upon the return to the Gold Standard, and was not characterised by the multitude of definitions of the money supply which now frame monetary discussion. The point of difference with monetarism in this respect is complicated by the history of periods when monetary aggregates did not change. As for monetary policy, the Cambridge School were primarily concerned with the behaviour of Bank Rate and the effect that changing interest rates might have upon spending and unemployment; there was no common view here; Robertson believed that no fall in Bank Rate would be sufficient to boost business confidence enough to generate more investment and an economic revival; from 1915 he had favoured public finance as the only effective route to revival. Hawtrey, in contrast, was the leading proponent of the 'Treasury View', that public expenditure must be at the expense of private sector spending and therefore should be avoided at all cost. He continued, throughout his life, to put forward this view; again he called for 'Bank Rate' policy believing that monetary control could be exercised via the rate of interest.

Moggridge and Howson write: 'Before the war Hawtrey had been the only "monetarist" member of the Cambridge School, the others playing down the role of money in the economy. Now Keynes . . . moved closer to Hawtrey's approach . . . he continued to share Hawtrey's interventionist approach to monetary policy' (Moggridge and Howson, 1974, p. 232). But even in the 1920s, Keynes did not acknowledge Bank Rate policy as a cure-all. He was very much aware of its limitations, recognising that there would need to be major changes in Bank Rate to provide any significant alteration to spending in both the inflationary conditions of the 1920s, and the extreme depression of the early 1930s (Howson, 1973, p. 463). It was not until 1932 that he seriously considered the kind of public works spending programme which others had been advocating in the 1920s and before.

SOME CONCLUSIONS

There is sufficient evidence to conclude that the Cambridge School is part of the family tree of monetarism. Indeed, on theoretical issues, it is closer to Friedman's work than is the recognised ancestry of the Chicago economists in the first half of this century; in approach, in emphasising the demand for money and its determinants, there is little difference between monetarism and Cambridge; this is also true of the monetary transmission mechanism. Where differences do appear is in relation to the *stability* of the demand for money; for although there was a tendency in the Cambridge School to treat the demand for money as stable in the long run, in the short run it may be highly unstable. Consequently on policy issues, given the economic conditions which prevailed in Britain when the Cambridge School was articulating its policy stance, there is some, but not total, common ground with monetarism. Monetary policy is certainly part of the policy armoury of the Cambridge School, particularly in the 1920s, but not the type of monetary policy which is restricted to a monetary stock target and acceptance of a monetary growth rule. Much more attention is devoted to bank rate policy as a short term, interventionist policy assisting in the control of cyclical fluctuations in the economy.

APPENDIX

Mayer's list of monetarist propositions

1. The quantity theory of money, in the sense of the predominance of the impact of monetary factors on nominal income.
2. The monetarist model of the transmission process.
3. Belief in the inherent stability of the private sector.
4. Irrelevance of allocative detail for the explanation of short-run changes in money income, and belief in a fluid capital market.
5. Focus on the price level as a whole rather than on individual prices.
6. Reliance on small rather than large econometric models.
7. Use of the reserve base or similar measure as the indicator of monetary policy.
8. Use of the money stock as the proper target of monetary policy.
9. Acceptance of a monetary growth rule.

10. Rejection of an unemployment-inflation trade-off in favour of a real Phillips-curve.
11. A relatively greater concern about inflation than about unemployment compared to other economists.
12. Dislike of government intervention.

REFERENCES

Bleaney, M. *The Rise and Fall of Keynesian Economics* (London: Macmillan, 1985).

Brunner, K. 'The Role of Money and Monetary Policy', *Federal Reserve Bank of St Louis Review*, 50 (1968): 9–24.

Cohen Council *Council on Prices, Productivity and Incomes* (First Report, London: HMSO, 1958).

Cross, R. *Economic Theory and Policy in the UK* (Oxford: Martin Robertson, 1982).

Eshag, E. *From Marshall to Keynes* (Oxford: Blackwell, 1963).

Fisher, I. *The Purchasing Power of Money* (New York: Macmillan, 1911).

Friedman, M. *Studies in the Quantity Theory of Money* (Chicago: Chicago University Press, 1956).

Friedman, M. 'A Theoretical Framework of Monetary Analysis', *Journal of Political Economy*, 78 (1970): 193–238.

Friedman, M. 'Monetary Policy: Theory and Practice', *Journal of Money, Credit and Banking*, February 1982.

Friedman, M. and A. J. Schwartz *A Monetary History of the United States 1867–1960* (Princeton: Princeton University Press, 1963).

Gordon, R. J. (ed.) *Milton Friedman's Monetary Framework* (Chicago: Chicago University Press, 1977).

Hawtrey, R. G. *Good and Bad Trade* (London: Constable, 1913).

Hawtrey, R. G. (1919) *Currency and Credit* (2nd edn, London: Longmans, 1923).

Howson, S. '"A Dear Money Man"?; Keynes on Monetary Policy, in the 1920's', *Economic Journal*, June (1973): 456–65.

Humphrey, T. M. 'D. H. Robertson and the Monetary Approach to Exchange Rates', *Federal Reserve Bank of Richmond Review*, May/June (1980).

Hutchison, T. W. *A Review of Economic Doctrines* (Oxford: Oxford University Press, 1953).

Keynes, J. M. *A Tract on Monetary Reform* (London: Macmillan, 1923).

Keynes, J. M. *The General Theory of Employment, Interest and Money* (London: Macmillan, 1936).

Laidler, D. 'Monetarism: An Interpretation and an Assessment', *Economic Journal* 91 (1981): March 1–28.

Lavington, F *The English Capital Market* (London: Methuen, 1921).

Macesich, G. *Monetarism* (New York: Praeger, 1983).

Marshall, A. *Principles of Economics* (London: Macmillan, 1890).

Marshall, A. *Money Credit and Commerce* (London: Macmillan, 1923).

Marshall, A. *Official Papers* (London: Macmillan, 1926).

Mayer, T. *The Structure of Monetarism* (New York: Norton, 1978).

Modigliani, F. 'The Monetarist Controversy or, Should We Forsake Stabilisation Policies', *American Economic Review*, 67 (1977): 1–19.

Moggridge, D. E. and S. Howson 'Keynes on Monetary Policy, 1910–46', *Oxford Economic Papers*, 26 July (1974), no. 2: 226–47.

Patinkin, D. *Essays on and in the Chicago Tradition* (Durham, North Carolina: Duke University Press, 1981).

Pigou, A. C. 'The Value of Money', *Quarterly Journal of Economics* 32 (1917): 38–65.

Pigou, A. C. *The Economics of Welfare* (London: Macmillan, 1920).

Pigou, A. C. (ed.) *Memorials to Alfred Marshall* (London: Macmillan, 1925).

Presley, J. R. *Robertsonian Economics* (London: Macmillan, 1978).

Robertson, D. H. (1915) *A Study of Industrial Fluctuation* (London: London School of Economics, reprint edn 1948).

Robertson, D. H. *Money* (Cambridge: Cambridge Economic Handbooks, 1922).

Robertson, D. H. *Banking Policy and the Price Level* (London: P. S. King & Son Ltd, 1926).

Robertson, D. H., Evidence to the Macmillan Committee, 8–9 May, 1930.

Robertson, D. H. *Lectures on Economic Principles* (London: Fontana, 1963).

Stein, J. L. (ed.) *Monetarism* (Amsterdam: North Holland, 1976).

Thornton, H. (1802) *An Enquiry into the Nature and Effects of the Paper Credit of Great Britain* (London: Allan & Unwin edn, 1939).

Tobin, J. 'A General Equilibrium Approach to Monetary Theory', *Journal of Money, Credit and Banking*, 1 (1969): 15–29.

10 Keynes's Economics: A Revolution in Economic Theory or in Economic Policy?[1]

BERNARD CORRY

INTRODUCTION

About 20 years ago the phrase 'we are all Keynesians now'[2] was commonplace. Keynesian economics was so in the ascendency that there was practically no alternative. 'National income analysis', as Keynesian economics was frequently called, *was* macroeconomics. There were isolated pockets of resistance but they were not to be found in the major centres of economics.

Now all this has changed, and to use Jerome Stein's terminology,[3] we now have 'three gospels' of macroeconomics – Monetarism, Keynesian and the New Classical Economics. It is difficult to assess the relative support for these three competing doctrines but my own guess is that Keynesianism is now clearly the minority view with its support coming largely from the older generation of economists. The 'gospels' clearly are competing doctrines because they present very different 'visions' of how capitalist market economics operate and have strikingly different policy implications. There are, of course, (almost) 57 varieties of Keynesianism, and attempts are now made to graft elements of other macro approaches into a Keynesian framework. Thus we have Keynesian models with rational expectations[4] and also the development of post-Keynesian economics[5] which is an attempt to use a much broader framework within the 'spirit' of Keynes.

It is not my intention in this paper to look at these varieties of Keynesianism nor at the subsequent developments. Nor shall I concern myself with the validity – in an empirical sense – of Keynesianism. Rather I want to look at what actually Keynes thought he was trying to achieve in the *General Theory* and whether that achievement warrants the use of the term revolutionary.

The paper is organised as follows; in section 1 we have a brief discussion of the notion of revolutionary thought and the allied concept of originality; section 2 outlines the case for arguing that Keynes was not revolutionary either in economic theory or in economic policy; section 3 then puts the revolutionary case; section 4 presents our conclusion, and also briefly tries to explain why the interpretation of Keynes offered here differs so widely from the standard treatment.

1. THE CONCEPT OF REVOLUTIONARY THOUGHT

I do not want us to get bogged down in essentialistic questions like 'What is the essence of revolutionary or original thought?' Nor do I want to rehearse yet again the 'Structure of Scientific Revolutions'[6] literature. I am not over-convinced of the value of such discussions. None the less, there are questions to be raised when we use terms like revolutionary or original and we have to look at some of them.

I think of the terms as being very close together and trying to encapsulate my own feeling, for a revolutionary idea in economics I would say that it is an idea that changes our 'vision' (in a Schumpeterian sense)[7] of how the economic system, or part of it works.

There are several possible answers to the question posed in the title of this paper;

(a) It may be argued that Keynes was neither revolutionary in terms of economic theory or in the design of economic policy;
(b) he was revolutionary in economic theory but not in economic policy;
(c) he was not revolutionary in economic theory but revolutionary in economic policy;
(d) he was revolutionary both in economic theory and economic policy.

I shall basically use this classification as a framework for the paper to be presented to you, and running ahead to the conclusion it is cell (d) into which I shall seek to place Keynes. That is to say, I shall argue that he was revolutionary both in terms of economic theory and policy. But I have to warn you that my reasons for this claim are somewhat different to those normally preferred.

There are several ambiguities in this classification that lie hidden there that must have provisional discussion, although they will also be exposed again as our story unfolds.

Ambiguity surrounds the very notion of 'revolutionary'. What do we wish to imply, what image is conjured up when we refer to a 'revolutionary idea' or a 'revolutionary thinker'? First, does revolutionary imply originality?

In general, I suppose, originality means the first statement of an idea, or an hypothesis or explanation of something. To be original is to originate an idea. Now I shall, in fact, argue that Keynes was original in this sense, but in general I do not see this notion of originality as digging up the quality of what we mean by original. It is surely not the first statement of an idea that is original but the realisation that the idea changes our 'vision' of how things operate or provides an explanation of an unhitherto unexplained event. To illustrate by an example from the history of microeconomics, I would argue that diminishing marginal utility originates not with the first statements of it (of which there were many!) but when it is first used to explain the empirical fact of a negative price-quantity relationship for most commodities. It is the realisation of the import of an idea, not its first statement *per se*, that makes it original.

A second ambiguity concerns the fact that an original idea may be wrong! And this is for several reasons. The idea may be 'analytically false', by which I mean that a certain alleged implication just does not follow logically from the structure of the model, or the implication from the new idea may turn out to be factually false.[8]

Unfortunately, or inevitably perhaps, economics with its half science, half non-science aura, dredges up two further aspects of this falsity issue. First of all it is often argued that a particularly theory may be 'right for its time' but not applicable outside its time period. For example, it may be argued that a sort of wages fund, advances, corn model is relevant to a pre-capitalist agricultural-based society but not to any other stage of economic development. Secondly, what is seen as 'original' or 'revolutionary' in past contributions may be a function of the current, today, state of that discipline. Both aspects occur in the interpretation of episodes in the history of economic thought – not the least, as we shall illustrate in a moment – in the interpretation of Keynes's contribution. Our second point above – that of today's economics influencing our views of past revolutionary or original contributions – is a most difficult one to handle. Time and again we observe changes in current thought forcing, wisely or unwisely, a re-evaluation of past contributions. It was, for example, under the direct influence of Keynes that earlier discussions of possible aggregate demand failures brought such writers as Malthus, Chalmers and Hobson[9] into a temporary home in the economists' hall of fame. Today in the light of the rejection of Keynes by Monetarists and New Classical economists we replace writers such as these with early statements of rational expectations, market clearing and the general nugatory character of government macro-interventionist policies, and researchers, so my spies tell me, are busily gleaning through dusty volumes at the British Library searching for original statements that general unemployment is a time when the work-force decides to take a vacation!

With these preliminaries aired, if not out of the way, let us now return to my original fourfold classification. To simplify, we can collapse it into two basic issues. Was Keynes a revolutionary, original thinker in economic theory? Was Keynes a revolutionary, original thinker in economic policy? We start with the theory issue.

Before getting into our analysis there are few other points that it is useful to clear out the way before embarking on an analysis of the vast literature on this subject.

In the first place we do have to note that Keynes himself was an avowed revolutionary and originator. He, like Jevons before him, stated explicitly his desire to revolutionise economics, and maximise the differences with the existing modes of thought. I have argued elsewhere that his passionate need for originality was a characteristic of the Bloomsbury group. The famous letter of Keynes to George Shaw is often quoted:[10]

I believe myself to be writing a book on economic theory that will largely revolutionise . . . the way the world thinks about economic problems . . . I can't expect you, or anyone else, to believe this at the present stage. But for myself I don't merely hope what I say, in my own mind I'm quite sure.

It may also have been connected with the androgynous nature of Keynes's personality. Virginia Woolf, for one, although she was probably quoting a firmly-held belief of the 'Bloomsbuggers',[11] thought that there was a strong connection between originality and androgyny. Of course, as with immortality, desire for originality and revolutionary status is no guarantee of successful accomplishment of that aim. But we do have to exercise extreme caution in evaluating revolutionary claims in those that openly profess them. The general inclination of such writers will be to emphasise, indeed maximise, their differences from the current paradigm, often by using the tactic of parodying the existing theories. In this they contrast with writers who temperamentally wish to play down discrete and sudden paradigm changes, and instead are at pains to assert continuity and the gradualist nature of theoretical change. Mill and Marshall are good examples of this approach, and in cases such as these we have to be careful not to fall into the opposite danger of underestimating the revolutionary and originality elements in their thought.

2. KEYNES WAS NOT A REVOLUTIONIST

Keynes was not a Revolutionist Theorist

There are two broad approaches to this claim, both of which have had their advocates over the years since the publication of the *General Theory*. Both these claims are separate from, although sometimes associated with, the claim that Keynes economics is just plain wrong!

The first approach of the non-revolutionists may be paraphrased under the slogan 'it had all been said before' and the method here is to take the basic individual elements in Keynes's approach and show their pre-Keynes origins. Taking the main elements of the Keynesian structure to be as follows:

1. The idea that output is (typically) demand constrained.
2. The consumption function and the multiplier.
3. The key role of expectations particularly with respect to private formation and the determination of interest rates.
4. Wages less flexible than prices.

Then the argument can be developed that each of these four elements, and in greater detail more elements could be added, had a long history pre-Keynes. What he did was to make them intellectually respectable via his own prestige and desire for originality.

A brief sketch of these pre-Keynesian and Keynesian histories would go something like this:

1. *Worries about aggregate demand*

The idea that changes in total spending would induce changes in output and employment goes back almost into pre-history. There are admittedly confusions as to whether it is real spending or nominal spending or both and there is a confusion between total demand and consumption. But, as Keynes pointed out in his attempt at a Keynesian lineage, we could here look at names like Petty, Berkeley, de Mandeville, Malthus, Chalmers, Lauderdale, Hobson etc.[12] This 'worries about demand' literature tends to follow the business cycle and peaks rather obviously in periods of depression. Thus we have bursts in the post-Napoleonic war period, in the late 1840s, in the 1880s, in the post–1918 period and in the 1930s. Interestingly enough though, we have not seen such a burst in the current depression. Much of this pre-Keynes demand literature is underconsumptionist or overproductionist in nature and does lead to the question 'was Keynes an underconsumptionist?'[13]

2. *The consumption function and the multiplier*

I suppose it is a reflection of how far away Keynes's thought was from neoclassical theory, and indeed *de facto* most economists' thought around the time of publication of the *General Theory*, that he did not emphasise, or even note, how far away the very notion of a consumption function was from orthodox neoclassical maximising theory. For an individual or household, income is an endogenous variable to be determined as part of the utility maximising process. The only constraints are the marginal rates of transformation between market and non-market work.

Nobody, certainly not Keynes, remarked on the important point that the very idea of a consumption function involved a 'rationing' model, until Clower's break-through paper.[14]

Before Keynes there is not much formal work on the consumption function, although a very clear statement of it is to be found in Lindahl and there was the Engels curve![15] It is obvious that the centre of interest only becomes the consumption function once divergences between ex ante saving and investment are thought, not just conceivable, but highly likely to occur.

The multiplier seems to have a much older history than its specific form in the consumption function.[16] It is clear, and acknowledged by Keynes, that he derived the concept entirely from Richard Kahn's seminal article,[17] but even before 1931 there appears to be a long lineage where the main elements of the concept – especially as a dynamic process – were clearly spelled out. Some of these early statements were admittedly rather vague references to extra spending being 'passed-on from hand to hand', but the notion of a dynamic process in the form of a geometric progression with a finite sum was established before Kahn. Indeed it may be argued that Keynes's presentation of the static multiplier in the *General Theory* was a retrograte step and inhibited for some years the proper understanding and importance of the concept.[18]

3. *The role of uncertainty*

It is sometimes stated that one of Keynes's major contributions – if not *the* major contribution – in the *General Theory*, was to place uncertainty at the very heart of macroeconomics reasoning. But what precisely does this vague claim amount to? The story goes somewhat as follows; neoclassical economics worked within an explicit (implicit) framework of perfect certainty, which implied a complete set of future markets ensuring automatic and continuous market clearing. Into this world Keynes placed uncertainty, not of the statistical probability type but rather of the 'every day is a new day' type. Genuine uncertainty where decisions are being taken today, based on guesses about the future state of key economic variables that are essentially unknowable. In Mort Sahl's language 'the future lies ahead'.[19]

Specifically there are two areas where Keynes emphasised the need to take particular account of uncertainty about the future. First of all, the very notion of the marginal efficiency of capital (MEC) is a subjective one since it involves the assessment of future rates of return to capital accumulation. Changes in expectations will affect rate of return estimates and hence shift the MEC schedule. These shifts, induced by market waves of optimism or pessimism, are much more important than the elasticity of the schedule with respect to interest rates. We thus see capital formation as the key to the macro-instability of market capitalism.

Uncertainty also enters into the demand for money, that is, Keynes's liquidity preference schedule. It is uncertainty with respect to bond prices that hinders the free movement of interest rates, in response to the changing relationship between the classical forces of productivity and thrift. So interest rates cease to act as the regulator of the desires to save and invest and the possibility of potential savings running to waste can be demonstrated.

Now was this aspect of Keynes new or had it all been said before? The 'nor new' proponents could certainly make a case. Keynes uncertainty seemed very close to the Knightian distinction between risk and uncertainty,[20] with uncertainty being essentially unpredictable in a statistical sense, and profit a reward for 'pure' uncertainty bearing. Moreover, the effects of swings in business psychology, or the propensity to invest, may also be called the 'Cambridge' theory of the trade cycle and is to be found in Marshall, Pigou and Lavington.[21]

The effect of uncertainty on the desire for liquidity and hence its effect on interest rates also is documented in the literature before Keynes.[22] And the other part of his interest analysis – the effect of money supply changes on interest rates, and hence the level of output, is even more prevalent in the history of monetary economics and, more relevant, it was part and parcel of the Marshallian monetary economics.[23]

4. *Wages and price flexibility*

We now come to what, for many observers of the Keynesian scene and of macroeconomics in general, is the real crux of the dispute. For these observers the major differences between Keynesian and other schools of macroeconomics all reduce to assumptions about labour market behaviour and in particular assumptions about the supply curve of labour. Moreover, since we are still, at this stage of our presentation, dealing with the critique of Keynes that argues 'it has all been said before', it is in the discussion of labour market behaviour that this critique is at its most vocal. Why is this? The argument may be put quite simply. In his specific analysis of the labour market – to be found in chapter 2 of the *General Theory*[24] – Keynes accepts the orthodox, neoclassical, theory of the aggregate demand function for labour. This means that with the assumption of profit maximising, competitive firms, and short-run diminishing marginal product to labour, the aggregate demand curve for labour is a negative function of the real wage rate. Thus, to obtain a result other than market clearing, Keynes had to specify something different from neoclassical analysis about the supply curve of labour. What he did was to suggest resistance to money wage cuts so that the traditional remedy for general unemployment – wage flexibility – was not an option. Now, the 'nothing new in Keynes' school argue, with more than considerable justification, if this is what Keynes is really about then, (a) it is not a theoretical breakthrough and (b) it was well known and frequently stated as a major cause of unemployment.

A sub-argument was that Keynes did, at least, provide some theoretical explanation of the well-documented fact that wages were generally less flexible than prices, so that real wages would tend to move perversely in a recession. Early interpretations of Keynes assumed that he had posited some sort of money illusion in the labour supply function,[25] but this gradually gave way to the relative wage hypothesis,[26] and subsequently wage resistance has been rationalised via implicit contract theory.[27] But, as is well known, money wage inflexibility was only Keynes's first, and unimportant, line of defence. He went on to say that even with money wage flexibility, there was no guarantee that this would ensure real-wage flexibility. Prices might simply follow money wages downwards and the beneficial effects of the deflation on interest rates via the rise in the real money supply, could be negated by speculative activity or even if this effect did operate, expenditure might be interest inelastic. The final twist of the knife seems to have come with the Pigou-Patinkin analysis of the real balance effect.[28] Keynes's supreme theoretical triumph, the proof of less than full employment equilibrium was either wrong once wage-price flexibility was allowed, or trivial if it was based on money wage inflexibility.

In summary the main arguments that Keynes was not original or revolutionary in economic theory are as follows:

(a) The building blocs of the Keynesian system were all there and well established before Keynes wrote the *General Theory*.

(b) In fact it was not the building blocs – for example, the consumption function, the marginal efficiency of capital, liquidity preference, and so on, that turned out to be of crucial analytic importance. Rather it was assumptions made about the working of the labour market.

(c) If Keynes allowed wage-price flexibility, which in fact he did, then he was analytically wrong in thinking that he had captured equilibrium involuntary unemployment.[29] If on the other hand he wished to remain with money wage inflexibility, he had rediscovered the obvious.

Keynes as a Non-Revolutionary in Economic Policy

We now turn to consider the case that, in terms of policy proposals, Keynes was simply reiterating a point of view that had had its advocates through many generations of economists and, moreover, that the very school of thought that Keynes attacked so vehemently in his theoretical work was absolutely in common with him when policy issues were under discussion. This argument takes the standpoint the Keynes's major contributions to the conduct of economic policy were twofold, one a positive, one a negative. They were:

(a) The advocacy of a policy of counter-cyclical public expenditure ('public works') to smooth the cyclical pattern of market capitalism. The theory behind such a proposal followed directly from Keynes's macro-model, and specifically from the theory of the multiplier. Keynes further argued that, in periods of depression, public expenditure should be deficit funded and would not 'crowdout' private expenditure.
(b) The rejection – and this was the negative aspect of his policy proposal – of wage cuts as a solution to general unemployment.

Now in what sense were the advocacy of counter-cyclical public works policy and the objection to wage cuts new?

Public works, as a means of dealing with unemployment, have long been advocated.[30] The history of such ideas goes back to, at least, Petty (see his *Political Arithmetic*), and was resurrected in most depression periods. So, for example, there are numerous pamphlets in each depression phase of the nineteenth century. But it is true that most of the early literature does not clearly distinguish public works as part of a general poverty programme from those designed specifically to deal with the downturn of the trade cycle. Moreover, the early schemes are basically of what may be termed 'the make-work' variety rather than as part of a general macro-strategy.

One of the first clear statements of the counter-cyclical aspect of public expenditure and a statement so often quoted – is the famous Webbs' minority report to the Royal Commission on the Poor Law (1908)[31] and elaborated in their *The Prevention of Destitution* (1911).[32] They were quickly followed, not simply by other unorthodox writers (if that is the correct description of the Webbs), but by orthodox Marshallians like Pigou.[33] Keynes, of course, had outlined the major elements of his macroeconomic policy in his Liberal Party pamphlet *Lloyd George Can Do It* written with Henderson.[34]

The objection to wage cuts, acting as a method of dealing with large-scale unemployment, does seem to be associated more uniquely with Keynes than the public expenditure aspect of his theory of economic policy. Certainly at the theoretical level very few writers before Keynes had doubled the efficacy of wage cuts as a solution, or at least partial solution, to the unemployment problem.[35] Indeed, one of the most enduring policy proposals in the whole history of economics has been this very proposition. The theoretical basis of it has changed from paradigm, but through thick and thin unemployment has been seen as the 'punishment' for asking too much, and employment the reward for not so doing. In pre-classical thought emphasis was placed in the supply curve of labour, it was assumed to be backward-bending in the relevant range, hence to increase employment and output, a fall in real wages was required and advocated. Classical economic thought switched to demand constrained situations in the labour market. The demand for labour, given the real wage, was determined by the wages fund which was assumed to be pre-determined and hence fairly constant in the short run. It thus followed that unemployment could be reduced by reductions to the average real wage. Even Marx's analysis incidently provided a similar relationship between the real wage and employment. A fall in real wages will increase the rate of exploitation and hence, for a given organic composition of capital, raise the rate of profit.

Neoclassical economic theory usually derives the real wage-employment relationship (although strictly it is a real wage-demand for labour relationship) from the notion of an aggregate production function which in turn is derived from the cost minimising behaviour of micro-producer decision units. The short-run aggregate production function, with the assumption of a given capital stock and state of technology, and hence, of diminishing marginal product of labour, is inverted to give a demand function for labour which is negative with respect to the real wage.[36]

So the policy view that a reduction in real wages will increase employment has a very long intellectual history. Now Keynes then came on the scene. He did not advocate money wage cuts as a solution to the unemployment problem. Was he therefore saying something very different? Well we are still, in this section, looking at arguments that Keynes was not a revolutionary thinker and the arguments here for his view must be rehearsed.

The first point frequently made is that many 'orthodox' economists had ceased to argue for wage cuts well before Keynes published the *General Theory*. Admittedly official policy seemed to still believe in the employment-creating possibilities of a general reduction in wages, but Pigou, for example, had ceased to advocate them as a feasible policy measure.[37]

Secondly, what exactly was Keynes's position on wage cuts? Did he really doubt the efficacy of real wage cuts? Was he not rather saying that it would be difficult, and socially devisive, to try to impose money wage cuts? And that if you suceeded it might not lead to real wage cuts because of the tendency for product prices to follow money wages downwards. So nominal wage flexibility was the theoretical equivalent of an increase in the real money supply, and the result was just as easily, or more easily, achieved by increasing the money supply. But, in general, a reduction in money wages would increase employment, so what was he saying that was really different? This then is the essence of the 'Keynes was not a Revolutionary' argument as far as the objection to wage-reduction policy is concerned. I shall have a good deal more to say about this issue when we turn to the case for Keynes as a Revolutionary.

Summary of section 2: Keynes as a Non-Revolutionary

In terms of economic theory, the possibilities and consequences of effective demand failures has a long history. The particular building blocs of Keynes's version of demand failures were also well established before the *General Theory*. Subsequent work in the structure of Keynesian economics showed that the crucial element was nominal wage inflexibility, and this is not a matter of a theoretical revolution but an agreed empirical fact about the way in which the labour market works.

In terms of a revolution in policy, the focus on public expenditure and effective demand, and specifically the focus on counter-cyclical public works expenditure, once again has a well-documented pre-Keynes history.

On the question of wage cuts, the orthodox school were themselves ambiguous and anyhow Keynes, on balance, thought that they would increase employment.

3. KEYNES AS A REVOLUTIONARY

Once again we shall proceed by first looking at economic theory and then at the advocacy of economic policy.

Keynes as a Revolutionary Theorist

As I have already mentioned, Keynes certainly thought that his *General Theory* was revolutionary, and he saw this revolution as having both a negative effect and a positive effect. Negatively he wanted to destroy certain existing doctrines, or if not destroy, argue that they were of very limited real world applicability, being only relevant to periods of full employment. It was for this reason that Keynes used the title *General Theory*. The two existing doctrines that he threw over were of course, Say's Law and the Quantity Theory of Money. From the *Tract on Monetary Reform* (1923)[38] Keynes had expressed doubts about the traditional analysis of a monetary economy. In the *Treatise*[39] he extended these doubts and began the elements of an alternative analysis, and it was as the *Treatise* was completed that Keynes realised that he was not to *modify* the classical analysis but rather *totally throw it over*. The process was a difficult one that he describes so well in the preface to the *General Theory*,

> The composition of this book has been for the author a long struggle of escape, and so must the reading of it for most readers if the author's assault upon them is to be successful, – a struggle from habitual modes of thought and expression. The ideas which are here expressed so laboriously are extremely simple and should be obvious. The difficulty lies, not in the new ideas, but in escaping from the old ones, which ramify, for those brought up as most of us have been, into every corner of our minds.[40]

Now, as we would expect, Keynes had difficulties on both counts. To persuade his colleagues to give up the past, and to persuade them to accept his new ideas. Age seems to have been the dominant factor in both counts – we see a similar picture in current macroeconomics with the Keynesian 'old guard' accused of being incapable either of comprehending the faults in their analysis or of getting to grips with the modern new classical macroeconomics. In particular, what upset

Keynes was not that the *General Theory* might be wrong, but that the older generation had simply not understood what he was trying to say. His exasperation with Dennis Robertson[41] has been referenced frequently, but he wrote in similar tone to Pigou and Beveridge.[42]

I do not have time here to dwell on the negative aspects of Keynes's revolution, nor are they germane to the direct concern of this paper. Let us instead concentrate on what Keynes was trying to achieve, that, in his view, was new. Something that had not been worked out successfully before. What was this? Here it seems to me that the answer is fairly simple, direct and Keynes never wavered from it, or had any doubts its importance or its originality.

It was to work out a theory of the determination of output, primarily with reference to the short period, that is where the capital stock is fairly constant, but his analysis was also applicable, or so he thought, to the long period. His complaint was that the orthodox tradition from Ricardo through to Marshall had no *theory* of the determination of output as a whole other than, perhaps, that it was constant at the full employment level,

> Alfred Marshall, on whose *Principles of Economics* all contemporary English economists have been brought up, was at particular pains to emphasise the continuity of his thought with Ricardo's. His work largely consisted of grafting the marginal principle of substitution on to the Ricardian tradition, and his theory of output and consumption as a whole, as distinct from his theory of the production and distribution of a *given* output, was never separately expounded. Whether he himself felt the need for such a theory, I am not sure. But his immediate successors and followers have certainly dispensed with it and have not, apparently, felt the lack of it. It was in this atmosphere that I was brought up. I taught these doctrines myself and it is truly within the last decade that I have been conscious of their insufficiency.[43]

Looked at this way, we can see that Keynes was trying to complete a piece of the Marshallian research programme. Marshall had analysed short-period equilibrium at the firm and industry level and here was Keynes doing the equivalent at the macro-level – at the level of total output. Just as Marshall had industry equilibrium when demand-price – a negative function of output – equalled supply-price – a positive function of output, so Keynes had total output equilibrium when aggregate demand-price equalled supply-price. And the effective demand was aggregate demand at the point of equilibrium.

The stability conditions that Keynes imposed on his macro-model may also be viewed as the application of Marshall's stability conditions to the volume of output as a whole. Recall that Marshall's condition for the stability of micro-market equilibrium was that

$$
\begin{aligned}
\text{for } Q_a < Q_e \qquad & D_p > S_p \\
\text{for } Q_a > Q_e \qquad & D_p < S_p \\
\text{for } Q_a = Q_e \qquad & D_p = S_p
\end{aligned}
$$

where Q_e = equilibrium output, Q_a = actual output, D_p = demand price S_p = Supply price.

Keynes's macro-stability conditions may be written as:

$$
\begin{aligned}
\text{for } Y_a < Y_e \qquad & AD > AS \\
\text{for } Y_a > Y_e \qquad & AD < AS \\
\text{for } Y_a = Y_e \qquad & AD = AS. \text{[44]}
\end{aligned}
$$

The stability of Macro-Equilibrium in Keynes's System

I have argued that Keynes's main theoretical concern was to provide a theory of the level of output. He further assumed that the stability conditions were satisfied, and hence output so determined would give a stable equilibrium, in the sense that a change in one of the exogenous variables or system parameters would be needed to change that equilibrium. Now this fitted in with another aspect of Keynes's programme, and that was to explain the 'real world' situations of an economy stuck at less than full capacity output equilibrium. Keynes, in the title of his revolutionary work, spoke of the *General Theory of Employment* not, you will note output, which is the variable we have emphasised so far. Why? Well naturally it was employment or the lack of it that was Keynes overwhelming concern, not just cyclical variations around a notional full employment trend but longish periods of general unemployment that could be described as less than full employment equilibrium, in the sense that market forces as they operated in the real world would not easily or quickly right the system back to full employment.[45] We shall deal in detail with Keynes's view of the labour market in the next part of this paper, but just note at this stage that Keynes wanted to account for a system where aggregate output was in equilibrium in the sense that, given the constraints, output decision-makers were optimising and, at the same time, the labour market was not in equilibrium.[46]

Keynes's treatment, though, of what we could call disequilibrium equilibrium, does leave open certain questions about his stability analysis. The main question is whether he was explaining stable equilibria that were randomly shocked to new equilibria or whether his theory was also intended to explain the cyclical path of capitalism. Before Keynes, although there is an element of truth in his assertion that classical and neoclassical macroeconomics had a built-in assumption of full employment growth, there was also a fairly voluminous literature on cycles in output and employment.[47] Was Keynes simply making a further contribution to this literature as it is sometimes alleged? The issue is complicated, and one feels that Keynes himself had not quite made up his own mind. He certainly did not think that he was providing yet another explanation of an economy subject to regular fluctuations, but trending at full resource utilisation. Indeed he regarded it as rare that even in a boom full employment would be achieved. The main thrust of the *General Theory* is not about periodic cyclical movements, but about the determinants of equilibrium output, with this equilibrium output having no necessary connection with full employment output. Admittedly he does make application of his analysis to the question of the trade cycle (see chapter 22, 'Notes in the Trade Cycle') and he does begin that chapter by stating, 'Since we claim to have shown in the preceding chapters what determines the volume of employment at any time, it follows, if we are right, that our theory must be capable of explaining the phenomena of the Trade Cycle'. He goes on to say that 'the regularity of time-sequence and of duration which justifies us in calling it a *cycle*, is mainly due to the way in which the marginal efficiency of capital fluctuates'.[48]

Keynes's basic explanation of these fluctuations in the marginal efficiency of capital is really one of swings in entrepreneurial expectations from optimism to pessimism, and in this sense Keynes's theory of the cycle is in the tradition of what we earlier called the Cambridge Theory of the Trade Cycle. But to repeat, I do not think that Keynes's main interest was in the trade cycle as such, it was rather to have a formal theory of the determination of output and hence of employment. And it is to the relationship between output theory and employment theory, and hence the labour market, that we must now turn, for it is here that we shall seek to show Keynes's genuine revolutionary contribution to economic theory.

Employment and The Labour Market

In the section where we discussed the case for considering Keynes as a non-revolutionary, it was pointed out that the interpretation of Keynes is that he accepted the 'classical' demand function for labour, and hence really only differentiated his analysis of the labour market by trying to reject the 'classical' supply function for labour. This interpretation of Keynes is very common, and is written into most so-called Keynesian macro-models. Indeed, it does seem to be conformable to what Keynes actually wrote in chapter 2 of the *General Theory*.

I now wish to argue that:

(a) If this was indeed what Keynes intended it is completely incompatible with his basic macro-model.
(b) If one looks carefully at chapter 2 of the *General Theory* there are hints, which are made absolutely explicit in his 1939 paper 'Relative Movements of Real Wages and Output',[49] that he had rejected the classical demand for labour analysis.

We must look carefully at both points. Point (a) suggests that he himself had not really thought through his analysis of the labour market. Keynes's basic model is extremely simple – really devoid of the complex analysis and taxonomy to be found in Pigou's *Theory of Unemployment*.[50] Output is an increasing function of investment (including the net trade balance) and specifically of the form

$$Y_t = KI_t$$

where K is the multiplier and consumption is $I\,[K-1]$. Note that current investment $[I_t]$ is largely dependent on what expectations were about the marginal efficiency of capital and about interest rates today, N periods ago. In this sense investment and hence output is exogenous in that current events and their effects on our expectations about the future have no effect on current investment.

With output determined, and for a given state of the technology of production – that is the form of the aggregate production function – there is a fixed relationship between output and employment. So the sequence of events in Keynes's vision is:

Effective demand → output → employment; and unemployment is found as the residual from labour supply minus employment.

Now this is clearly counter to the classical reasoning of a demand for labour schedule that makes employment (as the dependable variable) a function of the real wage (as the independent variable). The classical sequence is:

Real wage → employment → output.

Perhaps a diagram will help to explain the difference.

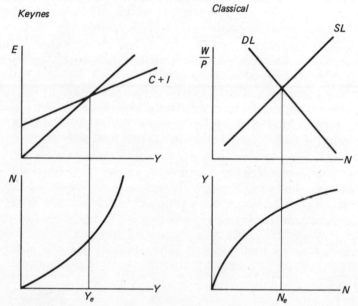

E = expenditure, Y = output, Y_e = equilibrium output, N = employment, N_e = equilibrium employment, DL = demand for labour, SL = supply of labour, W/P = real wage.[51]

FIGURE 10.1

To put the contrast in a nutshell, in a classical system employment is determined in the *labour market*, in Keynes it is determined in the *output market*. Keynes completely reversed the casual sequence of the classical analysis. He downgrades the labour market; it really has no role to play other than, given the supply of labour, to determine the volume of unemployment.

Given that current output and employment has been determined by decisions taken in the past, based on what entrepreneurs though what 'today' would look like, there is no reason, other than pure accident, why the volume of output so decided should generate jobs for all those seeking them. The labour market will rarely be in equilibrium, in the sense of full employment, even in boom times. Capitalist organisation will normally produce unemployment due to lack of effective demand. Moreover, even though disequilibrium will be the norm for the labour market, there will be no tendency for correction because output is 'stuck' at its equilibrium.

Now Keynes's approach is fundamentally different from the classical analysis and, I believe, very different from most interpretations of Keynes. It certainly deserves the adjective 'revolutionary'.

I now turn to point (b). Is there really an inconsistency in Keynes between his '*General Theory*' and his analysis of the labour market in chapter 2? As we shall see when we turn to look in detail at his 1939 paper, it is the output model that Keynes was advocating, but most commentators assume that he accepted the classical demand for labour in his *General Theory* – hence, for example, he would have to admit (or plead inconsistency) that a fall in real wages would increase employment in a regime of unemployment. But I must confess that I find this interpretation hard to swallow. Let's look at chapter 2 again. He certainly begins by stating that a classical postulate is that 'the wage is equal to the marginal product of labour',[52] and further, that in the classical world this postulate 'gives us the demand schedule for employment'. He then states that 'we shall maintain the first postulate as heretofore'.[53] But when he then goes on to explain what he means by this postulate it is very different from the classical interpretation and perfectly in line with his output model.

'It means' he writes, 'that, with a given organisation, equipment and technique, real wages and the volume of output (and hence of employment) are uniquely correlated, so that, in general, an increase in employment can only occur to the accompaniment of a decline in the rate of real wages'. Note that this quotation just denotes correlation. There is no suggestion of cause and effect. But Keynes continues:

> thus *if* employment increases, then, in the short period, the reward per unit of labour in terms of wage-goods must, in general, decline and profits increase. This is simply the observation of the familiar proposition that industry is normally working subject to decreasing returns in the short period during which equipment etc. is assumed to be constant; so that the marginal product in the wage-good industries (which governs real wages) necessarily diminishes as

employment is increased. So long, indeed, as this proposition holds, *any* means of increasing employment *must lead at the time to a diminution of the marginal product and hence of the rate of wages measured in terms of this product.*[54]

This quotation, it seems to me, *does* imply causation and it is from employment to the real wage. Not the classical demand for labour function. If you feel that the matter is still ambiguous and not as clear cut as I wish to imply, then you only have to turn to the 1939 paper where Keynes's position is crystal clear. Keynes's *Economic Journal* article was a response to articles in the same journal by Dunlop and Tarshis.[55] They had tried to test empirically Keynes's (and the classical) contention that there was a negative correlation between real wages and output – and hence employment. Their results seem to conflict with Keynes's relationship – they found rather, as has most subsequent research,[56] that output and real wages are positively correlated. They further assumed that their results 'refuted' a key element in the structure of the *General Theory*. Keynes's reply to them is obviously then of the utmost significance. He accepts their results and states that it is incompatible with what he had assumed in his own analysis, but this does not worry him at all as it must have done if he had really accepted that first 'classical postulate'. Far from being worried:

> If, however, it proves right to adopt the contrary generalisation, it would be possible to simplify considerably the more complicated version of my fundamental explanation which I have expounded in my *General Theory*. My practical conclusions would have, in that case, *a fortiori* force.[57]

And this for obvious reasons; it got away from the allegations of money illusion in the labour supply function, it reduced the fears of rapidly rising marginal costs and prices as an engineered expansion of demand made progress.

Keynes as a Revolutionary Policist

In section 2 where we looked at the view that Keynes was not a revolutionary figure in the practice of economic policy, the argument was made that his policy advocacy rested upon the twin towers of counter-cyclical public expenditures and the opposition to general wage reductions as a method of reducing unemployment. We pointed out, as have many critics of Keynes, that neither of these views were unique to Keynes. We must now consider these matters further. First the question of counter-cyclical policies; just as Keynes's analysis was not primarily about explanations of the trade cycle, although it did throw some light on it, so his main policy proposals were not about, or made for, an economy trending at full capacity but with a cycle imposed or built into it. The main policy implication of Keynes's *General Theory* was that an economic system, driven solely by capitalist market signals, would rarely produce enough output to employ all those who sought work. The policy implication is the need for permanent macro-control and intervention if full employment is to be maintained and Okun gaps minimised. Now this is a very different policy message from traditional trade cycle policy. Moreover, Keynes was not sanguine about the ability to control private capital expenditure via monetary policy particularly in conditions of depression.[58] His main instrument for macro-stability at a high employment output was direct public expenditure through public or private agencies, mainly on what he termed 'social capital', by which he meant capital projects that would not be undertaken if purely market signals were used.

The revolutionary nature of Keynes's policy message did *not* lie in 'how to cure a slump' as is often supposed, but rather in 'how to avoid slumps'. Now this is not just a subtle difference of language but really points, in my view, to a fundamental change in our way of thinking about the macroeconomic stability of capitalism. Keynes was not over-optimistic about the ability of an economy to pull itself rapidly out of a depression even with 'correct' economic policies. The way to prosperity from depression was slow and difficult; the message rather was 'don't get into severe recession', take measures before the economy is stuck in a low output, low employment, trap.

On the question of wage-cuts and employment, Keynes was clearly arguing something very different from the classical analysis. He was prepared to admit the possibility that at a new, lower, level of wages, the increase in the real money supply may lower interest rates and hence may stimulate investment, but there were an awful lot of 'maybe's' involved. Keynes's main concern though was not this aspect, but much more crucially, that the dynamics of the system, out of equilibrium, might well generate large instabilities. How decision-takers react to falling wages and prices is anybody's guess, and any semblance of a real-balance effect can easily be frustrated by the rising burden of fixed debt and consequent bankruptcies that deflation brings. Deflation as a cure for unemployment has a very hollow ring about it!

4. CONCLUSION AND SOME REMARKS ON INTERPRETATIONS OF KEYNES

I have tried to argue, and I hope, convince you, that Keynes was a truly revolutionary thinker. To recall, by 'revolutionary', I mean a set of ideas that fundamentally change our way of thinking about how the world works and Keynes did just that. He took the employment decision of traditional labour market analysis and placed it firmly in the output market. He abandoned the classical demand for, and supply of, labour approach and reversed the classical sequence of real wage to employment. This gives us a fundamentally different vision of how capitalist market economies operate. I must emphasise that I am not here concerned with the correctness or otherwise of this alternative vision but rather to persuade you that it *is* a different vision.

Likewise, this Keynesian vision forces a fundamental rethink of the correct macro-policy strategies to avoid the under-use of labour – the great curse of capitalism. Planning for full employment has to become a central and continuous concern of economic policy.

Now, apart from one or two notable exceptions,[59] our interpretation of Keynes's vision is very different from what may be termed the orthodox treatment. As we have already noted, there are many varieties of Keynesianism – perhaps our version should be labelled 'unrepentent Keynesian'. But the most common theme that emerged from the early interpretations of Keynes was what was to be known as the neoclassical synthesis. Technically, the debate about 'Keynes versus the classics' lost its drama of genuinely competing 'paradigms' or 'visions' and became one of the econometric arguments about the particular forms of the IS and LM curves. Admittedly, it has been argued that this form of the debate is in the spirit of Keynes[60] but obviously it is rather far removed from the interpretation presented here. What trimmed the revolutionary sails from Keynes's original vision was the treatment of the labour market – this really is our central point – and a major influence in this process came with Modigliani's seminal paper.[61] This was the first formal treatment of the labour market in a 'Keynesian' model, and set the pattern for most subsequent work. The demand for labour function is unambiguously neoclassical with the causality from the real wage to employment. And this was the pattern set for the standard macro-textbooks upon which generations of economics students were reared.[62] The resultant product, frequently referred to as the neoclassical synthesis, was most appropriately named for it had much more in common, both in terms of economic theory and economic policy, with classical analysis than with Keynes.

Parallel with this interpretation, this emasculation of Keynes, there did develop what is termed 'macroeconomics with quantity rationing' with signal contributions from Patinkin, Clower; Leijonhufvud, Barro and Grossman and many others,[63] but even these approaches, whilst they did allow for situations off the labour demand curve, and hence found no clear relationship between the real wage and employment, none the less still incorporated the classical demand curve for labour. It is this step which has been taken in so many interpretations of Keynes that seem to me to miss the revolutionary character of Keynes's contribution to economics.

I stated at the beginning of this paper that it would not be our concern here to assess the validity of Keynes's theory. However, it does seem to me that recent economic events, not just in the United Kingdom economy, but throughout the capitalist system, exhibiting as they do a rather rapid increase in the unemployment rate which then bottomed out to high but fairly stable levels of unemployment, is exactly the situation Keynes was concerned with. This is in spite of large variations in wages, prices, growth rates, and so on. It is surely this phenomenon – of a low level employment trap – that was Keynes's overwhelming desire to explain and help us avoid. We seem to have ignored his message.

NOTES

1. Part of the research for this paper was undertaken whilst I was the holder of a Senior Research Fellowship funded by the Economic and Social Research Council. I am grateful to the Council for this support. In an earlier paper on Keynes (Corry, 1978) I was mainly concerned with Keynes conscious desire to be a revolutionary thinker and the way in which, as part of his tactics, he gave a rather bizarre account of the history of macroeconomics. In this paper I am only concerned with the revolutionary and original nature of the *General Theory* and I wish to emphasise this aspect of his work much more than I did in the earlier paper. My assessment of Keynes, whilst not the common or usual one, follows very

much the contributions of, for example, Weintraub (1958), Davidson, (1978), and Wells (1960, 1974, 1978).

2. The phrase is usually ascribed to Milton Friedman.
3. Stein (1982).
4. See Taylor (1980) as an example.
5. See Eichner (1979).
6. Kuhn (1970).
7. Schumpeter (1954), especially chapter 4.
8. Examples of a theory being discarded because it is factually false seem to be very rare in economics. One might assume that any theory that predicts a secularly falling wage share has been falsified but it is surprising – perhaps not – what alibies are produced!
9. Chalmers (1832); Malthus (1951); Hobson and Mummery (1956).
10. Corry (1978) p. 4.
11. Rose (1978) p. 188 (see also Hession, 1984, chapter 6).
12. These are the writers referred to in the *General Theory*, chapter 23, as having particular 'Keynesian' insights. All references to the *General Theory* are to the *Collected Writings of J. M. Keynes*, vol. 7.
13. This is an interesting question that we cannot deal with here. Much may depend upon our interpretation of the term 'underconsumption' or the allied term 'overproduction'. It may be argued that Keynes's hypothesis of a declining marginal propensity to consume hinted at underconsumption, but the fact that he had consumption reacting passively to income changes in his model precludes consumption changes acting as an independent force in economic disturbances (for more on this see Bleaney, 1976).
14. Clower (1965, 1967).
15. Lindahl (1939).
16. Hegeland (1954).
17. Kahn (1931).
18. Plus the fact that Keynes changed his definitions of saving and investment, so that those who had thought they had mastered the *Treatise* were utterly confused by the *General Theory*.
19. Sahl (1965).
20. Knight (1957).
21. Pigou (1914, 1927), Lavington (1922); Marshall (1926).
22. Hahn (1956).
23. See Eshag (1963).
24. Keynes [1836] 1973, chapter 2.
25. Leontief, 1948.
26. Trevethick (1976).
27. Azariadis (1976).
28. Pigou (1941), D. Patinkin (1965).
29. As Johnson put it, 'underemployment equilibrium in Keynes's system depends on wage rigidity' (Johnson, 1964, p. 142).
30. Garraty (1977).
31. S. Webb and B. Webb (1908). (Report referred to in Webb and Webb, 1911.)
32. S. Webb and B. Webb (1911).
33. Pigou (1914).

34. Keynes (1973), vol. 7.
35. Although it was never too clear whether they were discussing real or money cuts in wages or both.
36. For a typical exposition see Cuddington *et al.* (1984), chapter 1.
37. Pigou (1933).
38. Keynes (1973), vol. 4.
39. Keynes (1973), vols 5 and 6.
40. Keynes (1973), vol. 7, p. xxii.
41. See especially Presley (1979) and Danes (1981).
42. Keynes (1973), vol. 8, p. 00 and p. 00.
43. Keynes (1973), vol. 7 p. xxv. This quotation is to be found in the prefaces to the German and Japanese editions of the *General Theory*. It is not to be found in the English edition.
44. This 'Marshallian' inheritance has not received much comment but see Chick (1983).
45. This is exactly the sort of situation that much of the world is in today (1985) and has been for some years. To argue whether this situation represents equilibrium or disequilibrium does, I must confess, strike me as rather trivial.
46. Here we see the affinity between Keynes and the more recent 'rationing' literature (see, for example, Cuddington, *et al.* (1984), chapter 2).
47. See, for example, Haberler (1946), Link (1959).
48. Keynes (1973), vol. 7, p. 313.
49. Keynes (1973), vol. 7, pp. 394ff. This paper first appeared in the *Economic Journal*, March, 1939.
50. Pigou (1933).
51. This diagram is taken from Wells (1978).
52. Keynes (1973), vol. 7, p. 5.
53. Keynes (1973), vol. 7, p. 17.
54. Keynes (1973), vol. 7, p. 17–18. My italics.
55. Dunlop (1938); Tarshis (1939).
56. For recent surveys of the empirical relationship see Neftci (1978), Sargent (1978), Drobny (1985).
57. Keynes (1973), vol. 7, p. 401.
58. Keynes (1973), vol. 7, chapter 22.
59. Those writers referred to in note 1.
60. Jackman, (1974).
61. Modigliani (1944).
62. As examples see Klein (1947), Derburg and MacDougall (1960), Ackley (1961), Bailey (1962), Allen (1967).
63. See Cuddington *et al.*, Part I (1984).

REFERENCES

Ackley, G. *Macroeconomic Theory* (New York: Macmillan, 1961).
Allen, R. G. D. *Macro-economic Theory* (London: Macmillan, 1967).
Azariadis, C. 'On the incidence of unemployment', *Review of Economic Studies*, vol. 43 (1976).

Bailey, M. *National Income and the Price Level* (New York: McGraw-Hill, 1962).

Bleaney, M. F. *Underconsumption Theories* (London: Lawrence & Wishart, 1976).

Chalmers, T. *On Political Economy in Connexion with the Moral State and Moral Prospects of Society* (Glasgow: Collins, 1832).

Chick, V. *Macroeconomics after Keynes: A reconsideration of the General Theory* (Oxford: Philip Allan, 1983).

Clower, R. W. 'The Keynesian Counterrevolution: A Theoretical Appraisal', in F. P. R. Brechling and F. H. Hahn (eds) *The Theory of Interest Rates* (London: Macmillan, 1965).

Clower, R. W. 'A Reconsideration of the Microfoundations of Monetary Theory', *Western Economic Journal*, 6 (1967).

Corry, B. A. 'Keynes place in the History of Economic Thought', in A. P. Thirlwall (ed.) *Keynes and Laissez-faire* (London: Macmillan, 1978).

Cuddington, J. P. O. Johannson and K-G. Lofgren *Disequilibrium Macroeconomics in Open Economies* (Oxford: Blackwell, 1984).

Danes, M. *Dennis Robertson and the Construction of Aggregate Theory* unpublished PhD thesis, London University (Queen Mary College) 1981.

Davidson, P. *Money and the Real World* (London: Macmillan, 1978).

Dernburg, T. F. and D. M. MacDougall *Macroeconomics* (New York: McGraw-Hill, 1960).

Drobny, A. D. *Real Wages and Employment: A Theoretical and Empirical Analysis* PhD thesis, Cambridge University, 1985.

Dunlop, J. G. 'The Movement of real and money wages rates', *Economic Journal*, 48 (1938).

Eichner, A. S. *A Guide to Post-Keynesian Economics* (New York: Macmillan, 1979).

Eshag, E. *From Marshal to Keynes* (Oxford: Blackwell, 1963).

Fender, J. *Understanding Keynes: an analysis of the General Theory* (Brighton: Wheatsheaf, 1981).

Garraty, J. A. *Unemployment in History* (New York: Harper & Row, 1977).

Gilbert, J. C. *Keynes's Impact on Monetary Economics* (London: Butterworth, 1982).

Haberler, G. *Prosperity and Depression* (New York: United Nations, 1946).

Hahn, L. A. *Common Sense Economics* (London: Abelard-Schuman, 1956).

Hegeland, H. [1951] *The Multiplier Theory* (New York: Augustus Kelley, 1984).

Hession, C. H. *John Maynard Keynes* (New York: Macmillan, 1984).

Hobson, J. A. and A. F. Mummery [1889] *The Physiology of Industry; Being an Exposition of Certain Fallacies in Existing Theories of Economics* (New York: Augustus Kelley, 1956).

Jackman, R. 'Keynes and Leijonhufvud', *Oxford Economic Papers*, 26, no. 2 (1974).

Johnson, H. G. *Money, Trade and Economic Growth* (London: Allen & Unwin, 1964).

Kahn, R. F. 'The Relation of Home Investment to Unemployment', *Economic Journal*, June, 1931.

Keynes, J. M. *Collected Writings of J. M. Keynes* vol. 7 (London: Macmillan & Cambridge University Press, 1973).

Klein, L. *The Keynesian Revolution* (London: Macmillan, 1947).

Knight, F. H. [1921] *Risk, Uncertainty and Profit* (London: LSE Reprints of Scarce Tracts, 1957).

Kuhn, T. S. *The Structure of Scientific Revolutions* (Chicago: University of Chicago, 1970).

Lavington, F. *The Trade Cycle* (London: King 1922).

Leontief, W. 'Postulates; Keynes' *General Theory* and the Classicists', in S. E. Harris (ed.) *The New Economics* (New York: Knopf, 1948).

Lindahl, E. *Studies in the Theory of Money and Capital* (London: Allen & Unwin, 1939).

Link, R. G. *English Theory of Fluctuations 1815–1848* (New York: Columbia University Press, 1959).

Malthus, T. R. [1836] *The Principles of Political Economy* (New York: Augustus Kelley, 1951).

Marshall, A. *Official Papers by Alfred Marshall* edited by J. M. Keynes (London: Royal Economic Society, 1926).

Minsky, H. P. *John Maynard Keynes* (London: Macmillan, 1976).

Modigliani, F. 'Liquidity Preference and the Theory of Interest and Money' *Econometrica*, 12 (1944).

Neftci, S. N. 'A time series analysis of the real wage-employment relationship', *Journal of Political Economy*, 84 (1978).

Patinkin, D. *Money, Interest & Prices* (New York: Harper & Row, 1965).

Pigou, A. C. *Unemployment* (London: Williams & Norgate, 1914).

Pigou, A. C. *Industrial Fluctuations* (London: Macmillan, 1927).

Pigou, A. C. *The Theory of Unemployment* (London: Macmillan, 1933).

Pigou, A. C. *Equilibrium and Employment* (London: Macmillan, 1941).

Rose, P. *Woman of Letters: A Life of Virginia Woolf* (London: Routledge & Kegan Paul, 1978).

Sahl, M. *The Hungry Eye* (recording, 1965).

Sargent, T. J. 'Estimation of Dynamic Labor Demand Schedules under rational expectations', *Journal of Political Economy*, 86 (1978).

Schumpeter, J. A. *History of Economic Analysis* (London: Allen & Unwin, 1954).

Stein, J. L. *Monetarist, Keynesian and New Classical Economics* (Oxford: Blackwell, 1982).

Taylor, J. B. 'Aggregate dynamics and staggered contracts', *Journal of Political Economy*, 88 (1980).

Tarshis, I. 'Changes in real and money wages rates', *Economic Journal*, 49 (1939).

Trevethick, J. A. 'Money, Wage, Inflexibility and the Keynesian Supply Function', *Economic Journal*, 86 (1976).

Webb, S. and M. Webb *The Prevention of Destitution* (London: Longmans, 1911).

Weintraub, S. *An Approach to the Theory of Income Distribution* (Philadelphia: Chilton, 1958).

Wells, P. 'Keynes Aggregate Supply Function: A Suggested Integration', *Economic Journal*, 69 (September, 1960).

Wells, P. 'Keynes Employment Function', *History of Political Economy*, 6 (1974).

Wells, P. 'In Review of Keynes', *Cambridge Journal of Economics*, 2 (1978).

Index